AFRICAN
TRADITIONAL
RELIGIONS

In Contemporary Society

Edited by Jacob K. Olupona

A New ERA Book

PARAGON HOUSE
St. Paul, Minnesota

Published in the United States by

Paragon House
www.ParagonHouse.com

Copyright 1991 by International Religious Foundation except for the following:

"The Sacred in African New Religions," by Bennetta Jules-Rosette, copyright 1989 by Sage Publications. Reprinted from *The Changing Face of Relgion,* 1989, by permission of Sage Publications.

All rights reserved. Except for use in reviews, no part of this book may be reproduced, stored in a retrieval system, or transmitted in any form or by any means, electronic, mechanical, or otherwise, without the prior written consent of the publisher.

A New Ecumenical Research Association Book

Library of Congress Cataloging-in-Publication Data

African traditional religion in contemporary society / edited by Jacob K. Olupona. — 1st ed.
395 p. cm.
Papers presented at the conference "The place of African traditional religion in contemporary Africa," held in Nairobi, Kenya, on Sept. 10-14, 1987, sponsored by the Council for World Religions.
"A new ERA book."
ISBN 0-89226-077-7 : $24.95
ISBN 0-89226-079-3 (pbk.) : $14.95
1. Africa, Sub-Saharan — Religion — congresses. 2. Africa, Sub-Saharan — Religion — Study and teaching— Congresses. I. Olupona, Jacob Obafemi Kehinde. II. International Religious Foundation. III. Council for World Religions.
BL 2462.5.A38 1990
299.6 — dc20

89-77137
CIP

This book is
dedicated to
Wande Abimbọla

Table of Contents

Introduction
    Jacob K. Olupọna   1

1. "Insiders" and "Outsiders" in the Study of African
    Religions: Notes on Some Problems of Theory and Method   15
    David Westerlund

2. Major Issues in the Study of African Traditional Religion   25
    Jacob K. Olupọna

3. The Place of Traditional Religion in Contemporary
    South Africa   35
    Gerhardus Cornelis Oosthuizen

4. The Place of African Traditional Religion
    in Contemporary Africa: The Yoruba Example   51
    Wande Abimbọla

5. Flowers in the Garden:
    The Role of Women in African Religion   59
    John S. Mbiti

6. The Role of Women in African Traditional Religion
    and Among the Yoruba   73
    Joseph Akinyẹle Ọmọyajowo

7. The Talking Drum: A Traditional Instrument of Liturgy
    and of Mediation with the Sacred   81
    Georges Niangoran-Bouah

8. Religious Politics and the Myth of Ṣango   93
    Akinwumi Iṣọla

9. African Traditional Socio-Religious Ethics
    and National Development: The Nigerian Case   101
    Friday M. Mbon

10. The Encounter Between African Traditional Religion
    and Other Religions in Nigeria   111
    Joseph Ọmọṣade Awolalu

11. Traditional African Religion and Christianity   119
    Vincent Mulago

12. Revitalization in African Traditional Religion   135
    Rosalind I.J. Hackett

13. Tradition and Continuity in African Religions:
    The Case of New Religious Movements   149
    Bennetta W. Jules-Rosette

14. Perseverance and Transmutation in African Traditional
    Religions   167
    Evan M. Zuesse

Contributors   185

Index   187

Introduction

Jacob K. Olupona

IT IS QUITE EVIDENT that African traditional religion plays an important role in shaping the character of African society and culture today. Yet, this tradition continues to suffer from lack of acceptance and inadequate understanding of its central tenets and essence. The two monotheistic traditions, Islam and Christianity, to which most Africans have converted over the century, have developed a hostile attitude to this tradition; Islam relegates it to *al-Jahilliyya*, the time of barbarism, and Christianity views it as pure paganism.

It is in response to these trends that the Council for World Religions (CWR) agreed to bring together scholars, leaders, and practitioners of African traditional religion to engage in a dialogue, to exchange ideas, and to discuss issues of common concern. This is part of the CWR's ongoing efforts to promote intra and inter-religious dialogue and harmony among world religions. The conference, "The Place of African Traditional Religion in Contemporary Africa," took place in Nairobi, Kenya, on September 10–14, 1987. To maximize results, the CWR invited several eminent scholars and practitioners to prepare written papers on chosen topics from the perspectives of their various disciplines and traditions. The essays collected in this book deal with most of the issues and themes addressed at the conference.

This volume of fourteen chapters examines the nature, structure, and significance of African traditional religion(s) as dynamic changing tradition(s). It analyzes and interprets several significant aspects of African religions and explores their possible contributions to national development and the modernization process. It also discusses the impact of social change on African religion today. The contributors are scholars from several disciplines (anthropology, sociology, history of religions, theology, literature and the arts); yet, in analysis and interpretation of their data, they all take transcendence and the sacred in African thought very seriously. The newness of this approach is in treating African traditional religion not as a fossil but rather as one of the most important building blocks of modern African life. The conference highlights such issues as the place of the African sacred drum as a living institution, the use of proverbs as a resource for our understanding of African religious attitudes and cosmologies, and the importance of the role and image of women in Africa. This work is significant in that it defines a new way of studying and viewing African traditional religion. It argues that deeper understanding must be based on a sensitivity to the structural logic of specific cultures, and that there must be multi-disciplinary study of the meaning of religious statements and actions. In this endeavor, the thoroughly researched data presented by a wide range of scholars serve as an excellent introduction and orientation to African religious experience and spirituality—powerful forces which must be reckoned with in any serious study of African societies today.

The following is an overview of the individual essays in this volume. In the first chapter David Westerlund presents an essay on " 'Insiders' and 'Outsiders' in the Study of African Religions: Notes on Some Problems of Theory and Method," in which he compares the approaches of the historian of religion and the anthropologist. Westerlund questions whether Western scholars should be taken less seriously than African scholars, regardless of methodological approach, or whether both Western and African academics (Christian, Muslim and secular) should be regarded as outsiders when compared with the actual practitioners of traditional religion. He also raises the issue of nomenclature in African traditional religion and asks whether, in view of the diversity and multiplicity of these traditions, it is more appropriate to speak of African religions in the plural or in the singular as it is commonly done. It is in his discussion of the appropriate methodology for the study of African religion that Westerlund has perhaps made the most useful contribution to the conference. It is well known that phenomenological and comparative historical approaches to the study of religion are quite new in African universities and that African traditional religion has largely been approached from theological and social-functionalist approaches. Westerlund opts for a phenomenological approach which enables scholars to deal empathetically and sensitively with African religions while remaining faithful to their own personal convictions.

In "Major Issues in the Study of African Traditional Religion," Jacob K. Olupọna deals with emerging themes in the understanding of African traditional religion. He notes that eminent historians of religion in the

West have, in the past, neglected the study of primal traditions, especially African traditional religion, as they were considered of little significance in the congress of world religious traditions. Such an erroneous position, he claims, has given way to more scholarly and empathetic study of African religions today. He then suggests that a primary objective of the study of African traditional religion is to locate it within the wider framework of the discipline of the history of religion (*Religionswissenschaft*). The paper focuses on four major themes as illustrative: transcendence and the sacred, method and theory, the significance of the historical approach, and resilience and adaptability. Olupọna argues that the Western notion of transcendence and the sacred hardly matches the African traditional religious worldview, yet most discussions of African traditional religion by both Western and African scholars themselves have been heavily influenced by Western theological thinking. He therefore suggests that a phenomenological-hermeneutical interpretation of African religions should be encouraged. Also, Olupọna observes that methodology and theory suitable for the study of African religions have received attention in recent times. He also suggests that an interdisciplinary study which combines phenomenological description and anthropological investigation will provide us with a more accurate interpretation of the essence of African religious beliefs and worldviews. Further on the methodological issues, Olupọna remarks that, normally, African scholars do not take the historical dimension seriously when writing about African traditional religion. Such neglect, he says, has created the impression that the religion is static and unchanging. He then observes that in the history of religions, diachronic analysis can no longer be neglected. Such analysis normally leads to issues of continuity and change in African traditional religion. The author observes that encounters of African traditional religion with Islam and Christianity have altered the fortune of the former so much so that African religions no longer remain in pristine form anywhere in Africa. He then discusses the effect of religious change, such as conversion, on African religion and society.

Gerhardus Cornelis Oosthuizen, in his paper "The Place of Traditional Religion in Contemporary South Africa," looks at the nature and essence of traditional religion in modern South Africa. He compares the African religious worldview to the modern scientific worldview and argues that the former goes beyond the one-dimensional approach of the latter in so far as it is more concerned with all aspects of the human person. The African worldview, he claims, is similar to the post-modern scientific worldview and, like it, acknowledges that there is more to knowledge, experience, and analysis than the rational dimension which the scientific worldview makes central. African sensitivity to the non-rational, therefore, will surely enhance our current search for depth. Oosthuizen emphasizes that, for the Africans, objectivity entails personal involvement in issues, and he argues that Africans are more comfortable with participation and developing relationships in religious practices than in mere mental digestion of scriptural and catechetical knowledge, and logical arguments. This explains, he argues, why indigenous churches, often patterned after an African traditional worldview, have been much more successful than Western churches in gaining converts. Oosthuizen also notes that African traditional religion essentially promotes a strong sense of community and is oriented towards human beings rather than things. He also revisits the old issue of the African concept of time and restates the controversial opinion that Africans make little reference to the future. However, Oosthuizen's argument provides a new answer that for the Africans time consists of events, but the advent of world religions, Western education, and scientific knowledge meant an introduction of a new concept of time into African thinking. This disjunction of concepts of time, Oosthuizen claims, has led to the present situation of urban disorder and anomie which Africans now experience. In addition to examining the relationship of African religion to nature, Oosthuizen also considers the role of traditional healing processes in contemporary southern Africa. He observes that traditional healers/diviners have recorded many successes even in areas where Western medicine has failed woefully. He believes that their knowledge of the social order and their religious awareness of their society enable them to attain such a high degree of success in their profession. He also compares the Western medical/healing practices with the indigenous ones and concludes that the two complement each other. Both should be merged in Africa's health care delivery system. In his conclusion, Oosthuizen observes that the African traditional system has a lot to offer humanity and that the post-modern worldview which the West is currently formulating will have an ally in traditional African culture.

In the next paper, Wande Abimbọla, an Ifa priest and Professor of Yoruba Culture, discusses "The Place of African Traditional Religion in Contemporary Africa: The Yoruba Example." His thesis is that in spite of the persistent presence of Islam and Christianity among the Yoruba, the traditional religion still holds sway among the people. He uses Ile-Ife, the Yoruba sacred city, to illustrate his thesis, that the Yoruba people are still adherents of the cults of Orìṣà, that they take part in the observance of traditional festivals, and that they patronize traditional herbalists and Ifa diviners. Abimbọla observes that although certain aspects of the Orisa cults are being gradually forgotten by the people, yet as many as 60 percent of the people still claim to be adherents of Yoruba Traditional Religion in Ile-Ifẹ, among these are Muslims and Christians alike. The author proceeds to state, however, that economic and sociological motivations lie beneath Yoruba participation in some of the traditional festivals and cults, rather than strictly religious ones.

He also observes that Muslims and Christians participate in traditional Yoruba festivals today simply out of their desire to be associated with the wider social group and its past heritage. While Abimbọla does not necessarily underestimate the fundamental religious motivation for observing the traditional rituals and cultic practices, he tends to emphasize the socio-political and economic functions of religions, both to the collectivity and individuals. Here he points out ways in which the individual may use traditional magic and medicine when he/she comes face-to-face with such ultimate concerns as sickness, ill-luck, witchcraft, and even death.

The next two chapters discuss various aspects of women and religion in Africa. John Mbiti's essay serves as an excellent introduction and orientation. It focuses on the role of women in three areas of African life and thought: mythology, proverbs, and prayer. Each African society has its own mythologies which explain various aspects of reality; women are always mentioned in the mythologies of creation and the origin of evil and death in the world. Just as in the Genesis myth, several of the African myths credit women with the origin of evil. However, Mbiti cautions us that some other myths do not blame women for the loss of the primordial paradise. Mbiti also emphasizes the use of proverbs as a resource for our understanding of the religious nature and worldview of African peoples. He regrets that the study of the religious significance of proverbs has scarcely started. Proverbs, he argues, pertain not only to wisdom literature but also refer to interesting liturgical events, sociological experiences, and cultural issues. While several proverbs point to the vulnerability and weaknesses of women – jealousy, envy and hate – they are often an expression of male prejudices, and such male prejudices, he pleads, should be discouraged. Prayer, the third area Mbiti touches upon, deals with what women do in terms of participating in the liturgical life of African peoples. He is of the opinion that women's prayer lives have been highly distorted by the patriarchal nature of African societies. Contrary to this distorting notion of the male-controlled oral tradition, he cites a few noteworthy cases where women, both practically and symbolically, are the central pivot of prayer life in their societies.

Joseph Akinyẹle Ọmọyajowo, in "The Place of Women in African Traditional Religion and Among the Yoruba," looks at the images of women in Africa past and present. He argues the probability of a feminine deity in African religion in the past and plumbs the meaning of this likelihood for our understanding and study of the nature of African traditional religion. Citing several cases from the Yoruba of western Nigeria, he argues that, at best, Yoruba tradition is very ambivalent on the gender of significant Yoruba deities, such as Oduduwa, the god-king and mythical primogenitor of the Yoruba race. Ọmọyajowo then focuses on the significance of women's festivals in social protests and control and examines their role in maintaining social cohesion and integration in several Yoruba societies. Ọmọyajowo also compares the Yoruba notion of women with that of the Western tradition, especially the Judeo-Christian tradition, and indicates that the Hebrew concept of a deity who is exclusively masculine and Paul's insistence that women should have no public role to play in worship are indeed foreign to African ideas of the deity. But he admits that the biblical notion must have influenced African scholars' interpretations of the place of women in African religion.

The above transition raises another problem in the study of African religion: the impact of social change in African religion. Ọmọyajowo shows that some of the Yoruba deities who were originally conceived as females have since changed into males, perhaps as a result of the changing social system of the Yoruba people.

Several issues emerge from the two papers on religion and women which remain controversial and would require research. But perhaps the two most important issues which should be mentioned outright are the connection and association of women with witchcraft in several African societies and the issue of women and purity. It is observed that, when a girl reaches puberty and menstruates for the first time, this is acknowledged, praised, and ritualized. Yet menstruation taboos are common in several African societies. It should not be forgotten, however, that almost all cultures throughout the world have elaborate beliefs and practices about menstruation; and African practices no doubt are part of this larger tradition. In all African cultures, menstruation is associated with women's secret power—often expressed also in witchcraft as antithetical to men's secret power: one of the ways in which women exert force and power mystically in the universe and on men. It was suggested during the lively discussion on this topic that it could not be that the biological nature of women is sinful, but rather that blood, which is a symbol of life, has some potency, which can itself destroy. It may be that people like to put this potential threat/power at bay, to control, so to say, that which is highly charged with the sacred.

George Niangoran-Bouah's essay, "The Talking Drum: A Traditional Instrument of Liturgy and of Mediation with the Sacred," draws our attention to the relatively new discipline of drumology as a useful source of valuable information for African studies in general and African religions in particular. Niangoran-Bouah presents varying features of the talking drum, especially as found among the Akan of the Ivory Coast and Ghana. The drum as an important religious instrument provides liturgical texts with an invaluable repertoire of African beliefs about God and sacral kingship. The author traces the origin of the negative colonial attitude towards the drum in Africa to the misconception that it was an instrument invoking demonic sentiments, a conception/judgment that persisted until the independence period in African countries. This misconception, no doubt, prevented a proper understanding of the drum's major role in the social life of the Africans.

The phenomenology of the talking drum is clearly revealed in Niangoran-Bouah's suggestion that, indeed, for the Africans the drum is sacred, created by god-like humans, and the drummer is a speaker and communicator of the sacred fixed text. It was also observed during the discussion that there is a sense in which the drummer can be compared to a poet. Just as the poet uses his voice to entertain people, so the drummer uses the drum to entertain. The drummer therefore must not be regarded as a technician alone; he is an artist in his own right. Even if the texts are fixed and unchanging, he still has to learn the words and also acquire the special skill of drumming. If he is not a good artist, the message cannot be reproduced fully. In addition, on the issue of the language of the drum being fixed, it was observed that while there may be some sets of phrases, proverbs, and wise sayings that form the drummer's repertoire, the drummer is free to improvise in-between in order to make his message fit the particular occasion.

Akinwumi Iṣọla, a specialist in oral literature, focuses more narrowly on the missionary interpretation of Yoruba oral tradition. He uses data from his own research on a well-known Yoruba deity, Ṣango, to correct the distortion created by European accounts of African religion. In particular, Iṣọla picks on Hetherselt, who allegedly distorted the Ṣango myth in his book *Iwe Kika Ẹkarun Ni Ede Yoruba (Yoruba Readers' Book V.)* Iṣọla infers that Hetherselt's misrepresentation was probably deliberate since his book, meant to be used in missionary schools, was designed to discredit Yoruba deities. Moreover, he noted that the distortion was known only among the educated elite. The non-literate adherents did not know of the existence of Hetherselt's version. Iṣọla then states what he believes to be the most accurate interpretation of the myth of Ṣango especially as revealed by certain ODU IFA (Ifa divination poems) each of which gave details of particular aspects of Ṣango's life history.

Iṣọla's paper raises certain fundamental issues. First, records may not represent the final truth, as we normally believe. He therefore appeals to students of African culture and religion to revisit their records, especially those written by Christian missionaries, and correct their misrepresentations of African religion. Second, the author encourages African scholars to do service to their cultural and religious heritage by going back to reliable sources, such as the accounts of the elders, to find facts that would correct the incorrect accounts that have been given to the literate world.

In his work, "African Traditional Socio-Religious Ethics and National Development: The Nigerian Case," Friday Mbon argues that African social ethics could promote sound socio-economic growth and overall development of contemporary African societies. He condemns the Africans' borrowing and adapting of alien values, as such attitudes often impede development and growth. He remarks that African value-systems are communal, and that they tend to protect the individuals from antisocial behavior, in opposition to Western ethical systems which he claims are self-centered and materialistic. While no one doubts Mbon's stand on the necessity for traditional socio-religious ethics, some participants challenged the view that the African dilemma arises solely from the imposition of Western secularism. It was argued that, indeed, at one time, Western societies themselves experienced the same destruction of their traditional values by the all-conquering forces of urbanization and technology. Unfortunately, the West did not have the advantage of warnings that are now available to the developing nations which are experiencing similar transformations and challenges. Each society, whether Western or African, would have to recover its cultural heritage and call on the power of its traditional ethical standards to respond to the inevitable societal transformations caused by those phenomena. Mbon accurately perceives an urgent responsibility confronting the African nations and has even prescribed a remedy that warrants our serious consideration.

Joseph Ọmọṣade Awolalu focuses on "The Encounter Between African Traditional Religion and Other Religions in Nigeria." He presents an historical overview of this interaction and observes that from the beginning of history until Islam and Christianity came into Nigeria, traditional religion had primacy of place. Thereafter, a great encounter took place between the indigenous religions and Christianity in southern Nigeria, and between Islam and indigenous religions in northern

Nigeria. Awolalu traces the different responses to this encounter with Islam and Christianity. He shows that, indeed, Islam was more tolerant of African traditional religion than Christianity. But of course the rise of African churches parallel Muslim accommodations during this period. But tolerance was extended only until the 19th century when a radical change occurred in northern Nigeria in the form of the Jihad of Uthman Dan-Fodio. The consequences of this jihad were adverse for indigenous religion. A dramatic change came again with the attainment of political independence in 1960 when many nationalists disassociated themselves from imperialism, including the foreign religion, and re-embraced traditional religion. One indicator of this new wind of change was that the Department of Divinity at the University of Ibadan had to change to the Department of Religious Studies to accommodate the study of African traditional religion.

Perhaps the highest point of this second stage of encounter was Nigeria's hosting the Festival of Arts and Culture (FESTAC) — in 1977 in Lagos, at which traditional religion was given official recognition by allowing its practitioners and scholars to present their view points during the debates on African culture. Awolalu argues that Nigeria is now in the third stage of encounter. With the rise of militant Islamic and Christian fundamentalism, both religions have become totally intolerant of traditional religion.

There is no doubt that Awolalu has chosen one of the most contemporarily central areas of the phenomena of religious change in Africa which obviously deserves a separate conference. From his presentation re-emerge some of the long-time unresolved issues in the study of African traditional religion: the term "African traditional religion" in the singular, which one of the participants described as an ideological construct, and who, considering the heterogeneity of African cultures and religions, suggests instead should be called "African religions." Regarding the relationship between religions today, it was argued that the healthy interaction between one religion and another is fast becoming a thing of the past. There is, unfortunately, an increasing antagonism between various religious believers as witnessed in the 1970s and 1980s in the Maitatsine Muslim uprising and the destruction of churches in northern Nigeria in 1987. Fundamentalist Christian and Muslim groups demand a stricter adherence to certain normative interpretations of Christianity and Islam respectively.

Vincent Mulago's essay on "African Traditional Religion and Christianity" focuses on the essence of African traditional religion on its own merit and in its relationship to Christianity in contemporary Africa. He focuses on three major themes: the essential elements, the primacy of life, and the meeting of African traditional religion and Christianity. He sees the essential elements of African traditional spirituality in, among other things, the preservation and maintenance of life and the anthropocentric nature of societal ethics. Mulago makes valuable observations about the primacy and centeredness of religion in the life of the African people, arguing that religion has a significant role to play in the present and future life of the people. On the issue of African traditional religion's encounter with Christianity, Mulago takes a Christian (Catholic) theological position. He acknowledges that there have been serious conflicts between African traditional religion and Christianity, but argues that everything that is positive in the religion has as its source the Supreme Being. Likewise revelation, too, has as its source the same Supreme Being. There can be no possible opposition between the essential elements of African traditional religion and revelation because both have the same source. In conclusion, Monsignor Mulago cites Pope John Paul II's speech in Nairobi in 1980, which holds that the real model of development is not that which glorifies material values, but that which recognizes the power of the spiritual; and this model is in conformity with African culture.

The relationship between religion and social change is the focus of Rosalind Hackett's paper. Hackett examines the ways in which traditional religious beliefs and practices find new forms of expression, new avenues of survival, and new channels of continuity in the modern world. She calls this process revitalization. She applies several sociological concepts in her analysis of the empirical data collected mainly in Calabar, Cross River State, Nigeria, to illustrate continuity and change within the structures of traditional African religions. Rather than see African beliefs and practices as fossils that are permanently unchanging, she paints a more dynamic picture of them.

The attempt to revitalize African religion, to create a tradition that can be universalized and can contend with prevailing socio-cultural changes in contemporary Africa, is identified as a conscious effort on the part of certain individuals – scholars and practitioners alike. Evident throughout the entire paper is a process one might identify as routinization. Through such organizations as Traditional Medicine Societies (herbalists), African religion is made accessible to the public, incorporating some of the trappings and benefits of modern society. Perhaps the most classic example of such institutionalization is the Orile-Orisa (literally the abode of the deities) association at the Ọbafẹmi Awolowọ University, Ile-Ifẹ, Nigeria. It is an association of Ifẹ intelligentsia committed to Yoruba traditional beliefs. The association succeeded in incorporating the worship of Yoruba deities into the religious calendar of the university. Sorting out the implications of this new process of revitalization Hackett leaves to future researchers. However, it is her conclusion that African traditional religion will not survive in its present form, although there will not be a total demise of its beliefs and tenets.

In "Tradition and Continuity in African Religions: The Case of New Religious Movements," (NRMs), Bennetta Jules-Rosette, a sociologist, observes that NRMs have a more volatile membership in non-Western societies in recent times than in the West. She remarks that this is partially due to the influence of leadership and succession crises within the NRMs movement, structural changes resulting from tensions arising from the interaction of the movements and larger society, and the influence of non-Western culture. Jules-Rosette identifies three main types of NRMs found in African regions: the indigenous or Independent Churches, Separatist Churches and neo-traditional movements. Unfortunately she left out Islamic NRMs. These movements, she observes, manifest a mixture of both traditional religious worldviews and historical and modern elements. There is no doubt that NRMs are enjoying a proliferation in numbers and increase in membership. Jules-Rosette observes that several sources provide the impetus for the rapid growth of NRMs, while the indigenous churches present the most rapid response to Christianity.

Jules-Rosette then examines the nature of NRMs in light of several well-known sociological theories, especially from the perspectives of Emile Durkheim, Max Weber, and E. Troeltsch. Troeltsch's famous church-sect topology is rejected as unsuitable for Africa's NRMs. She also cautions that the Western model, particularly one that distinguishes between sacred and secular domains, can hardly fit the analysis of NRMs in Africa. She examines the ways and means by which NRMs have responded to secularization and noticed four cultural responses: neo-traditionalism, revitalization, syncretism, and millenarianism.

On the future of NRMs, she predicts that, contrary to the criticism by scholars that the movements may not remain stable for too long and will continue to manifest signs of schism over leadership and succession issues, nevertheless, historical evidence seems to show that they have considerable energy for survival, especially through their international and ecumenical outlook. Finally, Jules-Rosette examines the cultural and social contributions of Africa's new religions, and observes that most of them have had considerable cultural and social influence on the larger society. Several of their protests against the mission's authority and against foreign liturgy have resulted in unexpected social consequences for society, the emergence of themes such as liberation and social emancipation of the masses. The movement, for some, has become the source of alternative lifestyles and has led to the solution of new cultural and social patterns of life.

Evan Zeusse, in "Perseverance and Transmutation in African Traditional Religions," focuses on the deep spiritual structures which will continue to shape African spirituality even when the specific religious units will have disappeared. He identifies three levels in traditional African religion that constitute its enduring quality: deep spiritual structure, folk practices, and intellectual rationalizations.

Zeusse emphasizes the centrality of relationship in Africa's deep spiritual structure. In his opinion, the concepts of the Supreme Being and personhood are germane to the idea of relationship. Close relationships give rise to power, and power presupposes hierarchy at the top of which is the Supreme Being. Zuesse observes that to be human is to belong to a society by participating in its rituals, ceremonies, and obligations. It is to the credit of African societies that even the non-human realm is embraced. The ability to live within this network of relationships, Zuesse argues, guarantees salvation and, within the structure of relationships, transcendence and immanence have no oppositional quality.

The participants found many aspects of the conference beneficial, and they expressed their gratitude to CWR for the invitation to participate. More CWR conferences, they remarked, would truly create new opportunities for dialogue between religious groups in Africa. The American and European participants expressed their happiness at the opportunity to meet African scholars and to discuss in an intensive way such a variety of topics of deep personal and professional interest.

A few gaps remain that need to be filled in future conferences on African traditional religions. We regret the absence of Muslim scholars. The few who were invited could not attend. Also, themes such as witchcraft, the nature of evil, ancestor worship/veneration, possession, trance, ethics, etc., should be given more attention. It was also suggested that a case study approach should be encouraged, especially if academic objectives are sought. Future conferences could be more focused and include people with a wider variety of backgrounds (anthropologists, sociologists, historians, Muslims, drummers, and sculptors). More traditional practitioners should also be invited, along with religious studies academics, who in Africa tend to be Christian theologians and ministers.

I express our gratitude to the CWR Director, Dr. Frank Kaufmann, and his assistant, Mr. Jeff Gledhill, for their support and efforts in making the conference a success. The publication office of CWR has been most helpful in expediting the publication of this volume. I also express thanks to H. Justin Watson, Steve Wright and Robert Brooks, the CWR editors I worked with. I wish also to thank Diane Beck of Amherst College, Massachusetts, U.S.A., who typed the final chapters of the book and Professor Ọlabiyi Yai of Ọbafẹmi Awolọwọ University, Ile-Ifẹ, Nigeria and the staff of the Center for New Religious Movements, Selly Oak Colleges, Birmingham, U.K., for translating into English the French papers presented.

1

"INSIDERS" AND "OUTSIDERS" IN THE STUDY OF AFRICAN RELIGIONS

NOTES ON SOME PROBLEMS OF THEORY AND METHOD

David Westerlund

RESEARCH ON AFRICAN RELIGIONS has been carried out mainly by scholars of religion and by anthropologists, even though historians, philosophers, sociologists, and others have made important contributions. This paper will be concerned only with the two groups of scholars mentioned first. The aim of the paper is to compare the different study perspectives that characterize works by scholars of religion and by anthropologists. More specifically, I will discuss the interests and outlooks on life that form the background of these differences. By contrasting different research traditions, such more or less "hidden" presuppositions can more easily be discerned. Although my general reflections do have a wider application, studies by, on the one hand, scholars of religion in anglophone African countries and, on the other hand, by Western social anthropologists will be in particular focus. It may be stressed, for example, that I will not refer in this paper to works by German and Austrian anthropologists (ethnologists), which differ essentially from works by, among others, British social anthropologists.

Among scholars of religion who have studied African religions, the comparative or religio-phenomenological approach has been predominant. Most anthropologists, on the other hand, have preferred to study African religions in a more limited cultural context. The predominant view among scholars of religion seems to be that religion should be regarded as a phenomenon *sui generis*. With the "intrinsic value" of religion in mind, they argue that, in principle, it is legitimate to study religion separated from its cultural context. In particular, a "decontextualization" of religion is a characteristic of broad comparative studies.

In the comparative research carried out by scholars of religion, there seems to be a search for a transcultural "spiritual unity," a tendency to emphasize similarities rather than dissimilarities. For example, in his book *African Traditional Religion*, E.G. Parrinder states that there is a great homogeneity in the religious sphere, that the resemblances between African peoples and religions are far more important than the differences.[1] Similarly, E.B. Idowu argues that there is "a common Africanness about the total culture and religious beliefs and practices of Africa."[2]

For anthropologists who apply a "holistic" approach to their study of African religions, the phenomenological approach must seem uninteresting and misleading. Apparently, most anthropologists do not regard religion as an entity *sui generis*, and in some holistic anthropological studies, African religions have been reduced to mere epiphenomena. In social anthropological research on religion the sociological "reductionism" of E. Durkheim has been particularly influential.

For scholars of religion who conceive of religion as something *sui generis*, the anthropological concentration on the social function of religion need not in itself be controversial. The difficulties arise when the sociological analysis becomes deterministic, and the religious phenomena are explained as mere reflections of social conditions. Naturally, scholars of religion do not regard it as their task to "explain away" religion. A good example of an anthropological study which focuses interest on the social function of religion, but without denying its intrinsic value, is E.E. Evans-Pritchard's classic *Nuer Religion*.[3] This book has in general been very well received by Western scholars of religion.

In my own study of African research on African religions I have concluded that African scholars of religion have usually shared this appreciative view of Evans-Pritchard's book. G. Lienhardt and M. Griaule are other anthropologists whose religio-anthropological or religio-ethnological works have been well received by African scholars of religion.[4] These anthropologists, like most scholars of religion, conceive of religion as something more than a product or reflection of, for instance, social and economic conditions.

The positive assessment of a fairly limited number of studies by Western anthropologists has, however, influenced the research of African scholars of religion only to a limited extent. The presentation of African religions that is found in studies by these scholars differs essentially from the presentation in Western anthropological works, particularly those which are based on "reductionist" concepts of religion. In books by leading African scholars like E.B. Idowu, J.S. Mbiti, and V. Mulago there is a pyramidal picture of African religions with God, the creator, at the top and under Him a number of superhuman beings such as divinities and nature spirits.[5] These beings are thought of as "intermediaries" between God and human beings. Due to their intermediary role God is clearly the highest and most important being, not only in areas where there is an elaborate cult of God but also in areas where the cult primarily concerns the intermediary beings.

With regard to the belief in the spirits of ancestors, which is widespread in many African agricultural areas, scholars of religion tend to emphasize its religious role and not, as in many anthropological works, its social function. Like divinities and nature spirits, the spirits of ancestors are thought of as intermediaries between God and man. Comparisons are sometimes made with the intermediary role of saints in Christian churches. Moreover, African scholars of religion usually pay much less attention to phenomena which have been labelled magic, witchcraft, and sorcery than do Western anthropologists, who interpret them within a basically sociological framework. Anthropologists have also been criticized for overlooking, or at least for not paying enough attention to, both the importance of the belief in God in African religions, as well as the importance of religion in general.

It is not possible, within the limited scope of this paper, to give a more detailed account of research by scholars of religion and anthropologists. However, these notes may be sufficient to indicate the great differences between the various study perspectives. In the light of these notes I will discuss the significance of different presuppositions.

Among anthropologists the term "ethnocentrism" is a derogatory one. It may be asked whether it is possible to avoid being "ethnocentric" when studying a foreign culture. Regarding the study of African and other religions, however, the religious affiliation of the scholars concerned, or lack of it, is of greater significance than their ethnic backgrounds. If a comparison is made between the following groups of scholars who have carried out research on African religions: (1) Western anthropologists, (2) Western scholars of religion, and (3) African scholars of religion, it can be concluded that the clearest dividing line is not between the Western academics and the Africans but between the anthropologists and the scholars of religion. It is illuminating to compare, for example, the research results of the Ugandan anthropologist O. p'Bitek with the results of African scholars of religion such as Idowu and Mbiti. Despite the former's vehement criticism of Western anthropology and its connection to colonialism, his studies of African religions, in which the social role of religion is strongly emphasized, are more akin to works by Western social anthropologists than to works by African scholars of religion.[6]

Ultimately, the choice of whether to study religion "as such" or "holistically" depends on the individual scholar's worldview and interests. Concepts of religion as well as presentations of African and other religions are influenced by the basic anthropological (in the proper sense of the word) and ontological views of the scholar. With few exceptions, scholars of religion have been religious believers themselves, and their interest has been in studying *homo religiosus* rather than social or economical man. Hence the tendency to "decontextualize" religion. The majority of African as well as Western scholars of religion are Christians. In his historical survey of research in comparative religion, E.J. Sharpe concludes that "liberalism, both theological and political, provided the ground in which it was able to flourish."[7] Apparently, most phenomenologists of religion have been influenced by liberal Protestant theology or by Catholic modernism. They have, therefore, reacted not only against "reductionist" anthropologists but also against conservative theologians. Paradoxically, it might be easier for conservative theologians, to whom Christianity alone is irreducible, something *sui generis*, and all other religions are "illusions" or "devilish inventions," to accept secular, "reductionist" analyses of non-Christian religions, than it is for more liberal scholars who conceive of *all* religions as entities *sui generis*.

In books on African religions written by African scholars of religion, it can be seen that the authors are influenced by their African background of belief. In addition to the more general belief in God and various spirits, some of them apparently believe in phenomena like witchcraft and sorcery.[8] With such a point of departure African scholars seem better prepared than their Western colleagues to "see with the believers' own eyes." Precisely the striving for an "inside view," a hermeneutical emphasis on description and understanding, based on empathy, is typical of the phenomenological perspective.

However, the fact that the great majority of African scholars who have studied African religions are Christians has also influenced their presentations of these religions. Being spokesmen for a theology of continuity, according to which Christianity is the "fulfillment" of African religions, they have tended to "Christianize" these religions in certain respects. In particular, this "Christianization" has concerned the role of God. The above-mentioned tendency to emphasize similarities, rather than dissimilarities, between various African religions, which is reflected, for instance, in the frequent references to "African religion" or "African traditional religion" in the singular, can also be interpreted in a Christian theological perspective. Obviously, the influence of nationalism cannot be overlooked either. The "harmonization" of different African religions is in accordance with important political goals. In the light of current political and religious conditions in pluralist African countries, it is not difficult to understand the fairly strong position of religious studies. The comparatively weak position of anthropology in Africa can also be understood against the backdrop of political and religious conditions. The holistic and "tribally oriented" research of anthropologists, which presents African religions as entities bound by local culture, is, politically and religiously, hardly opportune. In countries where national unity and not, as in South Africa, the unity of the "tribes" is the stated goal, the unifying perspective of comparative research on African religions may serve a more or less explicit political function. The civil religions which exist in religiously pluralist African countries, albeit as unofficial phenomena, are based on the unifying elements in African religions as well as in Christianity and Islam.

Unlike scholars of religion, Western anthropologists often have an atheistic or agnostic outlook on life. For scholars who do not presuppose the existence of a specific religious domain, which differs from and is partly independent of other domains, but regard all religions as illusions, it is natural to use some secular theory in order to explain why other people are religious believers and practitioners. According to Durkheim and other scholars influenced by him, it is not possible to reach a "deeper" understanding of religion if it is "isolated" from the social system.

I will not give detailed examples here of how different secular theories, based on the thinking of Durkheim and other Western, secular theorists, such as Marx and Freud, have influenced anthropological presentations of African religions. Instead, a quotation from an article by K.W. Bolle may illustrate a type of criticism of anthropological theorizing that can be found in works by scholars of religion, although the wording is usually more moderate: "The doings of anthropologists

have encumbered our minds with pomposities and monstrosities pre-
tending directly or indirectly to clear up our understanding of religion.
These monstrosities, without any relation to any actual life or experience
of anyone, least of all the tribal or non-literate or primitive, savage
peoples studied, have fostered every torture of the mind, from animism,
pre-animism and primitive mentality to various shades of functionalism,
cultural materialism and liminality—a long series of cruel irrelevancies
that have invaded and occupied and mutilated all our studies."9

Like many other scholars of religion, who react against "depersonal-
izing" theories, Bolle is primarily interested in the beliefs and practices
of the religious believers themselves and the *meaning* these beliefs and
practices have *for them*. He criticizes anthropologists who search for
"unconscious" patterns based on the assumption that religious believers
themselves do not understand why they believe or act in one way or the
other." The separation into categories of conscious/unconscious, among
all borrowed scientific vocables, has probably caused more evil, more
malicious slandering of peoples and traditions, during our lifetime, than
any other methodological approach."10

However, this criticism is not only directed against anthropological
research but contains also a measure of self-criticism. "What we see in
anthropology is a disease all of us have come to suffer from. We have
learned to generalize about human beings and their orientations as
human beings and forgotten the terms for thinking about human beings
humanly."11 A similar self-critical undertone can be discerned, for instance, in the anthropologist W. MacGaffey's conclusion concerning the
attitude of anthropologists about human beings whose cultures they
study. "We deem it essential to preserve a difference between us, an elite
no matter how small, who see the world as it really is, and them, who
see it only through a glass, darkly."12 Although structuralist approaches
have been of little significance in anthropological research on African
religions and cultures, it may be of interest in this context also to refer
briefly to the historian J. Vansina's criticism of the structuralist studies
of L. de Heusch. According to Vansina, structuralist analyses presuppose the "incredibly arrogant assumption" that "myth is a veiled nar-
rative that can be decoded only by foreign researchers, not by locals who
have grown up in the culture studied."13

As a scholar of religion in a faculty of humanities, I share the view of
Bolle and others, that the "inside" perspective, i.e., the self-understand-
ing of the human beings studied, *their* conceptions of man and of reality,
is of central interest. Others, however, may prefer to put the main
emphasis on "outside" perspectives. It should be remembered, also, that
in a sense all scholars are "outsiders." A complete "inside view" can only

be presented by the actual believers themselves, and a scholarly striving to depict such a view as faithfully as possible entails certain methodical problems.

In monographic studies based on field work, the documentary or "inside" parts have frequently not been clearly distinguished from the theoretical parts, which is unfortunate. For example, in many anthropological studies of African "symbolic systems" it is difficult to discern whether it is the African believers or the anthropologists themselves who regard certain phenomena as "symbols." It may, certainly, be argued that the borderline between description and explanation is fluid, that certain presuppositions affect the description too. However, this does not make it less important to try to differentiate the one from the other. On the contrary, one should aim at as "pure" a description as possible. The ideal form, which of course cannot always be used, is to reproduce verbatim questions and answers or other kinds of information in the original language as well as in translation.

A good example is L. Bartels' fine study of *Oromo Religion* (1983).[14] In this book the author has published a wealth of texts or documents in the form of direct accounts by various informants, and his own sparse reflections or comments are clearly distinguished from these invaluable documents. Bartels' book is also a model in that it provides some information about all the key informants; and after the texts, which are presented, the names of the informants are given. In many anthropological studies based on field research such information is lacking, which not only may conceal the heterogeneity of the cultures or religions studied but also makes any check of the sources impossible.

For scholars of religion who carry out comparative research on African religions and rely mainly or exclusively on scholarly literature, it is important to apply the method of source criticism. In broad comparative studies of African religions little attention has been paid to the distorting effects of secular and religionist theories in the sources used. As emphasized by J.G. Platvoet, it is essential to study not only books but also the authors and their biases. "Such a laborious, double study is not compatible with an unlimited comparative study of religions because of the sheer size of the work-load which it entails."[15]

In some recent comparative studies of African religions, the limitative approach advocated by, among others, Platvoet has been adopted. Two examples are E.T. Lawson's *Religions of Africa: Traditions in Transformation* (1984) and N.Q. King's *African Cosmos: An Introduction to Religion in Africa* (1986).[16] In these books the presentation of African religions is limited to a few selected examples.

In addition to facilitating the criticism of sources, a limitative approach also renders possible a consideration of the historical dimension of African religions as well as of their cultural integration. These are both important questions, but I will limit myself to some notes about the latter. In some comparative studies, as indicated above, the authors have tended to overemphasize the transcultural aspects of African religions. In studies of African Christianity, on the other hand, its cultural "contextualization" is, paradoxically, often stressed. Like Christianity, Islam, and other religions, African religions have different cultural forms in different parts of the continent. Although many anthropologists have tended to overemphasize the cultural aspects of African religions, scholars of religions may have something to learn from them with regard to the problem of cultural integration.

Of course, studies of African religions in their local cultural contexts need not be based on secular concepts of religion. While recognizing the error of religionist or theological "reductionists," who have failed "to realize that the differences in the beliefs of different cultures are at least as important as their similarities," E. Ikenga-Metuh in an interesting recent book on Igbo religion dissociates himself from secular, "reductionist" theories as well. In the introduction to this monograph he states that "overall, I have discussed beliefs and rituals as essentially religious phenomena, and have rejected any attempt to reduce them to mere psychological or sociological phenomena, or explain them away with evolutionary or other false assumptions."[17]

For methodical reasons I referred above to Bartels' book *Oromo Religion* as a model. Unlike many scholars, Bartels has declared explicitly his own presuppositions. In *Oromo Religion* he mentions that he is a Vincentian Father and how this has influenced his research. Yet it must be concluded that he has succeeded better than most scholars of religion in avoiding a "Christianization."

As a priest and theologian, Bartels is apparently a representative of a radicalized theology of religion. In Africa, S.G. Kibicho is one of the spokesmen for a radical African theology, which may strengthen the striving for the "inside view" of African religions and thwart the effects of what Ikenga-Metuh refers to as "theological reductionism."[18] Kibicho rejects the idea of Christianity as the "fulfillment" of African religions or the conception of these religions as a *preparatio evangelica*. "I feel that this attitude towards African traditional religion...is a relic of the old prejudiced, evolutionary view of African religion."[19] Moreover, a critique of the "Christianization" of African religions, particularly the religion of the Akan in Ghana, which reflects the idea of "fulfillment," can be found in a recent book by K. A. Dickson.[20] Previous attempts to fit African religions into the framework of a Christian model is also criticized by, among others, J.S. Ukpong. Dickson and Ukpong argue, for example, that the "mediumistic" religionist theory, according to which lesser divinities are intermediaries between God and human beings, does not seem to be applicable to the religions of the Akan and the Ibibio, respectively.[21]

To sum up, it should be emphasized that "inside" and "outside" views are ideal views. As scholars we are all "insiders" *and* "outsiders," although we may choose to put the stress on either "inside" or "outside" perspectives. Among scholars of religion, who as a rule are religious believers themselves, the striving to present an "inside view" has been predominant. Yet it cannot be denied that many works of such scholars have been highly influenced by theological theories (often implicit ones). As a consequence, they have "Christianized" African religions. Anthropologists, on the other hand, who usually are not religious believers, have frequently applied Western, secular theories in order to explain African religions. In other words, they have "secularized" African religions.

In my opinion, the striving for the "inside view" should, continuously, be given the highest priority in the humanistic, scholarly study of African and other religions. Thus, the aim should be, as it were, to "Africanize" African religions. However, since we cannot fully escape our position as "outsiders" or "reductionists," we should declare openly our own worldviews and interests. In this, as in many other respects, Bartels' *Oromo Religion* may serve as a model.

Notes

1. E.G. Parrinder, *African Traditional Religion*, 3rd ed. (London: Sheldon Press, 1974), 11.
2. E.B. Idowu, *African Traditional Religion: A Definition* (London: SCM Press, 1973), 103f. See further D. Westerlund, *African Religion in African Scholarship: A Preliminary Study of the Religious and Political Background*, Studies published by the Institute of Comparative Religion at the University of Stockholm 7 (Stockholm: Almquist & Wiksell International, 1985), 48.
3. E.E. Evans-Pritchard, *Nuer Religion* (Oxford: The Clarendon Press, 1956).
4. G. Lienhardt, *Divinity and Experience: The Religion of the Dinka* (Oxford: The Clarendon Press, 1961) ; M. Griaule, *Conversations with Ogotemmêli: An Introduction to Dogon Religious Ideas* (London: Oxford University Press, 1965). For more examples, see Westerlund, *African Religion in African Scholarship*, 27.
5. See e.g., Idowu, *African Traditional Religion*; J.S. Mbiti, *African Religions and Philosophy* (London: Heinemann, 1969); V. (gwa C.M.) Mulago, *La Religion*

Traditionelle des Bantu et leur vision du Monde, 2nd ed. (Kinshasa: Faculté de Theologie Catholique, 1980).

6. For a discussion of p'Bitek's research on African religions, see Westerlund, *African Religion in African Scholarship*, 60 ff.

7. E.J. Sharpe, *Comparative Religion: A History* (London: Duckworth, 1975), 138.

8. For some examples, see Westerlund, *African Religion in African Scholarship, 38.*

9. K.W. Bolle, "The History of Religions and Anthropology: A Theoretical Crisis," *Epoché, Journal of the History of Religions at UCLA* 7 (1–2), 1979, 4.

10. *Ibid.*, 8f.

11. *Ibid.*, 4.

12. W. MacGaffey, "African History, Anthropology, and the Rationality of Natives," *History in Africa* 5, 1978, 110.

13. J. Vansina, "Is Elegance Proof? Structuralism and African History," *History in Africa* 10, 1983, 313.

14. L. Bartels, *Oromo Religion: Myths and Rites of the Western Oromo of Ethiopia — An Attempt to Understand*, Collectanea Instituti Anthropos 8 (Berlin: Dietrich Reimer Verlag, 1983).

15. J.G. Platvoet, *Comparing Religions: A Limitative Approach*, Religion and Reason 24 (The Hague, Paris and New York: Mouton Publishers, 1982), 12.

16. E.T. Lawson, *Religions of Africa: Traditions in Transformation*, The Religious Traditions of the World series (San Francisco: Harper & Row, 1984); N.Q. King, *African Cosmos: An Introduction to Religion in Africa*, The Religious Life of Man series (Belmont: Wadsworth Publishing Company, 1986).

17. E. Ikenga-Metuh, *African Religions in Western Conceptual Schemes: The Problem of Interpretation (Studies in Igbo Religion)* (Ibadan: Pastoral Institute, Bodija, 1985), ix, xii.

18. *Ibid.*, ix.

19. S.G. Kibicho, "The Continuity of the African Conception of God into and through Christianity: A Kikuyu Case-study," *Christianity in Independent Africa*, ed. by E. Fashol-Luke et al. (London: Rex Collings, 1978), 380.

20. K.A. Dickson, *Theology in Africa* (New York: Orbis Books; London: Darton, Longman, and Todd, 1984).

21. *Ibid.*, 55ff, 67f; J.S. Ukpong, "The Problem of God and Sacrifice in African Traditional Religion," *Journal of Religion in Africa* 14 (3), 1983, 197f.

2

MAJOR ISSUES IN THE STUDY OF AFRICAN TRADITIONAL RELIGION

Jacob K. Olupọna

THE EMINENT HISTORIAN of religion and theologian, Wilfred Cantwell Smith, once stated that scholars interested in the study of non-Christian religions should devote their time and energy entirely to the study of the living world religious traditions (Oriental and Far Eastern religions) such as Islam, Hinduism, and Buddhism; and that the study of primal religions should be shelved, as these traditions have no relevance to contemporary society.[1] Cantwell Smith has been criticized by several of his colleagues, who are equally outstanding scholars of religion. He has since changed his mind and views about the primal traditions. One such critic, the Scandinavian scholar Åke Hulkrantz, remarked that Cantwell Smith's observation unveils the general apathy toward preliterate religion and culture. He aptly observed that this must change.

"These religions are of course of utmost importance, but they constitute a part of the many religions which, in different places and at different times, have accompanied humanity. Any phenomenology of religion which does not take into closer account religious forms among preliterate people gives a false picture of the religious world."[2]

Furthermore, Hulkrantz predicted that "...historians of religion will come increasingly to observe the 'primitive religions' in their multiformity."[3]

True to this prediction, primal religions, especially African traditional religion, during the last few decades have been the field of interest of several scholars. New information about African religion has appeared in anthropological and "history of religions" publications. Indeed, its importance in and contribution to the *religionswissenschaft* (history of religions) has now been well-documented.[4] In spite of these modest contributions, the study of African traditional religion remains obscure and unclear to a number of people. Increasingly African religion is challenged to join other participants in the parliament of world religions, to make her modest contributions to contemporary discussions on interfaith dialogue.

There are three main reasons for this state of affairs. First, being mainly an oral culture, the advent of Christianity and of Islam has swept away evidences of its vitality, nature, and scope. To the extent that the beliefs, doctrines, and rituals of these two monotheistic religions filtered into the remnants of the traditional religion, they have changed the perspective of the people. The second reason for present misconceptions is that African traditional religion is so diversified in nature and scope that it represents different things to different ethnic groups. Yet we know that it maintains a unity, as certain themes run through all the religious traditions irrespective of where they may be found. The third reason is that the study and interpretation of African traditional religion have been influenced by Western thought and ideas. These have formed the central categories through which the beliefs and practices are studied, interpreted, and understood.

Given the situation described above, I think the time has come for a rethinking of our analysis and interpretations of the central themes contained in the tradition.[5] We need to do this in order to locate traditional religion in the wider context of the history of religions and to show resources that may be useful in its dialogue with other religious traditions. This paper, therefore, aims at providing some reflections upon central issues and themes in the study and understanding of African traditional religion. The recurrence of these themes and issues in virtually all major studies of African traditional religion, and in the history of religions, is a proof of its predominance and significance. However, the themes must not be taken as fully representing the extent of the traditional religious life. Because of the limitation of space, we intend to focus on four major issues: namely, transcendence and the sacred, method and theory, the place of history, and resilience and adaptability. To be sure these are not exhaustive, as will be made clear from this paper.

Transcendence and the Sacred

The issue of transcendence and the sacred is a major one in African traditional religion. A Westerner visiting Africa for the first time would notice very quickly that Africans possess a religious system quite distinct from his own in many respects. If he were to take time to investigate what this is all about, he would notice, among other things, a strong belief in a Supreme deity and at the same time a belief in a multitude of deities presumed to be lesser in authority than the Supreme deity. If our visitor had theological inclinations he might ask for published materials by prominent African scholars to help clarify this confusion between deities, and what would appear to be a diametrically opposed view. It is most likely that our Western friend would find out that the books he has picked up contain profuse debates, or citations of such debates, in defense or denial of polytheism or monotheism as the true nature of African traditional religion. He may end up more confused than when he started.

The pattern of theistic beliefs among African people have no doubt generated several controversies among scholars, Europeans and Africans alike. This debate reached its climax in an era when intense theological debate was going on in Europe about the status of religion among primal people vis-à-vis those who practice the so-called "higher" religions. We do not have to repeat the motifs that have influenced the outcome of such studies on African religion, however; what should interest us are the unforeseen consequences of this action on the study of African religion. First, most of our discussions on the transcendence and the sacred in African traditional religion have, by and large, been influenced by Western theological discourse. If "theology is human discourse on God" and "...its primary task is to describe to that religion's followers the object of their faith, to conceptualize it rationally, and to develop an ethics in correlation with what it judges to be the truth,"[6] one then sees why a profuse debate on the theistic content and nature of African traditional religion has persisted until today. Perhaps what is lacking here is our failure to recognize that religion, as an experiential phenomenon, is essentially pretheoretical and does not begin as an intellectual enterprise. The great religions of the world occurred to their founders first and foremost as a series of unique experiences over a period of time before they were embodied in written documents. Canonical authorities for adherents came into being after the deaths of the founders. As a result of this confusion between religion as a unique phenomenon on the one hand and religion as an intellectual exercise on the other hand, African scholars have perhaps been too slow in capturing the real essence of the African religious life. It seems to me that the basic question with which we should begin in any meaningful study of African religion is the following: "How did the Africans themselves experience their world in a fashion that we can call religious?" Benjamin Ray once remarked that "The debate about African 'monotheism' might have ended long ago if both sides had recognized that African Supreme beings are like but unlike western concepts of God."7

The African experience of God is one in which the sacred and the profane tend to be symmetrical. The ordinary human experience is mimetic of the transcendence and the sacred. Eric Voegelin once characterized this form of experience in his classic *Order and History* as "...a society symbolized as a cosmos."8 In such society, the whole of the human existence is grounded in, and "expressed by means of the cosmological myth."9 Voegelin further remarked that "...cosmological symbolization is neither a theory nor an allegory. It is the mythical expression of the participation, experienced as real, of the order of society in the divine being that also orders the cosmos."10

Another historian of religion, Ninian Smart, also underscores the relevance of the mythic approach in understanding the religions of mankind in general. He noted that "Common as it may be to define religion by reference to belief in God or gods, etc. (a procedure which runs up against troubles in any case in regard to, for example, Theravada Buddhism), there may be merit in looking at the focus or foci of religious activities through the medium of the mystic, that is in a context where such entities are acting, not just so to say quietly existing."11

From my own field work experience and from the above observations, I shall propose that a phenomenological-hermeneutical investigation and interpretation of the mythological thought of the Africans would reveal the essence of the religious worldview. This approach has the advantage of allowing the materials "to speak for themselves" and would save the scholars from imposing a preconceived theistic formula on the materials being studied.

Method and Theory

The above naturally leads us to the second significant issue, problems of method and theory in the study of African religion. In the last few decades, there has been a growing interest in the theoretical and methodological issues in the study of religion. In several African universities, there are now compulsory courses at undergraduate and postgraduate levels in this area. This state of development has arisen as a result of, first, a shift in emphasis from a narrow theological focus to a broader historical and scientific study of religion. And second, the fact that religious studies now involves not just traditional belief systems but also secular ideologies such as Marxism, humanism, and other meaning-giving systems. Indeed this enterprise has been labelled "worldview analysis,"[12] rather than religious studies.

In recent times, the study of African traditional religion has tended towards phenomenological-anthropological models. That is, a focus on field work-based materials and a critical appraisal of the materials from phenomenological and anthropological perspectives. The procedure by which phenomenological investigation is accomplished has been described as a two-tiered process of "morphological phenomenology" and "hermeneutical phenomenology."[13] The first signifies the classification of various types and structures that arise from an examination of the data, and the second means discovering "...the essence of meaning residing tacitly within the situation of the phenomenon."[14] Unlike theology which deals with dogma and the truth-claims of beliefs, hermeneutical-phenomenology is "...a descriptive science and it avoids evaluating the religious values of the data being analyzed."[15] Anthropology of religion, on the other hand, is that branch of anthropology concerned with religious phenomena and data. While there is no consensus among anthropologists as to what it considers its proper aims and objectives, most anthropologists of religion are concerned with the functional and symbolic analysis of religious phenomena. In essence, the modern historian of African religion must utilize the anthropological model to elucidate his search for symbolic meaning and functions of the phenomenon under investigation. Obviously this would be a different interpretative enterprise from one which is concerned with extremely remote texts and rites unavailable through the very tradition that produced them.

My contribution here proceeds with the premise that the methods of modern anthropology of religion and hermeneutical-phenomenology, despite their different philosophical assumptions, have some fundamental characteristics in common. Yet, an adequate interpretation of African religion seems to lie in the approach that transcends the limits of both methods. By integrating the findings of both methods in the analysis of African religion, one should be able to deal more than adequately with the complexity of the material being analyzed. For instance, while the primary hermeneutical concern of the history of religions would be to "understand" the religious character, qualities, and meaning of African religion, one cannot draw any hard and fast line between religion and the culture through which it is expressed. Hermeneutical-phenomenology has to be seen as a necessary starting point of any analytical discourse. The thrust of the discourse would in fact be sustained by evidence from the cultural life of the people. I would like to think that African religion, like other primal religions, expresses itself through all available cultural idioms, such as music, arts, ecology. As such it cannot be studied in isolation from its socio-cultural context.

The Place of History

The next main issue, then, is to discuss the place of history, and of society, in the study of African religions. Having examined the basic structure and meanings of the phenomena under study, it is important for the researcher also to proceed to show the historical process which has brought the religious phenomenon to its present situation. One must say then that the lack of an adequate diachronic analysis in most of the works on African religion has inhibited progress in that field. In the context of the contemporary study of religion (*religionwissenschaft*), emphasis is always on the history and phenomenology of religion. As Mircea Eliade once remarked,

> The ultimate goal of the historians of religion is not to point out that there exist a certain number of types or patterns of religious behaviour, with specific symbologies and theologies, but rather to understand their meanings. And such meanings are not given once and for all, are not 'petrified' in the respective religious patterns, but rather are 'open', in the sense that they change, grow and enrich themselves in a creative way in the process of history.[16]

Perhaps the most notable contributions so far to the historical analysis of African traditional religion come from the project initiated by Terence Ranger on the historical study of African religious systems. The project, sponsored by the Ford Foundation, initiated a newsletter which periodically issued information on current research and publications in east, central, and southern Africa. The publication also contained references to conferences on African traditional religions. One advantage of the project has been that several conferences have been held on the religious history of African traditional religion in key places in east and central Africa. The selected papers from the conference in Dar es Salaam were published in June, 1970.[17] The book remains the best available text on that issue until today. In spite of the fruitful impact of this historical project, similar studies have unfortunately not been replicated elsewhere in Africa. One would hope that a similar project on west Africa will take place in the near future.

The criticism expressed is not an indication that there has not been other serious work on the historical analysis of African religion; rather, it is an attempt to point out the challenges which exist with respect to the historical treatment of African religion. Researchers in this area must realize that primary and secondary sources such as government intelligence reports, missionary papers, travelling accounts, and other archival materials which can be judiciously used to chart the historical patterns of several aspects of African traditional religion are few and in some cases ethnocentric. This leads us to the next issue of major importance in the study and understanding of African traditional religion: the issue of resilience and adaptability.

Resilience and Adaptability

It is in the area of resilience and change that African traditional religion has demonstrated its most important contribution to contemporary knowledge. African traditional religion has been quite receptive to change. For example, its encounter with the two monotheistic religions which have come to Africa, Christianity and Islam, as well as with modernity, has transformed the religion and triggered various kinds of responses to the encounter. To take an example, Robin Horton[18] has postulated that there exist two spheres in a typical traditional (African) religious worldview — the microcosm and the macrocosm. In the microcosm, lesser deities limited to the local communities take charge of peoples' daily life. The concept of the Supreme deity, underpinning the "macrocosm," is not well developed. However, as a society's worldview is broadened in response to heightened international interaction through increased trade, communication, social, educational, and political changes, and as people become increasingly aware of and involved in the macrocosm, the microcosm becomes progressively less important. Simultaneously, there is a shift in religious focus from lesser "spirits" to the "Supreme deity," which becomes much more prominent in the affairs of the community. This more inclusive symbol provides the much-needed moral guidance in consonance with a new cosmopolitan worldview.

If Christianity and Islam were not present, Horton further argues, African traditional religion would have responded to changes within its communities. While several scholars in the past argued that changes in traditional worldview are due to the presence of Christianity and Islam, Horton argues that this conclusion is wrong and suggests that traditional religion was already actively responding to ongoing social change at the time of contact with other religions. This thesis reduces Islam and Christianity to playing a catalyst's role, stimulating, and accelerating social change already in progress.[19]

An enduring quality of Robin Horton's thesis is that it demonstrates that African traditional religion was not just a house of cards that collapsed at the instance of change, but that it has the potential to adapt to change on its own, in response to changes taking place around it.

Another significant form of religious change is that which occurs as traditional religion encounters Christianity and its products. In this process of religious acculturation, elements of the new religion and the old tradition are fused together to produce forms of religious syncretism. A fairly well-studied form of this is the new religious movement, often called Independent African Churches, in which biblical and African worldviews are combined in meaningful ways to the converts.

In conclusion, there is no doubt that few African scholars have concentrated their efforts on describing and analyzing the various forms of religious change in Africa. But what they have done has added much to the existing knowledge of the tradition. Much still has to be done, however, to unearth the structure and process of the continuous interaction between traditional religion, its environment, and the society at large. This seems to be the way in which traditional African religion makes its contributions to contemporary society.

Notes

1. Wilfred Cantwell Smith, "Contemporary Religion: Whither and Why?" in Mircea Eliade and Joseph M. Kitagawa (eds.) *The History of Religions: Essays in Method-ology* (Chicago: University of Chicago, 1959), 37-38.
2. Åke Hultkrantz, *The Study of American Indian Religions*, Christopher Vecsey (ed.) (New York: The Crossroad Co. and Scholars Press, 1983), 94.
3. *Ibid.*
4. See for example the following works: Benjamin Ray, *Religion, Symbol, Ritual, and Community* (Englewood Cliffs, New Jersey, 1976); David Westerlund, *African Religion in African Scholarship: A Preliminary Study of the Religious and Political Background* (Stockhold, Almgrist, and Wiksell International, 1985).
5. In a similar tone, the Belgian anthropologist and historian, Jan Vansina, called for an appraisal of recurrent themes in the African traditions to enable historians and social scientists to properly analyze African oral traditions. See "Oral Tradition and its Methodology," J. Ki-Zerbo (ed.), *General History of Africa*, Vol. 1 (London, 1981).
6. Michael Meslin, "From the History of Religions to Religious Anthropology: A Necessary Reappraisal," *The History of Religions: Retrospect and Prospect*, Joseph M. Kitagawa (ed.) (London: Macmillan, 1985), 33-34.
7. Benjamin Ray, *African Religions: Symbol, Ritual and Community*, 52.
8. *Ibid.* Voegelin, *Order and History*, Vol. II (Louisiana State University Press, 1956), 5.
9. *Ibid.*, 13.
10. *Ibid.*, 13.
11. Ninian Smart, *The Phenomenon of Religion* (New York: Herder and Herder, 1973), 79.
12. See Ninian Smart's work, *Worldview: Cross-Cultural Explorations of Human Beliefs* (New York: Charles Scribner's, 1983).
13. Walter I. Benneman Jr., O. Yarian and Alan M. Olson, *The Seeing Eye: Herme-neutical Phenomenology in the Study of Religion* (University Park and London: The Pennsylvania State University Press, 1982), 14.
14. *Ibid.*, 14.
15. *Ibid.*, 15.
16. Mircea Eliade, *Australian Religions: An Introduction* (Ithaca: Cornell University Press, 1973), 200.
17. T.O. Ranger and I.N. Kimambo (eds.), *The Historical Study of African Religion (with special reference to East and Central Africa)* (London: Heinneman, 1972).
18. "African Conversion," *Africa* 41 (April 1971), 85-108.
19. *Ibid.*, 104.

3

THE PLACE OF TRADITIONAL RELIGION IN CONTEMPORARY SOUTH AFRICA

Gerhardus Cornelis Oosthuizen

THE MAIN EMPHASES in the African traditional worldview can be detected in their traditional religions, which have much affinity with postmodern era worldviews. This significant development should not be overlooked, and it is appropriate to give specific attention to it in this context.

It is difficult to speak about a single worldview in Africa, as cultural heterogeneity predominates, and continuous interaction takes place between the urban and rural. Another question is whether worldviews can still be contrasted in the late 20th century, with the homogenization process of secularism winning ground even in the most traditional cultures. Although less than a third of Africa is considered to be urbanized, the secularization/modernization process has intensified. Because a culture has thousands of different aspects, the real influence of those aspects which really matter could be weak. In spite of the fact that Africa's population surpassed the 500-million mark, its levels of urban population are low, even though the speed with which such urbanization is taking place, in relation to the total population resident in the cities and towns, is among the highest in the world.

Urbanization today is more extensive in Africa than in most regions in Asia — India and China included. This brings dramatic changes — cities are the centers of policy, economy, and development. Urbanization is more of a mental reconstruction than a material phenomenon. Cities are seen as the centers of modernization by some, but by others they are seen as destroyers of traditions and parasites on the rural population. Most of Africa has inherited a tradition which penetrated established, indigenous urban traditions. But one cannot say that Africa has either a modern or a traditional worldview — both are present in much of the makeup of Africa.[1]

In Africa, cultural heterogeneity predominates; even ethnic groups in Africa integrate with difficulty or do not integrate at all. In spite of ethnic identity becoming vague with minorities, significant aspects of ethnicity remain. Because urban and rural cannot be contrasted per se in Africa as there is still a certain rhythm between the two ways of life, no specific worldview predominates. There is the Islamic, the Christian, the traditional (or classical) religious African — all mixed worldviews, the former influenced by the traditional worldviews and all of them influenced by the secularization processes.

The outdated "modernist" worldview has not yet overwhelmed Africa in the sense that it has not yet established a deep-seated secularism and philosophical skepticism as in the West. This Western worldview is closed, essentially complete and unchangeable, basically substantive and fundamentally non-mysterious; i.e., it is like a rigid programmed machine. This mentally constructed self-propelled entity has brought all metaphysics, and religion as well, into doubt. This closed worldview is foreign to Africa, which is still deeply religious. Africa associates itself more freely with the post-modernist worldview, which is more open, incomplete, changing and which becomes more 'rational'. This world is not closed, and not merely basically substantive, but it has great depth, it is unlimited in its qualitative varieties and is truly mysterious; this world is restless, a living and growing organism, always pregnant with new developments for the future.[2] Action, event, and change are emphasized more than substance and fixity.

Within the context of the deterministic worldview of the physicists of the last decade of the 19th century, all the important problems posed by nature were thought to have been solved, and all the fundamental principles of the physical world were known. Tremendous new discoveries such as radioactivity, X-rays, and the quantum phenomenon, however, raised issues that could not fit into this neat conceptual scheme. Post-modern science then started, and it covered the whole range, the encyclopedia of science and not merely physics. There is today a new psychology, a new sociology, a new technology, a new look at religion, and so on. This implies that a new era has dawned.

The "new" has to do with new ways of thinking and perhaps also believing. Some of the most fundamental presuppositions of the so-called exact sciences have been set aside. Nineteenth-century physics had an incomplete concept of the depth of the universe which strengthened the rationalistic skepticism about metaphysical realities. It is accepted today that the physical world is in a sense mysterious, that it cannot be fully explained, that matter has aspects which are not fully understood. The powerful new ways of thinking and believing that have come into being do include intuition and feeling with regard to the investigation of reality. This approach is not foreign to classical Africa, which did not have the scientific and technological expertise, but which retained the holistic disposition to the environment—its world was never a closed machine-like entity in which feeling and intuition had no place. This disposition is important in any situation in which secularist superficialities threaten the very depth of human existence.

Being unconscious of the depth of reality led practically to a situation of total unconsciousness, dominating the modern period, of the mysterious aspects of nature. Having become conscious of the dimension of depth in matter-energy, in space-time, and in the process of life, the human being experiences more the miracle of nature and the tremendous sense of the mysterious.[3] This sense of the mysterious has always been present in classical Africa and is still present in the traditional religious context. This depth is the key which opens the door to being conscious of the deep metaphysical aspects of existence, where not only miracles but also worship are accepted. A return to metaphysics in the face of positivist and linguistic emphases reveals the new trend also in philosophical circles in the West. The reaction is against the hard intellectual approach with its cold emphasis on objectivity; room is made for the subjective, non-rational, creative approach. The old-fashioned, strictly absolutist, "rational" approach of modern science has become untenable. It is indeed fortunate that the traditional African religious approach retained the sense of depth in human existence.

New insights into the nature of matter have given the universe a new look, about which scientists often speak. Reference is often made to an "in-depth" investigation, i.e., at a molecular level, such as in the new genetics, virology, physiology, and so on. When scientists use the term "mystery" in connection with the unexpected aspects that post-modern science brings to the fore, it includes the unending number of questions which confront the human mind. Every piece of matter is inexhaustible, and the unending number of scientific questions seek answers which are often not to be found in the rational sphere. Post-modern society has thus to live the best it can with scientific uncertainties. This has made the post-modern approach much more modest than the "know-it-all," archaic, limited, rational approach of the outmoded modernist period which still rules the world of secularism. Natural science has, however, changed radically; it has become intensely human and personal, and with imagination, intuition, and creativity, it brings new horizons to man. This has established a kinship to the traditional approach in Africa, which is most intensely expressed in its traditional religions.

The Traditional Worldview of Africa

The traditional African worldview has great difficulty with the cold, rational emphasis of the modernist worldview at the expense of other dimensions in people's existence. Africa has its own specific approach to the physical and metaphysical world as expressed in its classical religions. This is why Africans wish to interpret the soul of this continent themselves — the modernist, superficial, secularized Westerner is incompetent to understand it.

The metaphysical world for Africans is a reality; through their religion, the experiences they have supercede the one-dimensional approach of the modernist worldview, which makes itself felt on this continent, especially in industrialized southern Africa.

In the post-modern world, a kind of transformation of consciousness has taken place; the continuing process of the in-depth penetration into the secrets of this planet and the universe has led to a questioning of the superficial approaches of the 17th to the 20th centuries. Also, the theories about the "primitive" mentality, as contrasted with the so-called "modern" mentality, have been reexamined. The standpoint of Lucien Levy-Bruhl (1857–1939) was that the thought processes of what he called the primitive peoples were more concrete in expression and less logical and abstract in form than the rational approach of the modern world. He designates this as "mystical thinking" and refers to the so-called "pre-logical" mentality in this connection. In this thinking no contrasts exist between soul and body, between soul and matter, with the result that there is, for example, a holistic approach to healing.

Furthermore, the law of participation prevails—everything is part of everything else, the group precedes the individual. The group again cannot exist by itself but exists in conjunction with the supernatural world.[4]

What Levy-Bruhl denigrates as "mystical thinking" is echoed by the post-modern scientists in the sense that thinking goes beyond the mere rational, that there are other dimensions in "knowing," in analyzing, in experiencing, which should be considered more carefully. The traditional approach has assisted the Africans not to lose their balance in the overly rationalized modern world. The modernist approach has great limitations when it comes to the deepest issues in human existence. Africans do not wish to integrate the cold rationalist approach into their worldview and even less into their religious disposition. The main problem was that they could not accept its one-dimensional approach. While the modern approach dehumanized, the post-modern scientific approach rehumanizes—it has a marked influence on what is human. The areas of study do not merely lead to additions to what people already know, but, on the contrary, great changes take place in the way they know. Not only do people's mental equipment and potentialities change and become extended, but receptive faculties which were lost or atrophied are restored or renewed, and new ones come to the fore. Modern society became the victim of inhibiting attitudes and concepts during the modern era. Intuition is again receiving scientific appreciation, and the importance of the non-rational and trans-rational is again receiving a place in the experience of human beings.

The basic scientific and technological approach has to remain if society wishes to establish an acceptable level of material existence, but Africa has a sensitivity at the non-rational level which could make a valuable contribution to humanity's contemporary search for depth. This approach is expressed in the religions of black Africa. In classical southern Africa, religion embraces everything and is directed at the essence of things. Here the human being, not matter, is the center of the world, with the metaphysical forces as the sustainers, of which the Deity (deities) is the most powerful, and these forces have a mystical relationship with the world and its environment. There is no question of the homogenization of human existence. Furthermore, behind everything is a brooding, mystical power present in humans and objects—in different degrees of strength and effectiveness. The difficulty arises when emphasis is put on this mysterious power as an effective means to achieve one's aims. It withholds determined involvement to change one's environment, as the emphasis on the effectiveness of magic is irreconcilable with realistic action directed toward economic development.[5]

Traditional Religious Reaction against Objectivity without Personal Involvement

Objectivity which does not emphasize personal involvement is unacceptable. The emphasis on the mental digestion of biblical knowledge in Sunday schools and catechism classes of the established churches is contrary to the approach in the traditional religions and indigenous church context, where, through participation, the beliefs are, one might say, inhaled. Belief in Africa is not an epistemological issue, not *fides* (belief) but rather *fiducia* (trust), a non-epistemological activity. It is not based on propositions but on relationships. In traditional African religion it is more a question of trust, more a matter of relationships than of propositions of logical arguments which predominate. In the traditional religion it is the deep sensitive attainment rather than cerebral acceptance which takes precedence. The whole human being is involved in observation, functioning as a feeling, willing, and thinking unit. This is also reflected strongly in the African indigenous churches.

In the traditional religious context the Supreme Being was never far away—God and the other metaphysical forces were never far removed; existentially the metaphysical forces were always behind everything. The official approach of the King or Chief in Africa was not easy because of his elevated position. It was difficult to make contact with the Divine, just as it was difficult to make contact with a chief. Furthermore, if the Divine were to reveal Itself as It is, people's autonomy would suffer in Its presence. The direct presence of the Divine is more than a human being can bear. This is why ancestors are approached rather than the Supreme Being, and this is in line with the traditional hierarchical structure. God is only formally a *Deus Absconditus* but not existentially such. He reflects himself through various mediators who transfer His gifts to the human being, such as healing, well-being, and so on. It was the emphasis on the rationality of God, an order in nature created by God, which accounted for the development of science. This has unfortunately led to the crowning of reason to the detriment of the other dimensions of existence which receive attention in the traditional African context. The emphasis in the African traditional religion is on the relationship with the ancestors who are concerned with practical needs and on upholding the deep sense of community.

Traditional Religion and the Sense of Community

In the context of traditional Africa, people are surrounded not by things, but by beings—the metaphysical world is loaded with beings.

Thinking in this context is synthetic rather than analytically orientated, which implies that everything is interdependent and in the end has religious value. The traditional approach does not have a place for something which is religiously neutral. Furthermore, the whole of reality is of primary concern. Nature is not objectified as in science; orientation towards totality is reflected in the intense feeling of community. In modernist thinking, the principle of identity prevails — there is no sharing of being. For the traditional person in Africa, a communal unity of essence is possible — an individual is never a mere individual, but is also the other (who is not merely another).

In traditional African religion, personality receives the highest priority, and personality presupposes relationships. One of the main reasons for the existence of so many indigenous independent house churches in South Africa is that they are substitutes for the traditional intimate family relationships in a situation where such relationships are eroded as a result of the rapid secularization processes. Humanity in Africa is basically family, basically community, with a strong emphasis on the traditional religion and its symbiotic union with ancestors and spiritual entities in the metaphysical world. In the traditional religious context, all the acts from birth to death and thereafter bind the person as a communal being to everyone around themselves, especially those who have passed on to the metaphysical world and those still to be born. The sacrificial meals are symbolic, emphasizing that the family/community has been brought together with the ancestors. Those who die enter a condition of collective "immortality" and can be propitiated through sacrifices made to them. In traditional African religion, ontological harmony is of primary importance. The ontology of classical Africa is basically anthropocentric. The person is the center of existence — not as an individual, but as family, as community. To be blessed implies having children and food, and to be healthy, but this is the case only if the whole community shares in it. Based on this approach, most of the indigenous churches are simultaneously welfare organizations.

The circle symbolizes this togetherness — in the houses, in dancing, singing, and in having meals in a circle. The classical African approach to being human based on personal inter-relationships is much more biblical than the individualism of the modern world. John Taylor emphasizes, "Learn from Africa how to see people as the Bible does."[6] According to this approach, people do not exist for their identity, but for their involvement.

Time in the Context of Traditional African Religion

Time is such a vital issue, a fundamental and obvious aspect of human existence, that it needs close attention. The modern linear concept of time has left the impression that human beings are approaching the future, that they control time. Thus for them, progress is based on the race to make the best of time—a ceaseless time tension has entered human existence. Post-modern instruments and discoveries broadened humanity's outlook regarding the extent of time as well as the unending depths of local or immediate time. A second has acquired great significance. An electronic computer does in a second what a large team of trained human beings took months and even years to accomplish. To speak about a millionth and even a billionth of a second is not unusual today. Post-modern science has led us to realize the depth of time even more as a result of the vast expansion of the starry heavens. After Charles Darwin, when the idea developed that time does not pass without deep-seated changes taking place, time has assumed a dynamic meaning.

In traditional African thinking, time consists of events, i.e., what has happened, what happens, and what will soon happen. In this approach, the future is not an event and thus plays a minor role, while in the secularized world, the future is at the center of the time concept. Basically, Africa emphasizes a two-dimensional concept of time, namely a dynamic present and a long past.[7] The future in this cyclic concept of time is greatly devalued. Events merely come and go. The past receives the main emphasis; here the human being finds his orientation; here lies his roots; here he finds security. Here is the world of the ancestors from which he finds direction. There is here no emphasis on final fulfillment or the "end of the world."

The future in traditional African thinking is a short period—in most African languages it goes no further than a few months. Modern secularized people are controlled by time. Their whole civilization suffers from a time misconception. They are always tense. Their whole being is directed to a non-existent future which they plan meticulously. It is their focus point, with the result that they hardly exist in the present. The present is only a necessary stepping stone to the future, because there lies their hinterland, their utopia. The traditional person in black Africa is not controlled by time, rather, they control it. Time for the Westerner is of primary importance; the event for the traditional African is important, not time. What is important is not the time factor in an event, but the event itself—not being on time for an event, but being part of it, even for a small fraction of it, is what matters. The intensity of an event matters, and this intensity is seen in the traditional religious activities.

Not all time has significance; living time, often from midnight to sunrise, is in traditional thinking more loaded with vital force than others. Such times are intense because of the events that take place, such as the execution of special acts or sacrifices. Great gatherings in the so-called "established and indigenous" churches usually take place during Easter. Such times are intense because the events are intense. Time is a stream of events and is measured where these events are the most powerful.

With the coming of Christian missions, western education, science and technology with its accompanying rapid social change and focus on a non-existent future, chaos entered the existence of the black people, especially in South Africa. Furthermore, it is still a traumatic experience that religion and the human being's daily life have been separated. The fact that established Christianity created the impression that religion and daily personal needs could be separated is one reason for the proliferation of the indigenous churches in South Africa, of which there were 30 in 1913, 800 in 1948 (with a membership of 9 percent of the black population), 2000 in 1960 (with 18 percent), and 3270 in 1980 (with nearly 30 percent).

Furthermore, the shifting of time from the past to the future created a dangerously unstable situation in Africa; a disharmony as a result of the formation of what L. S. Senghor calls a "half caste" culture. The change from the traditional concept of time to the emphasis on the future has led to social and political instability.[8] But the serious question is whether the secular world's distortion of the time concept—a linear movement dragging us forward and upward—should not be rectified and restored to what time really is, namely, a cyclical issue related to an event, where the quality and intensity of the event take precedence and not abstract time. That black Africa is concerned about the absence of planning—the future has to be worked for if one wishes to reap its benefits—does not imply that one should be controlled by time, that it should become a totalitarian phenomenon which controls all dimensions of existence as is the case in the modern techno-scientific world. The cyclical concept of time, which is closer to reality and which is embedded in traditional thinking in Africa, should receive closer attention.

Christian theology has most probably been misleading in accepting as the one and only biblical approach the linear concept of time, that the present and future predominates. Should this future be interpreted merely in a linear context? The prominent theologian Schillebeeckx, for example, speaks of "the biblical primacy of the future over the present and the past."[9] He adds that one should not look back to the Bible but to the future with the Bible, and that the present and the past will be oriented to a new reality which is still to come.[10] In the indigenous churches, their looking back to the Bible has given biblical emphasis existential value; it lives in their context, and the emphasis is not "on a pie in the sky" in the future but on the well-being of people in the here and now. The future has in this regard new possibilities and realities and is not merely a deterministic process. The mystery of the origin of life and existence was always wonderful for Africa, the mystery of what has happened. For the modern world, with its secularistic emphasis, the mystery of what has not as yet happened is all-important, and this is faced with great intensity. Our maturity in the modern society does not lie in knowing the wisdom of (and what mattered in) the past, but what should be constructed in the future with our unequalled creative and transformative power. The shallowness of our civilization, the things we work for and enjoy, the existential situation of the world we have produced, could hardly be termed stable and mature. Research has shown that there is often much more stability and sense of security among the traditionalists than among those who try to find their salvation in what is modern.

Traditional Religion and Interpersonal Relationships

In this era, science and technology have become intertwined — previously they were only closely associated with one another. As a result of the 18th-century technological revolution, humanity has made a conscious jump "forward." Technological efficiency has increased a million times over. Not only our environment, but the individuals themselves are being transformed. Attempts are being made to solve problems thousands and millions of times more difficult than any before. In seconds we grasp what took months and years previously. The present generation has created magical forces through cybernetic science-technologies, which have brought forth unequalled possibilities. A major transformation has taken place, not only in the scientific-technological sphere, but because a new "spiritualization" of science is taking place, another segment of humanity becoming involved. We are seeing a holistic approach and a return to emphasis on the non-rational. There is a new order of human experience. Only a small percentage of human beings realize what is taking place, and even fewer fully comprehend it. To this new approach the traditional African culture stands much nearer than the so-called modern culture does. Africa's contribution to the development of science and technology has been limited, but Africa's contribution at the human level could be decisive, i.e., by assisting in keeping humanity human, by assisting humanity in being triumphant over the machine, the computer, and man's other ingenious inventions and developments. With the personalization of people's existence and the emphasis on human relations, the African traditional approach as expressed in classical religions and relationships could make a vital contribution.

Traditional Religion and Nature

Africa has never been divorced from nature. Post-modern science is very conscious of the fact that humanity cannot live apart from nature. Africa has not discarded the holistic approach. The importance of the approach is being rediscovered in our time. For the post-modern physicists, the atom itself has become a mysterious world. Mystery refers here to what is unknown, incomprehensible, and even impenetrable for the human mind in its fullness. Post-modern science reveals here a wonderful sense of modesty not evident in most modern scientific approaches. "Mystery" refers to the quality of the unknown. The world has more in store than what strict rational analysis reveals. It has non-rational elements which can only be grasped by intuition. The accumulation and deepening of knowledge does not decrease or diminish the sense for the mysterious but intensifies it. This confronts the homogenization of human existence. There are many today who are disturbed by the obvious fact that Western culture is tragically out of step with the basic character of the universe. The universe is fundamentally not materialistic but relationally orientated. It is morally obligatory for human beings to be more concerned than they are today with relational values. The universe, the individual, and community life are dependent upon holistic driving forces. Conscious cooperation and individuality in the community are among the highest values in the human being's existence — not separation, total independence, razor-edged competition, and individuality for its own sake. Africa's deep-seated respect for the wholeness of life could make a significant contribution in the post-modern era.

Traditional Healing Approaches and Their Significance in Contemporary South Africa

Apart from the sense of community, family adherence, respect of elders inculcated in their children, the deep sense of the presence of metaphysical forces (and the sense of security this gives), the relief of tension through rhythmic acts and singing, assistance rendered to the unfortunate in their circle, etc., traditional religion gives attention to diseases which Western-trained doctors and psychiatrists are unable to handle. The therapeutic methods of diviners, for example, are receiving more and more attention in South Africa, even by those who had originally rejected them out of hand.

The traditional healer/diviner has, even according to many African professionals, greater success in the alleviation of psychological disturbances than Western-trained psychotherapists. Historically, the state and the mental health profession have not recognized the value of indigenous healers but persecuted them instead. Mkhize states, "It obviously creates a gap in literature if there is all of a sudden emphasis on their importance as healers without an attempt to articulate the basis of their success or efficiency."[11] The traditional healer, directed by the ancestors and other spirits from whom he/she receives power, utilizes this supernatural power for healing purposes. The traditional healer is "very conscious of social order and group cohesion, and particularly family harmony and group dependency."[12] He/she operates within the specific social pattern of the people and also within the context of their religious awareness, which gives him/her a priestly role, consulting the ancestors and discovering their wishes or their diagnosis of the problems. He/she does not merely consult with the individual, but almost invariably works with the family, special friends, or the group. These are usually present at consultations. The traditional healer/diviner has a wider role than just healing, but acts also as consultant on family and other relationships, as priest, and as one taking a great interest in ecological issues. In other words, he/she also has the daily needs of people at heart.

Such a healer/diviner goes through an extensive training course. Of great importance is that such healers/diviners share the worldview of their clients, that they have strong personalities, and that they are *au fait* with the particular techniques utilized in traditional therapy. Compared with the Western-trained psychotherapist, the traditional healer has also to prove that he/she has certain specific qualities — not only the necessary qualifications which are not easy to obtain, but also that he/she has certain proven powers of divination, an acceptable social status, and that he/she acts professionally. Even the attire of the diviner used in therapy sessions demonstrates the dignity and majesty attached to the profession. These have culturally determined symbolic meaning.[13]

Of great significance are the expectations with which the client enters into the therapy situation, as this often has a remarkable influence on the outcome of the consultation. The main expectation is to be understood, and many Western-trained psychotherapists have not the faintest idea of the African cosmology, with its ancestral and other spirit-influences, the various supernatural causes and the effects of neglecting ritual observances. Many of the activities of the traditional healer are psycho-therapeutic. These are provided with warmth, empathy, and genuine-ness in order to restore confidence, doing so in a familiar way to bring more comfort to the patient than the cold, clinical Western approach.

Modern medicine has proven to be effective in explaining the causes of sickness and in putting into action the curative processes. Because of this it has not fully detected, however, its weaknesses in the traditional African context and thus fails to rectify its limitations in this context. Conceptual models of sickness and health vary. The arrogance of the Western-oriented model when it comes into contact with other models can easily cause frustration. For Africans health does not merely mean a healthy body or a healthy mind.[14] Disease is not just a physical or mental condition but is a religious matter.[15] Sickness implies that there is an imbalance between the metaphysical and the human world as the flow of numinous power/life force has been disturbed. This accounts for the holistic emphasis in healing.

Traditional healers should be made aware of conditions which could be treated more effectively in hospitals, and the hospital should consult reputable traditional healers in therapy-resistant cases of culture-bound syndromes in African patients. In this way an effective traditional healer could become a primary health worker.

A theory of indigenous etiology should lead to the inclusion of the belief patterns of clients on their records.[16] Medicine and methods used in the treatment of patients should be brought more within the African worldview for those who still adhere to it. Their beliefs should not be ignored. A combination of facilities offered by Western-trained health professionals and traditional approaches should receive closer attention. In a society where the sense of community is strong, the diviners will continue to play a prominent role as they are specialists in social rela-tions — this cannot be said of the Western psychotherapist. There is thus a definite vacuum which the traditional healer fills effectively.

Among Africans in South Africa, healing can never merely be viewed along conventional Western mechanistic lines bounded by the limita-tions of its closed, rational approach, because African healing is rooted in a worldview which is larger and broader. While Western medicine has become divorced from religion, and a split has taken place in treating the body, mind, and soul by the physician, psychiatrist, and priest, respectively, and the social worker has been concentrating on the social problems, the diviner relates to all these issues as a trusted person in the community. Religion remains of major significance in healing pro-cedures among Africans in South Africa, especially among the tradi-tionalists, those from the independent/indigenous churches with their

prayer healers/prophets (offices which are replacements for the diviners), and to a large extent among those from the established churches.
In spite of the individualistic scientific approach of each and every
hospital in South Africa, a large section of both urban and rural patients
wish to have their illnesses treated in a way that is to a certain extent a
traditional medical approach.[17]

Furthermore, collaboration between traditional healers and Western-
trained professionals is not foreign to certain areas in Africa.[18] Schweitzer reports that the participation of traditional healers in the treatment
and management of mental illness greatly contributed to a clearer understanding of the psychopathology and psychodynamics of the major
psychiatric disorders which occur in African patients.[19] In other areas,
the Medical Councils frown upon traditional healers, but many patients
leave these hospitals in order to consult traditional healers from whom
they often find genuinely effective assistance.

The diviners are on the whole intelligent and highly perceptive members of their communities; they are the priests, the sociologists, the
social psychiatrists, and dignified persons who command respect. They
are more than healers, taking a holistic approach to the patient's situation in all dimensions of his/her existence. The traditional healer is a
psychotherapist, being as effective in alleviating psychological and be-
havioral disturbances as any other psychotherapist; but he/she is more
than this, as indicated already. These factors reveal some of the reasons
for the growth of this profession.

In the indigenous church context, the traditional churches have grown
in South Africa mainly because "they are churches in the true sense of
the word; they are hospitals and they are social welfare institutions."[20]
The liturgical approach, the healing procedures, the strong sense of
community in these tremendously dynamic independent church movements in South Africa, owe much to some of the approaches taken in
the traditional religious context, in spite of the fact that they have
rejected many aspects of the traditional belief system.

Conclusion

The African traditional approach with its holistic emphasis has much to
give to the modern world with its closed, limited, merely rationalist
disposition. In the traditional religions in South Africa, the human
being is not dehumanized, but his/her personality is of value to the
community. The sense of being together, being one, is vital. The
traditional religious approach has made worship in the indigenous
church context more existential—religion here has to do with people's

various dimensions of existence. Religious activities are not merely something one sits through lifelessly, but are dynamic and related to specific needs in the South African traditional religious context, and this exerts a particular influence on the indigenous churches, which are deeply involved in the needs and aspirations of their flocks. Religious activities have assisted in providing security in situations of discrimination, deprivation, and oppression.

The post-modern worldview, which will hopefully become more prevalent, will find ready rapport with the traditional African worldview. If technology and science could help Africa to develop without becoming an ideology on this continent, and if Africa retains its sensitivity to the depth of human existence, this continent could be at the forefront of the restoration of mankind's true humanity.

NOTES

1. A. O'Connor, *The African City* (Hutchison University Library, 1983), 15.
2. H. R. Schilling, *The New Consciousness in Science and Religion* (London: SCM, 1973), 44.
3. M. Born, *The Restless Universe*, 2nd ed. (New York: Dover, 1951).
4. L. Levy-Bruhl, *La Mentalite Primitive* (Paris, 1925).
5. P. Gheddo, *Why Is the Third World Poor?* (New York: Mary Knoll, Orbis, 1973).
6. J. Taylor, *Primal Vision* (London: SCM, 1963).
7. J. S. Mbiti, *New Testament Eschatology in an African Background* (Oxford: Oxford University Press, 1971), 24.
8. H-J. Margull, *Aufbruch zur Zukunft* (London: Gutersloh, Gerd Mohn, 1962).
9. E. Schillebeeckx, *God the Future of Man*, transl. N. D. Smith (London: Sheed and Ward, 1968), 35.
10. *Ibid.*, 35–36.
11. H. B. Mkhize, "A Study of *Umthandazi*," paper read at symposium on indigenous healing approaches, Medical School, University of Natal, May 24, 1986; cf., by same author, *Indigenous Healing Systems and Western Psychotherapies*, M.A. dissertation, University of Natal, Pietermaritzburg, 1981.
12. R. W. S. Cheetham, and K. A. Griffiths, "The Traditional Healer/Diviner as Psychotherapist," *S. A. Medical Journal*, Vol. 62, 11 Dec. 1982, 957.
13. M. Gelfand, *Medicine and Custom in Africa* (Edinburgh, 1964); also his *Witch Doctor: Traditional Medicine Man in Rhodesia* (London, 1964). See also E. Fuller Torrey, *The Hind Game: Witch Doctors and Psychiatrists* (New York: Emerson Hall, 1972); also I. M. Mkhwanazi, *An Investigation of the Therapeutic Methods of Zulu Diviners*, M.A. dissertation, University of South Africa, 1986.
14. H. Ngubane, *Body and Mind in Zulu Medicine: an Ethnography of Health and Disease in Nynowa Zulu Thought and Practice* (London: Academic Press, 1977), 28.
15. J. Mbiti, *Introduction to African Religion* (London: Heinemann, 1975), 134.

16. M. V. Bührmann, "Thwasa and Bewitchment," *South African Medical Journal*, Vol. 61, No. 23, 877–879.

17. Cheetham and Griffiths, 960.

18. R. D. Schweitzer, "Indigenous Therapy in Southern Africa," *Bulletin of the British Psychological Society* 33, 278–281.

19. Schweitzer, 148.

20. M. Stovall, *Indigenous Churches in Southern Africa* (Bloomington, Indiana: University of Indiana Press, 1976), 26.

4

THE PLACE
OF AFRICAN
TRADITIONAL
RELIGION IN
CONTEMPORARY
AFRICA
THE YORUBA EXAMPLE

Wande Abimbọla

Introduction

THE PAPER IS MOTIVATED by the need to investigate how much of the traditional religion is left with the access gained by Islam, Christianity, and modern trends into the traditional religious situation in Africa. It is to be noted and appreciated here that despite the devastating effects of Islam and Christianity on the autochthonous religion of the Yoruba, the religion continues to hold its own and is regarded in modern Nigeria as one of the three major religions in the country. It is in this connection that one can talk of the place of Yoruba traditional religion in contemporary Yorubaland and Africa at large. In this study we will concentrate on the place and significance of Yoruba traditional religion in the Nigerian plural religious situation. It should however be noted that the situation in Nigeria is similar to what obtains in many other black African countries.

The Beginning of Islam and Christianity in Yorubaland: Conflict and the Decline of Traditional Religion

Islam reached Yorubaland several centuries before the Jihad of Uthman dan Fodio, but Christianity gained access much later in 1842 through Badagry. The following Yoruba saying explains the situation.

> Aye la ba'Fa
> Aye la ba 'Mọle
> Ọsan gangan nigbagbo wọle de.

> We met Ifa in the world
> We met Islam in the world
> It was late in the day that Christianity arrived.

The Decline of Yoruba Religion: Ile-Ifẹ as a Case Study

In order to gain a thorough understanding of our subject matter, we have made an in-depth study of the religious situation in Ile-Ifẹ, a sizcable Yoruba community believed by the Yoruba to be their ancestral home. It is obvious from the study that the decline of Yoruba religion as a formal entity in Ile-Ifẹ and its environs has been very rapid during the last generation. It is estimated that Yoruba religion has lost about 40 percent of its adherents during the last half century, and that at present it can claim but 60 percent of the total population. However, it would be erroneous to conclude from this that traditional religion plays no significant part in the life of the Ile-Ifẹ community. To a striking degree, traditional practices have been retained by those who have embraced Christianity and Islam, and they still play an important role in the community generally. Four aspects of Yoruba religion are selected for examination: the retention of the cults, the observance of the festivals in honor of the orisa, the place of Ifa divination, and the role which traditional medicine still plays among the Muslims and Christians in Ile-Ifẹ and its environs.

It was estimated that about 34 percent of all Muslims and a slightly higher percentage of all Christians attended one or other of the festivals in honor of the local deities. A slightly lower proportion of members of the established Mission churches participate in the traditional festivals.

Some of the cults are already only imperfectly understood, and it was evident that the significance of others is fast being forgotten. In other cases, there was some indication of a confusion between two or more cults. A bewildering number of deities are worshipped in Ile-Ifẹ. To make some order out of such a complex pantheon of divinities is by no means easy. However, a broad division can be made between those deities of national significance to all the Yoruba, and those which have special relevance only to the ancient city of Ile-Ifẹ.

It was noticeable that the national deities were not widely worshipped. As in most cultures, the "high god," *Olodumare* or *Ọlọrun* as he is known among the Yoruba, is not given any image and does not have shrines. The gods of the Yoruba myths are not venerated to any significant degree either by the Muslims or the Christians. It is true that many of these deities have temples often like that of *oriṣanla*, which are quite imposing in structure. But these cults seem generally to be in the hands of particular families which act as priests and guardians of the shrines.

Traditional Cults That Persist to Date in Ile-Ifẹ and Its Environs

Despite the decline, it is to be noted that a good number of cults exist to date in Yorubaland. First, the cults which concern the ancestors, the so-called living dead, play a role of considerable importance. One writer on Yoruba religion has declared that the "great annual appearances of the *Egungun* are the chief communal ancestral rites of the Yoruba." This is largely true. In addition, there are many family ancestral cults of varying importance.

A second national cult widely observed is that in connection with the oracle divinity known as Ifa. Ifa is also used to designate a method of divination and has been described in detail by the present investigator. Ifa is frequently resorted to in times of stress and crisis by the Christians. The festival of Ifa is still popular in many areas. Another widely venerated of the national deities, however, is the *ogun*, the iron god whose devotees are considerable in number and for whom many families maintain a household shrine. *Ogun* has become the patron of those professions that have to do with iron, such as farming, hunting, blacksmithing, and driving. Most families therefore, can be, to some extent, connected with activities over which *Ogun* exercises patronage.

Our second group of festivals—those which were connected with Ile-Ifẹ itself—supported the theory that the sociological, rather than the religious, significance is uppermost. There are a good number of festivals which are in honor of mythical or historical figures who had played an important part in the historical traditions of the town. It is sometimes difficult to be sure whether we are dealing with myth, legend, or history, as for example, in the story of *Oduduwa*, the traditional founder of Ile-Ifẹ and the great ancestor of the Yoruba. Here, it seems probable that the myth enshrines some genuine historical event, namely the advent of a victorious warrior-leader who was eventually deified after his death. There is a tradition which has it that we are dealing with the displacement of an ancient culture by that of new conquerors represented by *Oduduwa*.

A second popular group of festivals centers around *Mọremi*, who by the virtue of her beauty, wisdom, and courage is said to have saved the people of Ifẹ from the troublesome and intractable *Igbo* invaders. Others are the cults of *Oluorogbo* and *Ẹla*. The oral traditions have it that *Oluorogbo* was the son of *Mọremi*, the great heroine of Ile-Ifẹ, who offered her son as a sacrifice in payment of a vow. In this connection, it is interesting that in Ile-Ifẹ the festival of *Oluorogbo* is independent of that of *Mọremi*. In point of truth, as maintained by Idowu, *Oluorogbo* and *Mọremi* have no cultic connection.

It may be argued with some degree of plausibility that the observance of some of the traditional festivals and, to a lesser extent, of the cults by the Yoruba in general is largely a sociological phenomenon rather than a religious one. This would not, perhaps, be the case with the adherents of the traditional cults. But among the Muslims and Christians, the basic reason for the worship of the deities and the veneration of the ancestors is economic. In which case some patron deity such as *Ogun* is worshipped to ensure professional success. There is also a sociological reason. The observance of these cults and festivals in connection with the past is a pointer to the national desire on the part of the Christians and Muslims to be associated with the wider social group and its past heritage. Such group loyalty is even stronger in the case of the cult of the ancestors in which the family nexus is extremely pronounced. The traditional elements which are retained by the Yoruba Christians and Muslims in Ile-Ifẹ and its environs may thus well be of more significance to the sociologist than to the investigator into the phenomenology of religions.

It is interesting to note that what is left of the followership and practice of the traditional religion in Yorubaland is recognized by the Nigerian government. It is also important to note that African traditional religion is given a prominent place in the higher institutions in the country. It is taught up to university level in order to maintain the religio-cultural identity of Africans in the face of the world.

The Significance of Yoruba Traditional Religion in Contemporary Nigerian Traditional Festivals

A lot of festivals abound in Yoruba traditional religion. A good number of them are in honor of the most important divinities of the Yoruba such as *Ọbatala, Ọrunmila, Ṣango, Ẹṣu, Ọya, Oriṣa-oko, Sọnpọnna*, and a countless number of others. The significance of the festivals is seen as pointed out earlier, in terms of local trade and the phenomenon of religious co-fraternity generated by the festivals. The devotees of these divinities, as well as the Christians and Muslims, trade in some items needed for the celebrations irrespective of their religious leanings. What matters here is not the issue of religious differences, but how to effect sales of commodities and make profits. Here it is to be noted that, in consequence of these festivals and other items, the issue of religious solidarity has become a phenomenon to be reckoned with in Yoruba religious history.

Moreover, it is to be noted that during the festivals and in consequence of family solidarity, which existed before religious differences came into the show, Muslims and Christians usually join in the celebrations. Interviews conducted show that a good number of those who celebrate festivals such as *Egungun* and *Oro* in most parts of Yorubaland are either Muslims or Christians. Thus the traditional festivals serve as instruments to weld together the deities and their devotees, the *ọba* and his subjects.

The Significance of the Cult of the Ancestors: Death and Burial Rites

Here we shall have a specific look at the significance of burial and funeral rites in contemporary Yorubaland. The phenomena of death and burial rites usually bring people of diverse beliefs together since people come from various walks of life irrespective of their religious leanings as sympathizers, mourners, friends, and relations. Thus, regardless of religio-social differences, people troop together to sympathize with the bereaved and to mourn the dead by showing a kind of solidarity. The Yoruba shed all religio-social differences in mourning the dead and regardless of the religious leanings of the deceased and his survivors. These phenomena serve, at least, to effect some kind of interim peaceful co-existence or inter-faith fraternity during the mourning period, burial, and funeral ceremony. Traditional and modern singers, drummers, and choral groups are invited from various places, regardless of their religious leanings, to add flavor and gaiety to the ceremony. In this

connection, it is not entirely religion that dictates which singers or drummers to invite. What is important here is the question of skill in the work
and the choice of the children and relations of the deceased. Funeral
ceremonies as occasions of religio-social differences, transcend religious
camp or particularity. It is an occasion that usually serves as a sure locus
of contact in a heterogeneous or pluralistic religious community.

On such occasions, children, relations, and friends come in groups,
in uniform regalia to celebrate the occasion. What takes priority now is
social integration rather than religious differentiation and disintegra-
tion. The occasion is usually one of religio-social interaction and equilibrium, mutualization, and socialization. On such occasions, people of
diverse religious convictions talk together, dance together, sing together, trade together, move together, and exchange pleasantries and gifts.
Thus the occasion of a funeral celebration can be regarded as one of the
best times to effect inter and intra religious fraternity in Yorubaland.

The significance of grandiose funerals in the Yoruba pluralistic society
should not be left out here. The Yoruba, regardless of their conversion
to either Islam or Christianity, still attach importance to grandeur during burial and funeral ceremony. The importance attached to the ceremony is one of the reasons why they lay high premium on plurality of
wives and multiplication of children who they think would be able to
support them when they grow old and feeble and accord them decent
and grandiose burial when they die. Christianity, in particular, had acted
as a check to the Yoruba inclination for multiplicity of wives through
the practice of one man, one wife, but it has not been able to achieve a
serious success. A good number of Yoruba Christians still marry more
than one wife. Here, the issue of tradition is rated higher than adherence
to Christian practices.

Magic and Medicine

Magic and medicine are features of Yoruba traditional religion which are
still influencing Yoruba contemporary society, despite the incursion of
foreign religions and the Western system of therapeutics. The Muslims,
Christians, and others patronize local herbalists in Yorubaland for one
problem or the other. The issue of religious difference is not considered
important when it comes to solving a problem — physical, mental, spiritual, and mystical. In this connection Dọpamu observes:

> But in view of improved medical conditions and accelerating technological
> progress, beliefs in Yoruba magic and medicine have persisted. Observations
> have shown that there are many Yoruba, literate and non-literate, who still hold
> tenaciously to the beliefs in magic and medicine, especially those that are

relevant to their present-day needs. Although they may rely on the English medicine or spiritual healing, they still augment this by the use of Yoruba magic or medicine.

Magic that helps in this regard includes the following: *madarikan* magic that protects one against one's enemies; *ajẹpọ* magic that enables one to vomit any poison taken; *ajẹra* magic that renders poison taken harmless. Then we have *oogun awọn agba* magic that neutralizes the effect of the witches; *awure* magic that effects good luck; *ataja* magic that helps sales; *ifẹran* magic that makes everyone love one another; and *awijare* magic that enables one to win a case.

Another category of traditional medicine relates to the cure of the various diseases and ailments. A good number of the traditional medicinal items have been found to be very effective in Yorubaland. Thus the government of the Federation of Nigeria has been called upon in recent times to give official recognition to the traditional systems of healing, such that both the traditional and the Western practices can co-exist in hospitals and health centers. It is interesting to note that many diseases especially related to mental and psychological disorders which cannot be cured in the modern hospitals are being treated in the herbal homes of the Yoruba traditional healers.

Today in contemporary Yorubaland and Nigeria at large, there is always the sustained and insatiable demand for magical benefits, the elimination of evil agents, a sense of access to power, protection, the enhancement of status, health, increase in prosperity, and relief from both physical and mental anguish in day-to-day life. These are the various worldly activities which require the reassurance of supernatural goodwill and favor. As long as these activities and functions variously appeared to be fulfilled through the application of Yoruba traditional magic, and as long as people continue to show anxiety with regard to their future, Yoruba religion through the agency of its traditional magic and medicine would continue to be relevant to the contemporary African society.

Concluding Remarks

In the preceding pages we have been able to demonstrate that, despite the competition between Yoruba traditional religion and foreign religions, the former has not been relegated to the background. It should be accepted that Yoruba traditional religion no longer holds sway over the entire population in terms of cultic activities, yet it influences the society in various ways as itemized above. It is a statement of fact that traditional religion, despite the entry of foreign faiths, has been the *sine qua non* of the existence of the Yoruba. Foreign religions and modern trends have not been able to relegate traditional religion to the status of a thing of the past. The religion is as relevant and meaningful to a good number of the Yoruba, Muslims, and Christians alike in contemporary Yorubaland as it was in the pre-Islamic and Christian era.

Notes

1. The Jihad of Uthman dan Fodio started in 1804. For further details see I.A.S. Balogun, *The Life and Works of Uthman dan Fodio* (Lagos: Islamic Publications Bureau, 1975).
2. This saying shows the historic sequence of the entrance of the three religions practiced by the Yoruba into their society. Islam entered Yorubaland since the 12th or 13th century A.D. probably from Mali, known to the ancient Yoruba as "Ilu Mọle."
3. Ile-Ifẹ is believed by the Yoruba to be their ancestral home. The Yoruba also regard Ile-Ifẹ as the cradle of mankind.
4. See Bọlaji Idowu Olodumare, *God in Yoruba Belief* (London: Longman, 1962).
5. The ancestral cult known as *Egungun* is one of the most important cults of Yoruba traditional religion. The Yoruba remember their ancestors annually with elaborate festivals involving carnivals embraced by the entire community including the Christians and Muslims.
6. See E. G. Parrinder, *West African Religion* (London: Epworth Press, 1961), 123.
7. See Wande Abimbọla, *Ifa: An Exposition of Ifa Literary Corpus* (Ibadan: University Press Ltd., 1976).
8. See Bọlaji Idowu, *op.cit.*, 101–106.
9. *Oduduwa* is believed by the Yoruba to be the mythical figure who created dry land from water in ancient Ifẹ. All the kings of the Yoruba who wear beaded crowns are believed to have descended from *Oduduwa*.
10. P.A. Dọpamu, "Yoruba Magic and Medicine and Their Relevance for Today," in *Religious Journal of the Nigerian Association of Religious Studies*, 4, 1979, 3–20.

5

FLOWERS IN THE GARDEN
THE ROLE OF WOMEN IN AFRICAN RELIGION

John S. Mbiti

Introduction

A BEAUTIFUL PICTURE OF WOMEN in African society is presented in a proverb from Ghana, which says: "A woman is a flower in a garden; her husband is the fence around it!" (*Bannerman*, 19). In this paper I wish to examine the place and the role of women according to African Religion. The paper draws on three areas: mythology, proverbs and prayers.

In the area of mythology we are confronted with the picture of women in the early state of human existence. This is not history. The myth is broader than history in explaining some aspects of society. It is a language depicting truths or realities for which history does not provide a full explanation.

Proverbs express wisdom acquired through reflection, experience, observation, and general knowledge. They are closely related to the culture of each given society. To appreciate, understand and apply the proverbs correctly, it is useful and even necessary for one to be part of the culture concerned, or to study it carefully. We are not able in this paper to go into depth, but quoting or examining some of the proverbs here will give us a working picture of what the religious wisdom of African peoples says about women.

Prayers take us into the spirituality of those who pray them. They show us, among other things, the inner person, the needs of the heart (such as joy and sorrow, gratitude and disappointment, expectation and anxiety), as the praying person stands 'naked' before spiritual realities. Prayers open up a real realm for women to express themselves. So we want to see what women say in prayer, and thereby to get a glimpse into their spiritual life as it may be nourished by African religion and as it in turn contributes to African Religion itself. Some of the prayers are specifically women's prayers in composition and use; others are common to both men and women.

Women in African Mythology

A large number of myths is to be found in Africa. Each and every African people (the word 'tribe' has sometimes bad connotations in recent years) has its own body of myths, stories, legends, and oral history. We want to concentrate here mainly on the myths dealing with the origin of human beings, since women are featured very prominently in these myths.

Some myths speak about an original Mother of mankind, from whom all people originated. For example, the Akposso (of Togo) tell that when Uwolowu (God) made human beings, he first made a woman on the earth and bore her the first child, the first human being (*Baumann*, 138, 180). The Ibibio of Nigeria hold that the human beings came from the divinity Obumo, which was the son of the mother-divinity Eka-Abassi (*Baumann*, 180). In eastern Africa a story is told about a virgin woman, Ekao, who fell to earth from the sky and bore a son; the son got married to another woman and founded human society (*Baumann*, 49, 246). Other examples are mentioned by Baumann (pp. 245–248).

The main idea here is to link human life directly with God through the woman. She herself is created by God and in turn becomes the instrument of human life. She rightly becomes the one who nourishes and passes on life. This is beautifully illustrated in a myth of the Tusi (of Rwanda). They tell that the original pair of human beings was in paradise. But both the man and the woman were sterile; they could not bear children. So they begged God to help them. God mixed clay with saliva and formed a small human figure. He instructed the woman to put the figure into a pot and keep it there for nine months. Every day the woman had to pour milk into the pot, mornings and evenings. She was to take out the figure only when it had grown limbs. So she followed these instructions and after nine months she pulled out what had now become a human being. God made other human beings according to this method, and these later increased on the earth (*Baumann*, 204). The pot is here the symbol of the mother's womb, in which a baby takes shape and after nine months it is born. The woman shares directly with God in a personal way, the secrets and mysteries of life and birth. This role of the woman is so important that it is pictured as having already started in the mythological time.

In other myths of man's origin, the woman is always or nearly always mentioned. In many cases even the name of the first woman is given in the myths; some myths mention only the name of the first woman and not of the husband. A lot of myths say that the first human pair was lowered by God from the sky to the ground (earth), such as the myths of the Akamba, Turkana, Luo, Luhyia and others in Kenya; those of the Baganda and Banyoro in Uganda; those of the Tusi in Rwanda, of the Bemba and Ila in Zambia, of the Yoruba and Igbo in Nigeria, and of many others.

In a few myths it is told that the woman was made by God out of the man's body, or after the man had been made. Perhaps behind these myths is the wish and practice on the part of males (men) to dominate women. For example, the Kwotto of Nigeria say that God made the first human beings out of the earth (soil). He made (created) first the husband, and, when he had become tired, he then made the wife (woman) who turned out to be weaker than her husband (*Baumann, 204*).

Fire is an important element in human life. In some myths it is the woman who either invented or discovered fire. Women are also credited with inventing or discovering foodstuffs and their preparations. Thus the cooking skills of the woman are attributed to her from mythological times. She is thus not only the bearer of human beings, but also their cook who provides them with nourishment.

The life of the first human beings is generally depicted as having been in a form of paradise. God provided for them; in some cases they lived in the sky (heaven) with him, or he was on earth with them. God gave them one of three important gifts: immortality, resurrection (if they should die) or rejuvenation (if they grew old). However, this paradise got lost: the earth and heaven separated from each other and God went to live up in heaven while men lived on the earth. In place of the lost gifts came diseases, suffering, and death. There are many myths which address themselves to this change of human fortune. Some speak about a message which God sent to the people, but which either did not reach them or was changed by the messenger on the way; or the message arrived too late: a faster messenger from God had brought another message (of loss, death). Myths of the lost or changed or later–arrived message are very widespread in eastern, southern, and parts of western Africa. The carrier of the good message (of immortality, resurrection, or rejuvenation) is often the chameleon. The carrier of the contra message is often the lizard, the hare, the weaver bird, or the frog.

In some cases the myths speak of a test which God put to the original human beings. They failed the test. So the misfortunes of death and suffering, and of God's separation from men came about. Other myths explain that this happened as a result of jealousies and quarrels within human families. Still, in other myths, the cause originated from animals like the hyena which, being (always) hungry, sought and ate the leather rope that had united heaven (sky) and earth. (See further in *Baumann*, *passim*, and *Mbiti*, I, 171–177.)

There are, however, considerable myths which put the blame for this unfortunate tragedy on the woman. Thus, for example, it was a woman who, in Ashanti myths (of Ghana), while pounding fufu (the national food) went on knocking against God who lived in the sky. So God decided to go higher up. The good woman instructed her children to construct a tower by piling up the mortars one on top of another. The tower almost reached him, leaving a gap which could be filled with only one mortar. Since the children had used up all the mortars, their mother advised them to take the bottom-most mortar and fill the final gap. As they removed this mortar, the whole tower tumbled down and killed many people. In one of the Bambuti Pygmy (Zaire) myths, it is told that God gave the first people one rule: they could eat the fruits of all the trees, except from one tree. The people observed this rule, until a pregnant woman was overcome by food desire and persistently urged her husband to get the forbidden fruit for her. Finally he crept secretly into the forest, plucked the fruit and brought it to her. However, the moon was watching all this and went and reported to God. God became so angry that he sent death to the people as punishment.

While the woman is in these and some other myths blamed for the misfortune that befell the first human beings, she is clearly not the main nor the only culprit. Indeed the myths which put the blame on her are proportionally few. They indicate that she shares in the causes and effect of suffering, misfortune, and death in the world. She is a human being like men and children. She is also faced with the mysteries of life at the other end. Just as she shares in the mysteries of life's beginning, so she shares in life's end.

Through the myths of origin, we get a picture of the woman as someone placed by God in a special position. She shares with him the creative process of life. In some ways her position and her role in these myths eclipse the position of the husband (male). She is in a real sense an agent of God. At the same time the woman shares in the misfortunes, suffering, and death which in various ways came into the world.

Women in African Proverbs

Here we shall consider the woman as seen and depicted in African wisdom, in the proverbs of the ages. There are infinitely more proverbs than myths. We find them in every African people. They address themselves to many themes and areas of life and knowledge. They are very concentrated in the sense that they put a lot of thoughts, ideas, reflections, experiences, observations, knowledge, and world views, into a few words. We shall quote only a few proverbs here and try to capture what they intend to put in a few words.

Women are pictured as being extremely valuable in the sight of society. Not only do they bear life, but they nurse, they cherish, they give warmth, they care for life since all human life passes through their own bodies. The following proverbs bring these points out clearly.

"Wives and oxen have no friends" (*Barra*, 2). This means that the wife is so valuable that she cannot be given over to even the best of her husband's friends to keep her as his own. For that reason, another proverb reminds us that "A woman must not be killed" (*op. cit.*, 62). She is the mother of life, and to kill the woman is to kill her children (real and potential); it is to destroy humanity itself. The woman should be handled with respect and not be treated as if she were a slave. So another proverb asks the husband: "Did you buy me with elephant tusks?" (*p'Bitek*, 6), if the husband is illtreating her. She thereby reminds him that he really cannot buy her; she is not a commodity for sale like elephant tusks or slaves.

Even an aged woman is a blessing to men. So another proverb says: "It is better to be married to an old lady than to remain unmarried" (*Kalugila*, 5). There are areas of human life which only the woman can fulfil. The unmarried man is lacking something as another proverb explains: "It is at five that man succeeds" (*Massek* and *Sidai*, 42). This proverb by the Maasai of Kenya and Tanzania means that a successful life needs "a wife, a cow, a sheep, a goat, and a donkey." This is a reminder that, even if one is rich, one is not successful as long as one lacks a wife.

The value of the woman begins already when she is born and not when she gets married. So it is stated: "A baby-girl means beautiful cows" (*Dalfovo*, 214). Already at birth the woman is destined to be married—so the people believe. In traditional African society this entails a bride-exchange in form of cattle, services, foodstuffs, family ties, or other expressions of the marriage contract. Furthermore, the woman will bear children and thus enrich her husband and the wider circle of relatives from both sides. So the Tsonga and Shangana people of South Africa (Azania) say: "To beget a woman is to beget a man" (*Junod*, 179). This saying carries with it the hope and expectation that, after marriage, the wife will bear both girls and boys.

The woman who is not married has practically no role in society, as far as traditional African world-view goes. It is expected that all women get married. So a proverb of the Lugbara (Uganda) states: "An ugly girl does not become old at home" (*Dalfovo*, 286). This means that the looks of a girl should not stop her from getting married. Otherwise this would deny her the role of womanhood.

This thought is bound up with the value attached to the bearing of children. The childless woman goes through deep sorrows in African society. It is said, for example, by the Gikuyu (of Kenya): "The woman who has children does not desert her home" (*Barra*, 60). This means that bearing children gives the woman the security and joy of a family, of being taken care of in her old age, of being respected by the husband and the wider community. So another proverb states that "the woman whose sons have died is richer than a barren woman" (*Barra*, 61). This means that people will excuse a woman (mother) for losing her children through death, but the one who does not bear is hardly 'excused.' Consequently people say: "A barren wife never gives thanks" (*Kalugila*, 20)—nothing else is as valuable as having children; they are the deepest cause for giving thanks. If a woman has everything else, except children, she would have no cause or joy to give thanks. The sentiment is expressed in African societies that the more children one has the better. So the Ghanaians say: "A serviceable wife is often blessed with the birth of a tenth child" (*Bannerman*, 19). Parental blessings often run along the lines of "May you bear children like bees! May you bear as many children as calabash seeds!" Today's economic and educational pressure will force a change in these sentiments, where parents feel the pressure to reduce the number of children they can support and educate adequately. Nevertheless, African society is carried away by the proverb which says: "The satiety of a pregnant woman is off-spring" (*Dalfovo*, 238). This means that motherhood is the woman's fulfillment.

The mother or wife is probably the most important member of the family; she is the center of familyhood. So it is said by the Akamba of

Kenya, for example: "He who has not travelled thinks that his mother is the best cook in the world." This proverb, while attacking a narrow horizon in life, shows how central the person of the mother is. This same sentiment is expressed in another proverb, from the Gikuyu of Kenya: "The baby that refuses its mother's breast will never be full" (*Barra*, 33). This means that other people may feed the baby or the person concerned, but their food would never satisfy as well as that provided by the mother, who also provides warmth and security.

The place of the mother is further indicated by comparing her with other women or wives, whether she is alive or dead. The Swahili of eastern Africa say categorically: "The stepmother is not a real mother" (*Kalugila*, 17). This sentiment is shared by other peoples and is expressed in various ways. For example: "Somebody else's mother, however good she may be to you, can never be better than your own mother," or "A sheep does not lament the death of a goat's kid," or "Your stepmother is not your mother," (*p'Bitek*, 10, 14, 11), all from the Acholi of Uganda. Their neighbors the Lugbara put it this way: "There are not two mothers," or "There is not another mother" (*Dalfovo*, 78, 108). From southern Africa we hear: "The mother's breast cannot get leprosy" (*Junod*, 159). All these and many other proverbs indicate that the mother's role cannot be one hundred percent duplicated, for what she means personally: she provides (or should provide) the best love and tenderness, warmth, care, bodily and emotional nourishment, and much more. All this begins already, when the person is still inside the mother's womb and lasts (or should last) until the mother has died, or indeed, it continues when she dies and becomes a spirit, a living-dead.

It also means that the love, the care and tenderness should be reciprocated by everyone towards his or her own mother, since everyone has a mother. So we hear admonitions like these: "A child does not laugh at the ugliness of his mother" (*Dalfovo*, 208) from the Lugbara of Uganda; or "The mother of the big he-goat has no horns" (*Kimilu*, 115) from the Akamba of Kenya. This last proverb indicates that all the "big" men (such as artists, generals, presidents, singers, bishops, doctors, professors, inventors, scientists and so on) are each born of a woman, of a mother who may not herself be regarded as a "big" person in society. She may not "have horns," but she gives birth to a "big" person in society and deserves respect and recognition for it.

Women are human beings and as such they also have their weaknesses. African society knows these weaknesses and speaks about them openly. One of these is jealousy, especially when several wives live together in a polygamous family. Three proverbs from the Lugbara of

Uganda illustrate this weakness clearly: "The tongue of co-wives is bit-
ter!" or "The tongue of co-wives is pointed" (which means that co-wives
can sting each other with their talking), and "A co-wife is the owner of
jealousy" (*Dalfovo*, 58, 59). Such domestic problems can affect the husband who has the task of pleasing each wife. So a Ghanaian proverb
asserts: "Polygamy makes a husband a double-tongued man" (*Bannerman*, 18). The husband's role is not easy if the co-wives do not get on
well with each other. He may be seen to favor one more than the others.
In this case he could be rebuked with a proverb like "This polygamist
ploughs one field only" (*Junod*, 179). This indicates that in fact the
husband may provoke the co-wives to show jealousy, when they realize
that he favors one of them more than the others.

However, the fact that jealousy may arise in polygamous families is
not basis enough to condemn polygamy as such. There are many happy
polygamous families, just as there are even more unhappy monogamous
families. Jealousy is not confined to polygamy. Indeed, there are proverbs that show and urge respect for polygamous families. For example,
the Lugbara (Uganda) remark "Uncriticized, are you the senior wife?"
(*Dalfovo*, 51). This is a reminder to people that the senior wife is the
focus of highest respect in the family; nevertheless, she is not so perfect
that she cannot also be criticized. In any case, she has more respect by
being a co-wife than she would have if she were the only wife in a
monogamous family. It is said in Kenya: "Axes carried in the same bag
cannot avoid rattling," to mean that, among other things, it is not so
terrible if co-wives "rattle" with each other. They belong together as a
family. Indeed, a proverb from the Tsonga of southern Africa can be
applied to support the "value" or even "necessity" of co-wives: "A pole
is strengthened by another pole" (*Junod*, 1910). If women in African
society would have found polygamy to be unbearable, the custom would
have died long ago. One proverb reminds us that in such families there
are mutual support, love, care, and friendship: "The way to overcome
cold is to warm each other" (*Junod*, 191).

There are also prejudices shown to women in African societies around
the world. Here are some examples of prejudice and condemnation
towards women. Among the Tsonga-Shangana people of southern
Africa, it is sometimes said "This woman is a fire," or "This woman is a
deceitful and ferocious crocodile" (*Junod*, 187). Even the beauty of
women may earn them remarks like "Do not desire a woman with
beautiful breasts, if you have no money!" (*Junod*, 187), to mean that
beautiful women are expensive to win and maintain. The Gikuyu of
Kenya say: "Women, like the weather, are unpredictable," and "Women

have no secure gourds, but only leaking, upside down ones" (*Njururi*, 1). The second of these sayings means that "women are given to letting out secrets. You can't trust women with secrets." The same point is expressed in another proverb of the Gikuyu: "Woman, remember that the mouth is sometimes covered with a branch" (*Barra*, 92), to mean that the woman does not know how to keep secrets, how to shut her mouth when it comes to letting out secrets.

It is thought that women ruin men. So the Maasai remind us: "The prostitute can make you useless" (*Massek* and *Sidai*, 32). This proverb is one-sided, in that it does not blame men for what they do to women! The Maasai also accuse the woman of being short-sighted by saying that "A woman cannot see her palm" (*Massek* and *Sidai*, 29). In Uganda the Acholi complain that "Women have no chiefs" (*p'Bitek*, 10), to mean that "women cannot allow another woman to be superior. In another sense, a chief is not a chief to his own wife or wives, or even to other women." Naturally, when the men occupy so many of the superior positions in society, what more is left for women? The woman is often blamed for disputes in a marriage, even though in most cases these disputes are caused by both partners. So there are proverbs in Tanzania, for example, which say: "A lazy wife does not miss going to her parents frequently," or "The good wife is at her husband's home, the other one is at her parents' home" (*Kalugila*, 19). But what happens to lazy men, or do they not exist? Women are also accused of domineering their husbands, whatever the realities may be: "No man is a hero to his wife" (*ibidem*).

African men complain that they cannot understand women. So the Ghanaians say "When women increase in wealth, they are silent. But when they fall into trouble, the whole world gets to know." In another saying we hear that "In a town where there are no men, even women praise a hunchback for being the fastest runner" (*Bannerman*, 19, 38).

There are men (and women) who fear women, considering them to be dangerous. So we hear proverbs like: "To marry is to put a snake in one's handbag," and even to take up contact with women is an evasive undertaking: "One does not follow the footprints in the water" (*Junod*, 177), which means that "following a woman is like following footprints in water" because "the way soon vanishes." It is even claimed that words of women have no legal value, as the women are not reliable: "Women have no court" (*Junod*, 175). Women are feared and said to ruin men. "Marriage roasts (hardens)" (*Junod*, 175), is said to mean that a man's heart hardens after marriage, because of his wife. Even beautiful women get a share of prejudice: "Beautiful from behind, ugly in front" (*ibidem*) – a proverb which warns that a person may look attractive or say nice words at first, but after getting married turns out to be really 'ugly' in a deeper sense.

f) In spite of these and other prejudices against women, there are many beautiful things said about them. Some of these we have already encountered. Men will fight over women, to show how much they value the women concerned. So in Ghana we hear that: "Two bosom friends that vie one and the same lady have chosen a common road to be each other's enemy" (*Bannerman*, 19). It is also from Ghana where we have the beautiful comparison and mutual complement between the wife and the husband: "A woman is a flower in a garden; her husband, the fence around it" (*ibidem*). So the women need all the protection and care that men can give them. For this reason the Lugbara say: "The man dies in the wind, the woman in the house" (*Dalfovo*, 57). The woman and the man belong together; they can and do love each other; they need each other. So in another Lugbara proverb we are told: "The woman is the rib of man" (*op. cit.* 237). This statement is parallel to the biblical crea- tion story in Gen. 2:21f., in which the woman, Eve, is said to have been made out of the rib of the man, Adam. The Akamba (Kenya) warn against the danger of remaining unmarried: "He who eats alone, dies alone," and this means that he leaves neither wife nor posterity to re- member him in the world of the living.

Women and Prayers

In traditional African life the women play a significant role in the religious activities of society. One of the areas where this role is promi- nent is in offering prayers for their families in particular and their communities in general. In many areas there were (and still are) women priests (priestesses). Almost everywhere in Africa the mediums (who are so important in traditional medical practice) are nearly always women. In most cases it is also the women who experience spirit possession. Traditional healing is a profession of both men and women, but it is more often the women practitioners who handle children's and other women's medical needs. In this paper we have space for only a few prayers which illustrate how actively involved the women are in the spirituality of African religion. The examples are cited out of my own book: *The Prayers of African Religion*, 1975.

A woman's morning prayer runs: "Morning has risen. God, take away from us every pain, every ill, every mishap. God, let us come safely home" (*Mbiti*, II, 31). In this prayer the woman (mother) brings before

God her family and hands it over to God, believing that he will keep away all evil. It is a prayer from the Pygmies of Zaire.

The Aro women of Sierra Leone pray in a litany for a sick child. They address it specially to the departed members of the family who are taught to participate in the healing process by conveying the request to God. The mother prays: "O spirits of the past, this little one I hold is my child; she is your child also, therefore be gracious unto her." The other women chant: "She has come into a world of trouble: sickness is in the world, and cold and pain; the pain you knew, the sickness with which you were familiar." The mother prays on: "Let her sleep in peace, for there is healing in sleep. Let none among you be angry with me or with my child." The other women take up their chanting: "Let her grow, let her become strong. Let her become full-grown. Then will she offer such a sacrifice to you that will delight your heart" (*ibidem*, 50). In this prayer we see how close to the spirit world the women feel. They enter into it, they solicit help from it. The physical and spiritual worlds mingle here in a harmony of "going" and "coming." The women depict here a deep sensitivity towards the invisible and spiritual realities.

A woman whose husband is away fighting in war prays for his protection and safe return. She prays not just for him alone, but for others who are with him. Like all similar prayers all over the world, this is one-sided, favoring one's own side. It comes from the Banyarwanda and pleads: "Let him be saved with those who went with him! Let him stand firm with them. Let him return from the battle with them..." (*op. cit.*, 83). In this way the women participate in fighting on the side of their husbands. The husbands would be encouraged to get this form of spiritual support from their wives.

Recognizing that menstruation is intimately linked to the passing on of life, many African peoples perform a ceremony to mark the first menstruation. At one such ceremony in Ghana, the Ashanti mother of the concerned girl prays that she may grow to full maturity and bear children. This is the wish of every mother for her children. "Nyankonpon Tweaduapon Nyame (Supreme Sky God, Who alone is great), upon whom men lean and do not fall, receive this wine and drink. Earth Goddess, whose day of worship is Thursday, receive this wine and drink. This girl child whom God has given to me, today the Bara state has come upon her....Do not come and take her away, and do not have permitted her to menstruate only to die" (*op. cit.*, 96).

In many parts of Africa it does not always rain enough. Rainmaking ceremonies are performed at which sacrifices, offerings, and prayers are made to God, beseeching Him to give more rain or to let it rain if the rain has delayed. Here is one such prayer made by the Maasai women

of Kenya and Tanzania. The woman leader intones one part while other
people who are present for the occasion sing or recite the other part:

> Leader: "We need herbs on the earth's back!"
> Others: "Hie! Wae! Almighty God."
> Leader: "The father of Nasira has conquered, has conquered."
> Others: "The highlands and also the lowlands of our vast country which
> belongs to thee, O God."
> Leader: "May this be our year, ours in plenty (when you grant us rain!)."
> Others: "O messenger of Mbatian's son" (*op. cit.*, 113).

This prayer is for the welfare of people, animals, and nature at large,
since all depend on water for their survival.

Women express gratitude to God after childbirth. Then they know
that life comes ultimately from Him and is sustained by Him. The following prayer is said by Pygmy women in a ceremony dedicating a baby
to God. The mother and father lift the baby towards the sky and pray:

> "To Thee, the Creator, to Thee, the Powerful, I offer this fresh bud, new fruit
> of the ancient tree. Thou art the Master, we thy children. To Thee, the Creator,
> to Thee, the Powerful: Khmvoum (God), Khmvoum, I offer this new plant"
> (*op. cit.*, 124).

The sorrows of being childless go very deep in the wife. There are
many prayers for help in such situations. From an affected woman of
the Barundi we get the following prayer, in which we feel with her the
agony of her spirit:

> "O Imana (God) of Urundi, if only you would help me! O Imana of pity,
> Imana of my father's home, if only you would help me!...O Imana, if only you
> would give me a homestead and children! I prostrate myself before you, Imana
> of Urundi. I cry to you: Give me offspring, give me as you give to others!
> Imana, what shall I do, where shall I go? I am in distress: where is there room
> for me? O Merciful, O Imana of mercy, help this once!" (*op. cit.*, 86).

Death also brings with it is own sorrows and problems, and many
prayers are offered in such times. The following prayer pours out des-
peration with the same forcefulness as the previous prayer:

> "My husband, you have abandoned me. My master is gone and will never
> return. I am lost. I have no hope. For you used to fetch water and collect fire-
> wood for me. You used to clothe and feed me with good things.... Where shall
> I go?" (*op.cit.*, 99).

This prayer comes from the Basoga of Uganda, but its echoes can be
heard all over Africa.

It is clear that women both participate in the religious activities of
society and make their own contributions for the spiritual welfare of

their lives, their families, and of society in general. Through prayers women express themselves as self-determining. The prayers are a small window that open into their spirituality which indeed is the spirituality of all human beings. As the women share with God in the great mysteries of passing on life, so they share also in giving human life a spiritual orientation. They are truly flowers in the garden. They give beauty, scent, and seed to life.

References

J. Yedu Banner, *Mfantse-Akan Mbebusem* (Ghanaian Proverbs), Ghana Publishing Corporation, Accra, 1974.

G. Barra, *1,000 Kikuyu Proverbs*, East African Literature Bureau, Nairobi and Macmillan & Co., London, 1960.

Hermann Baumann, *Schöpfung und Urzeit des Menschen im Mythus der afrikanischen Völker*, Reimer, Berlin, 1964 (2nd ed.).

A.T. Dalfovo, *Lögbara Proverbs*, M.C.C.J., Rome, 1984.

Henri Philippe Junod and Alexandre A. Jacques, *Vutlhari Bya Vatsonga. The Wisdom of the Tsonga-Shangana People*, Central Mission Press, Pretoria, 1957 (2nd ed.).

L. Kalugila, *Swahili Proverbs from East Africa*. Methali za Kiswahili toka Afrika Mashariki, Scandinavian Institute of African Studies, Uppsala, 1977.

David N. Kimilu, *Mukamba Wa Wo*, East African Literature Bureau, Nairobi *et al.*, 1962.

A. ol'Oloisolo Massek and J.O. Sidai, *Enjeno oo Lmaasai*. Wisdom of Maasai, Transafrica Publishers, Nairobi, 1974.

John S. Mbiti, I, *Concepts of God in Africa*, S.P.C.K. London, 1970.

Ngumbu Njururi, *Gikuyu Proverbs*, Macmillan and Company, London, 1969.

Okot p'Bitek, *Acholi Proverbs*, Heinemann Kenya Ltd., Nairobi, 1985.

6

THE ROLE OF WOMEN IN AFRICAN TRADITIONAL RELIGION

AND AMONG THE YORUBA

Joseph Akinyẹle Ọmọyajowo

Introduction

THIS PAPER WILL MAINLY FOCUS on the possibility of a feminine image of deity in our traditional religion and the functions of women in the religious system of the Yoruba race in a world that is so fundamentally masculine and in which women are not accorded any visibly prominent status in religious matters.

Generally and globally, the superiority of men over women has always been taken for granted. Women themselves seem to have internalized this image of female inferiority (a situation in which I have seen the women's liberation or feminist movements as no more than apologetic) and have therefore somehow taken male domination as the natural order of things.

The Oriental world keeps women behind the veil, and they continue to be denied the right to think for themselves. Jewish thought did not regard women as a necessity but merely as helpers to men. In this regard, Professor Ọmọṣade Awolalu's conclusion is that the woman surrenders to the standard of a man-made world in which she finds herself, and her husband becomes her keeper in every sense. According to him, the woman hardly decides anything on her own, even the small details of her daily life are settled by her husband.[1]

The Jews had a strictly masculine concept of God: We read of the God of Abraham, of Isaac, and of Jacob and not of Sarah, Rebecca, Leah, or Rachael.[2] In their synagogue assemblies, they never counted women to make a quorum. This prejudice was crystallized in the miracle of feeding performed by Jesus. The figure of five thousand was said not to include women and children. To Paul, it was an anathema for a woman to speak in the church; if there was anything she wanted to know, she should ask her husband at home. In Islam, women could only lead prayers for a congregation of women. In the mosque women are not to stand in the same row with men but separately behind the rows of men.

African Concept of God

The African concept of God is not altogether masculine. In many parts of Africa, God is conceived as male, but in some other parts, he is conceived as female; the Ndebele and Shona ethnic groups of former Rhodesia have a triad made up of God the Father, God the Mother, and God the Son. The Nuba of the Sudan regard God as 'Great Mother' and speak of him in feminine pronouns. The Ovabo of South West Africa say that "the mother of pots is a hole in the ground, and the mother of people is God."[3] Although called the queen of Lovedu in South Africa, the mysterious 'She' is not primarily a ruler but a rain-maker; she is regarded as a changer of seasons and the guarantor of their cyclic regularity.[4]

There may be more cases of a feminine image of God than we can easily identify here because of the difficulty created by the fact that most African languages have identical male and female pronouns. Be that as it may, we can safely conclude that African traditional religion is, generally speaking, less sexist in its masculine image of God than other religions. This may be the factor that makes it possible for men and women to perform sacerdotal functions in the worship of the deity and of his functionaries, the divinities, who are also in both sexes.[5]

The Akan of Ghana and the Igbo of Nigeria have a feminine image of the Earth Spirit. Although the Akan did not regard Asase Yaa (the

Earth Spirit) as a goddess, they nevertheless rank the spirit after the Supreme God and pour libations and sacrifice fowls to her. The Igbo accord worship to Ani (or Ala or Ale) as Mother goddess, or Queen of the under-world, who is responsible for public morality.[6] Ani is the most-loved deity and the one who is closest to the people. She helps them if they are troubled by other divinities, but punishes hardened criminals.[7]

The Yoruba Concept

Among the Yoruba of Nigeria, Oduduwa, its progenitor, is believed by certain traditions to be a female orisa (divinity). J.O. Lucas asserts that there is hardly any doubt that Oduduwa was originally a female deity. With her adoption as the progenitor of the Yoruba race, there seemed to have arisen a tendency to regard her as a leader and a hero in consequence of which later stories transforming her as a male deity, were invented.[8] This male-divinity tradition has become very strong in Ile-Ife, where originally the myth that Oduduwa was a female divinity (she was called Iya, male-mother of divinities) was well known. However, today, the popular tradition is that Oduduwa was the strong and powerful leader under whom the nucleus of a strand of the present Yoruba race migrated into the land from their original home. The import of all this is that the powerful progenitor of the Yoruba race was believed to be originally a female divinity; and it can therefore be argued that the Yoruba society was at one time based on a matriarchal system.[9]

Yemoja (literally Yeye-omo-eja; mother of fishes) was also a female Yoruba divinity representing water. The myth was that she had a good-for-nothing son who committed incest against her. The mother fled, and the wicked son pursued her until she fell backward as a result of exhaustion. Streams of water poured from her body and eventually united to form a lagoon. The divinities that emanated from her include: Olosa (lagoon goddess) Olokun (God of sea) Oya (goddess of River Niger) Osun (River Osun goddess) oba (goddess of River Oba) Orisa-oko (fertility god) etc., etc. The priesthood of Orisa-Oko is open to both male and female, but he actually has more priestesses than priests. His priestesses form a secret society of their own, and no man dare injure or offend any of them.

Among the Owe people of Kwara state the traditional religion, like in many other Nigerian communities, is an affair completely controlled by the adult male section. As Bishop John Onaiyekan pleads, Owe traditional society is very much patriarchal.[10] But there is the phenomenon of "Ofosi," women who are initiated into an esoteric and deeply religious society involving periodic and authentic spirit-possession. They are considered as wives of the divinity. Specifically, their part consists mainly in singing and dancing in honor of the 'Ebọra' divinity on the appropriate occasions. On such occasions they sing and dance round the town visiting the houses of elders and of their own leaders.

The progenitor of my home village Iṣarun, known as Oluaṣarun, (literally, the lord of Iṣarun) was originally a powerful hunter, who like most founders of Yoruba towns and settlements, was believed to have come from Ile-Ifẹ. He stopped over in many places including Benin, Ọba-Ile, Ilaramọkin, and Igbara-Oke and became deified after he sank into the earth while dancing during a festival.

What is relevant to our subject here is the fact that the divinity has always been manifested in a priestess commonly referred to be as "Aya Olua" (Olua's spouse). During special festivals (especially the Annual Yam Festival), the priestess would bring messages from the divinity to the entire community or to individuals within and outside the community. When possessed, the priestess would speak as if she is the divinity himself and has to be addressed in masculine pronouns.[11]

This pattern is common throughout Yorubaland. We did highlight it elsewhere when we said that the manifestation of possession by the spirit of a divinity occurs when the priestess has been seized with frenzy and thrown into a state of ecstasy for many days. She would not be referred to by her own name but by the name of the divinity manifested in her.[12]

Also of relevance to us is the phenomenon of singing and dancing by well-dressed women during celebrations (one example is in respect of Olua-Iṣarun). While the songs and dancing add glee to the celebrations, they have a veiled, but more significant effect of curbing recalcitrant and criminally minded members of the community, who during the year had broken the norms, conventions, and customs prevalent in that community. The songs are usually deliberately composed to highlight the crimes committed and expose the criminals. The singing groups, protected by the community's traditions, perform the "role of the people's court" to whose verdict the culprits and their relations cannot pretend to be indifferent and against which they have no appeal.

The popular Ọmọjao festival (in honor of Ọbalufọn divinity) in Akure shares the same features with Oluaṣarun but is more aggressive. The gaily dressed young women, armed with well-rehearsed abusive songs, move from house to house, naming names and coming down heavily on the social-miscreants within the community. One such song will suffice as an illustration:

In mẹrun sodo, In mẹrun sodo
Ọmọde mee bu ye rẹ
O gbideregbe, o gbideregbe
O gbideregbe lokelisa
Omo rẹ ki in mẹẹsukun
Ẹbi rẹ ki in mẹẹsunkun
In mẹẹ sunkun ẹkun debe.

Bow your heads and speak in whispers.[13]
It is forbidden for the youth
to abuse elders (or their mother)
She stole a goat, she stole a goat,
She stole a goat from Okelisa Street,
Her children stop crying,
Her relations weep no more.
Weep no more, your weeping can no
longer avail anything.

While Ọmọjao festival is celebrated in daylight, Ogun Obinrin (female celebration of Ogun festival) is common to every community within Akure Division and is celebrated during the night. Under the cover of darkness and the immunity graciously conferred by tradition, the women boldly call out in songs the names of the offenders in front of their respective houses and contemptuously pour opprobrious condemnation on them. In all this, women act as messengers of the deity to the community. Some of them act as cultic-functionaries who are set apart for the services of certain divinities. As such they are in categories of priestesses, diviners, mediums and medicine women. Like Orị̣a-Oko, some of them may even become deified and so attract worship (e.g., Ọya).

Significance

It may not be a wild assumption to conclude that in the traditional Yoruba society, with all its prejudices against women, religion, more than any other factor, plays a major role in ascribing status to women. Even with the prohibitions and restrictions[14] that are strongly supported (if not actually motivated) by the male-chauvinist attitude, that a woman should not aspire to tasks which would challenge the male authority at home and despite the thought that it is unsuitable for a woman to speak in public meetings, since such public roles belong to the man,[15] women cannot possibly remain passive in a society in which they have to come to terms with the tutelary spirits, if they must live a successful and peaceful life. Their special contribution to the general welfare and cohesion of the society can really be indispensable to the deity.

In every Yoruba community, there is an elaborate code of manners and etiquette, the observance of which helps to reduce the strains and frustrations of interpersonal relationships.[16] A breach of this code tragically disturbs the rhythm of the society and undermines the authority of the gods whose duty it is to ensure, if not enforce, strict obedience to the norms. With their ritual dances and singing, women warm the hearts of the gods and with their invectives, especially in the homes of the social non-conformists, they contribute a very significant and effective mechanism of social control. Disarmed by the traditional immunity enjoyed by the women, the victim is either compelled to mend his ways or take the easier way out—flee from that society. It is also the duty of the traditional ruler and chiefs to offer sacrifices to purify the community to remove the evil effect of the women's action.

Conclusion

We feel scandalized today by the brazen prevalence in our society of the most heinous crimes like ritual killing, cold-hearted murder, kidnapping, drug trafficking, armed robbery, witchcraft, embezzlement, bribery and corruption, to mention just a few, on scales unknown in history. Heightened by the undermining of such controlling factors as we have discussed, and other related effective measures, and with the super-imposition on our culture of ill-acquired alien habits in the name of religions, modernity, and civilization, the worst may not have been seen yet.

One's advocacy is not for a return to the "primitive" features of our traditional religions, but for a resuscitation of those noble aspects of our enviable culture which among other things, promoted cohesion within the society and for an amelioration of those traditional measures of social control whose strict enforcement might infringe upon the inalienable and fundamental human rights of the citizens.

Our conclusion, therefore, is that the Yoruba woman, in addition to her having an intimate experience of the deity, plays within the religious milieu a very functionally significant and dynamically relevant role in the social life of the Yoruba society. Firmly believing, like Professor Kofe Asare Opoku, that religion (which as cement, holds our societies together) binds man to the unseen powers helping him to form the right relationships with these non-human powers and to his fellow human beings,[17] I am persuaded that our patriarchal image of God and the globally low view of women in religious matters can only lead to a disparagement of the efforts of women in the achievement of those objectives.

But beyond the dynamic role already acknowledged, women would need to heed the challenge thrown by one of their number, Rose Zoe-Obianga, that women must be willing to fight against their own alienation (in whatever area — religious, political, social, or economic) and timidity. They must be willing to fight at the side of their own brothers, whose struggle could then become efficacious as they recognize their own true worth.[18]

Notes

1. J.O. Awolalu, "Women from the Perspective of Religion," in *ORITA: Ibadan Journal of Religious Studies* x/2 Dec. 1976, 95.
2. W.T. Davis, "Our Image of God and Our Image of Women," *ORITA, op.cit.*, 123–4.
3. J.S. Mbiti, *Concepts of God in Africa* (London: S.P.C.K., 1982), Impression, 92.
4. E.G. Parrinder, *African Traditional Religion* (London: Sheldon Press, 1962), 79.
5. Awolalu, "Women from the Perspective of Religion," 99.
6. Kofi Asare Opoku, *West African Traditional Religion*, (Singapore: Feb, 1978), 53.
7. Parrinder, *African Traditional Religion, op.cit.*, 53.
8. J.O. Lucas, *The Religion of the Yoruba*, CMS Bookshop (Lagos 1948), 92–94.
9. E.G. Idowu, *Olodumare: God in Yoruba Belief* (Longman, 1962), 23–25.
10. John Onaiyekan, "The Priesthood in Owe Traditional Religion," in A.A. Adegbola (ed.) *Traditional Religion in West Africa* (Ibadan: Daystar Press, 1983), 26.
11. The current Priestess made history a couple of years ago when she sent messages about sacrifices prescribed by the divinity to the writer, a very senior church minister. The embarrassed, most spiritually ambivalent citizens of the community strongly protested against such a frivolous message and threatened to discredit and depose the alien priestess.
12. J.A. Ǫmǫyajowo, "Women's Experience of God and the Ultimate — the African's Experience." Paper presented to the *Conference on God: The Contemporary Discussion*. Seoul, South Korea, August 1984, 3.
13. Heads are bowed while the leader of the group raises the song in order to conceal her identity.
14. There are many rituals women are not allowed to watch or witness, just as there are secret societies, the membership of which is reserved exclusively for men. Where both sexes share membership of a society, the women so allowed must have passed child-bearing age and are therefore ritually acceptable to the gods. Similarly, women, from the impurity associated with menstruation, are not usually "called" by the gods.
15. Marja-Liisa Swantz, "The Changing Role of Women in Tanzania," in *Christianity in Independent Africa*, (eds.) Fashole-Luke, Gray, Hadrian and Tasie (London 1978), 141.
16. N. Fadipe, *The Sociology of the Yoruba* (Ibadan University Press, 1970), 301.
17. Opoku, *West African Traditional Religion, op.cit.*, 11.
18. Rose Zoe-Obianya, "The Role of Women in Present-Day Africa," in *African Theology en Route* (eds.) Kofi Appia-Kubi and Sergio Torres (Maryknoll, N.Y.: Orbis Books, 1979), 148.

7

THE TALKING DRUM

A TRADITIONAL AFRICAN INSTRUMENT OF LITURGY AND OF MEDIATION WITH THE SACRED

Georges Niangoran-Bouah

Introduction

GENERALLY SPEAKING, the outsider who comes to Africa for the first time is surprised by the omnipresence of the drum in both religious and profane ceremonies. The drum is an instrument that everybody hears and sees; it is the instrument of kings.

In the beginning of the colonial period, both administrators and missionaries waged a merciless war against the drum for various reasons. For the former, the drum was the instrument that participated actively in political resistance by signaling over a long distance to the natives the western military campaigns, the punitive expeditions, the time and itinerary of the repressive forces.

Christian missionaries found in the drum an excuse to wage a war against African traditional possession cults. They took away and destroyed thousands of drums, convinced that this membranophone was the diabolic instrument that liberated satanic maleficent forces and energies.

Once more the drum was judged from the exterior and condemned without an effort to study and understand what it represented in the

African traditional worldview. By throwing into the fire and locking
into museums the most beautiful specimens in order to silence them, an
important access to an understanding of African traditional thought was
blocked. He who destroys and burns the Bible cannot know the origins
of Christianity. Similarly, he who burns the Quran has no access to an
understanding of Islam.

By so doing, the colonial administrators through their prejudice ignored the fact that the black African has deposited the sum of his
knowledge, his religious beliefs, and his attitude and behavior towards
the sacred in this art object. The drum is more than a book; it is a
fundamental institution.

Mediation with the Sacred

The Sacred. According to religious anthropology, the Sacred is that
which is connected to religion and that which inspires respect and deep
veneration. The Sacred is whatever goes beyond man and inspires his
respect, his admiration. From the Sacred generally emanates a particular
fervor, coupled with an element of fear of an absolute power and an
element of mystery. The sacred being or object enjoys a fascinating
power, often presented as being the locus of energy able to manifest
itself at any moment and anywhere.

For the traditional African, the Sacred is an organized and hier-
archized universe filled with invisible beings which include God, spirits,
the spirits of the ancestors, myths, legends, ceremonies, elaborate rituals, and cult objects.

It is this universe of absolute power, of mystery, of fascinating might,
that we are trying to reconstitute through what the African drums say.

The texts chosen to illustrate the point in this paper will not be
followed by commentaries, in order to allow the reader to find for
himself their philosophical, religious, or theological importance. The
poet is not wrong in saying;

> "Contemporary drum
> Of founding ancestors,
> Messenger coming
> From the beginning of time;
>
> Drum, wherever you are
> And whatever your state,
> Drum word,
> Memory of the Ancients,
> We implore you, speak,
> Talk to us in the African way

Of immemorial times,
Speak, speak to us
Of deep Africa
Of true Africa!" [1]

The Drum: Means of Communication. The drum is a musical percussion instrument belonging to the family of membranophones. Outside of these there are drums with splits or lips. Generally, African drums are sculpted from a special tree trunk, which must be blessed with an appropriate ritual which varies according to region and society. The wood for drums doesn't warp or give way, regardless of the environment.

However, there are drums made out of baked mud, of calabash, and even of metal. The drum may take any shape.

The Drum: Element of Mediation with the Sacred. Each human group adopts a medium for documenting its relationship with the sacred in such a way as to survive the hardship of time. Thus, some societies have books while others have drums. In fact, drums and books play the same role and have the same significance for their respective societies. For the *Akan* of the Gulf of Guinea, a drum text becomes the standard version of a historical event, of a personality, of an institution, and of fundamental beliefs preserved in the collective memory of the people.

In black Africa, the talking drum is in fact a precious element of communication. In the highlands, with a favorable direction of the wind, the language of a drum can be heard at a distance of forty kilometers.

For the Akan, the drummed documentation is serious; it is sacred and respected by the whole population. This is the reason that it is the preferred method of communication with gods, the spirits, and the ancestors.

Serer Myth about the Origin of the Drum[2]

The first creation happened by explosion. First, in the vegetal world, the first tree (the SOMB) exploded and grains of all kind gushed forth from the trunk to cover the earth with a vegetal rug. Then, in the animal world, the first animal (the Mbothior) exploded too, and from his body escaped countless eggs and little animals to fill the earth. The Supreme Being created woman first; man came afterwards.

In the first creation, there was harmony, at least in the beginning. The trees talked and moved. But one day a big conflict broke out among the trees, the animals, and men, starting a period of serious unrest. The jackal, spirit of perversion, led the revolt against the Supreme Being. At this time of peace between the three worlds: the world above, next to the Supreme Being, the world of the earth, and the underground world (of underground living beings — different from Dyanif, the village of the dead), there was a feast on the occasion of a birth, and all the animals were invited.

The hyena, the ambiguous animal — because it is at the same time a vivifying and voracious spirit — had missed the departure for the feast; it had counted on royal help. But the Spider-weaver was still there and accepted the responsibility for the transport of the hyena. This one, charmed by space, started to sing:

> "The weaver has woven a thread,
> We are crossing, we are crossing."

The voracious one ate with a heart full of joy. It drank, too, and fell asleep. So it missed the return. The Royal Eagle and the Spider-weaver had already left. The hyena started to cry. The Supreme Being, Rood Sane, was kindly. He gave to the hyena two heavenly objects: a long cord and a small drum. When the hyena would come down to the earth, it would start beating the drum. But its vibrations would be mortal, because the instrument came from God. First of all a special rhythm, a special drummed message had to be worked out.

Everything went according to plan. The hyena kept the drum of Rood and used it as a weapon to kill and devour. In the meantime, the hare observed it. It caught the protective language and decided to get the drum, which was easy at the moment when the hyena went hunting. The hare became master of the drum for some time.

Thanks to his intelligence, man understood the importance of the instrument and of its language and was able to get it into his possession and to use it without danger, for the benefit of man.

Among the Akan in Cote d'Ivoire and Ghana, the drum defines its origin itself by saying:

> "God in creating the world
> Has suffered to create.
> What did he create?
> He created the Drum.
> Divine Drum,
> Wherever you are
> In nature,
> We call upon you,
> Come."
>
> *(Abron drum text)*

The two versions agree; the drum is a creation of God, and from this fact, its origin goes back to the beginning of time, to the creation.

Sacralization of the Drum

As a rule, once the sculptor has finished his work, the work or cult object is submitted to a ritual for sacralization before its official utilization. In our days, this important and indispensable ritual is accomplished along with the sacrifice of animals.

> "Boa, Goddess earth,
> Boa, God Heaven
> Boa has sculpted
> A masterpiece drum
> To reward him,
> He was, against all expectation,
> Decapitated and with his own blood
> The ritual of sacralization was,
> As is custom, accomplished.
> God Heaven and Goddess earth
> Consider his case
> And do him justice."
> *(Baoule drum)*

Food Taboo of the Agni Drummer

In all countries of the world, the individual approaching the Sacred has duties and obligations. Let's listen to those of the Agni drummer mentioned by the drum:

> "The drummer
> Does not eat
> The lizard's meat.
> The drummer
> Does not eat
> The crocodile's meat.
> The drummer
> Does not eat
> The toucan's meat
> Which lives from raw eggs."
> *(Agni drum text)*

The Postulates and Principles of the Drum

A people can be understood deeply only through its world vision and its most intimate beliefs. For the Akan, the drum is not a simple membranophone, a percussion instrument, a rhythmic instrument which anybody can approach and manipulate as he likes without a foregoing ritual. The talking drum is called *tchreman*. The word is composed of *tchre* (to show, teach, and educate) and of man (assembly, nation, ethnic group, and country). Etymologically, *tchreman* (drum) designates an individual who instructs and educates his people. It was a teacher and educator. The drum was then the instrument through which the man of culture expressed himself. Without this instrument, man cannot deliver his message, and without man, the instrument alone cannot produce its sound and message. The drum, then, has its postulates and principles, products of its cultural environment.

1) The drum is an animated being. In this chapter, the drum is no longer only perceived as a material object of human conception and fabrication but also as an animated being endowed with a vital force and a spiritual principle.

> "While organizing the world,
> God-the-Creator
> Has suffered to create.
> What did He create?
> He has created the Word
> And the Word-carrier,
> Has created the drum and
> The drummer....
> Divine drum,
> Wherever you be
> In nature,
> We call upon you, come!
> Divine drum,
> We shall wake you up
> And make you heard."
>   *(Abron drum text)*

> "I am coming from my dream
> And find myself
> In the hands
> Of the drummer."
>   *(Abron drum)*

These texts go without commentary; in the spirit of the authors, the drum exists well as a living being. Consequently, it is invoked, addressed, and invited as an animal or a man.

2) The drum speaks. As a living being, a drum can speak. The drummed message is produced by striking the membrane with the sticks. The hand, the membrane, and the sticks are the organs of the drummed speech. This is exemplified in the following poetry of the Baoule and Essuman ethnic groups:

> "The thumb,
> Finger with mouth,
> Wake up and speak!

> The thumb armed with
> Sticks for drumming
> Is more loquacious and
> More eloquent
> Than a human being
> Sleeping; wake up
> And come!"

For the last text, the thumb and the sticks are visualized as constituting a whole entity different from the human being.

Because the drum is more eloquent and loquacious, and because it is sacred, it is used in communication with God, with local deities, with cosmic deities (sun, earth, moon, Venus), with the ancestors, and with the spirits during important events. Such events include the enthroning of a new chief, the funerals of dignitaries, the feast of the generations and of the age groups, the new yam festivals, and the new year festival (also called *abissa*).

3) The drum is memory. In the case of the membranophone, the instrumentalist is not an artist in the sense of inventing or improvising the texts which he communicates. He is a technician who digs out documents recorded in the past. The drum is a memory which, on request, restitutes completely a memorized text.

4) The language of the drum is unchangeable. Indeed, once the drummed texts have been conceived and accepted by the king and his council of elders and by the drummers, they are disseminated throughout the kingdom. They must not undergo any unilateral modification. Modifying them would be tantamount to a violation of the very essence of the drum language. To prevent the practice of unilateral modifications, the Abron drum says: "If a drummer does his job badly, he is in trouble."

In the past, the drummer who unilaterally tampered with an approved text and thus rendered it voluntarily incomprehensible, was publicly punished by the death sentence. Fear of fines and especially of the death penalty compelled the drummers to be serious and competent.

5) The texts of a talking drum are as reliable as those of the written word. The texts are authentic (not manipulated), conventional (known and accepted by the sages, scholars, and drummers of the country), first hand (conceived by the founding ancestors or by a target group of the pre-colonial history), and, finally, signed (each drummer signs the documents which he disseminates by his name and genealogy).

The Universe of the Sacred

The Creation According to the Drum

"Odoumandan (God)
When creating the world
Has suffered to create.
What did he create?
He has created the Ossein
(master of the word),
Created the drummer and the drum,
And created Otchre Kwaou Aba,
Chief executioner."

(Abron drum)

"God-the-Creator
Has created Heaven,
And he has created the Earth.
He has created the night,
And has created the day,
Alone
Absolutely alone.
God has created the water
And has created the crocodile."

(Agni drum)

"Edanga
When creating the world
Has created the seer and
Created the artist
Who has allowed
The seer to create
The dance of possession."

The Adan Pantheon

God. The name of God changes according to the regions (Anangaman, Edanga, Edangaman, Odoumankaman, Odangaman, Odomunga), and according to his aspect to be clarified (Nyankonpon, Nyame, and Awoupadi).

"The creator
Was already there
In the beginning of time."

(Abron drum)

"The origin of God
Is unknown
Because it remains
Unknown to God Himself"

(Foumassa drum)

1) Proof of the existence of God

"If you notice
That in the morning
A bird remains sadly
Sitting on a branch:
This is because it has not yet
Said good morning to God."

(Agni drum text)

2) Attitude and behavior of humans towards the Eternal One

"Man has always
Been servant of God;
The one who listens to my word
And follows my advice,
If he wishes to have silver,
He will have it.
If he wishes to have gold,
He will have it."

"Almighty God,
I adore you,
As the tongue
Behaves in
The mouth."

(Abron drum)

"The human being has always
Been servant of God.
Creator, I salute you!
God, good morning,
Good morning, Lord!"

(Abron drum)

"Great God
Infinitely mighty
You who give us life
We glorify you,
Bless us!"

(Agni drum)

The Divinities, the Genius, the Spirit, and the Spirits of the Ancestors

The Cosmic Divinities

God Sun

"Oh you bright sun
Who gives life
To the world
Give me the strength
To sing to you all the years!"

(Agni drum text)

L'Etoile Venus

"Kotoklo
Beautiful star
Whose disappearing
Brings the day.
Give me the strength
To sing to you
All the years!"

(Agni drum)

Goddess Earth

"Planet earth, we will
Cause you a wound
By digging a grave;
The earth taken off will
Come back to you
Earth, there is a death,
I announce it to you!
We bury a corpse
We bury a brown coffin
And we do this by
Human solidarity.
Earth, wherever you are,
I implore you come!"

(Abron drum)

"The earth is mother
Of the Stone,
If there is something to eat
And to drink, take care
That she has her part."

(Abron drum)

"Oh you good earth
Who nourishes us
The year has come to its end.
We glorify you,
Bless us!"

(Agni drum)

God Sky

"Sky, sky,
What has happened
So that you be
In darkness?
Sun, if you lifted up a stick
To hit and kill the moon,
You would have done her evil
For nothing!
Sun, you have gone to the Moon,
And mistaken your way.
This is why you are wrong
You are wrong, you are wrong,
You are wrong."

(Abron drum)

Goddess Moon

"Beautiful moon
Who brings together
The joyful troupes
Give me the strength
To sing to you all the years!"

(Agni drum)

Earthly Divinities

The Genius and the Spirits

1) Tano

"The river crosses the path
The path crosses the river
Which of the two elements came
    before
The other?
We have constructed the path in
The direction of the river
The river has always existed
The river comes from the creator
Konkon Tano,
Brefia Tano,
Principal divinity
Of the king of the Ashanti
Tano king of the waters
Tano, you alone have been able to
Oblige the Divinity of Pra
To consume the Afasie yams
With patience,
One always reaches the goal.
Tano king of the waters
Fiampon, I greet you,
Salut, Salut, Tano king of the waters,
Majesty, I salute you."

(Agni drum)

2) The sorcerer, eater of the souls

"Sorcerer, I salute you.
Sorcerer, I salute you!
Our victims are but
Men of value!
We don't have anything to do
With wretches.
Sorcerer, I invoke you
When the night comes,
I rise
To wake you up.
When the day comes,
I rise
To wake you up.
Sorcerer, I greet you...."

3) Bird of bad omen

"Bird Ateba
Messenger of the dead
Be greeted"

(Agni drum)

Religious Thoughts

1) Bad luck

"When someone else
Has bad luck
One has to share
His pain."

(Baoule drum)

3) Death

"God has created death
And has allowed death to kill him.
This was at the beginning
Of creation.
This is the cause
Of our suffering.
Death,
What ordeal!
You have suffered and
Terribly suffered.
Death,
What ordeal!
You have suffered and
Terribly suffered.
Death,
Peace to his soul!
Our compassion, Majesty."

(Ashanti drum)

2) The dying

"It often happens
That the dying one
Is present
At the funeral
Of the healthy one."

4) Spirit of death

"When death
Chooses a victim,
She does not exchange him
Against money.
When death
Chooses a victim
She ends up killing him.
If death had been
A human being,
One would have bought her
To cut off
Her head."

(Baoule drum)

Heroes and Ancestors

1) Heroes of historical legends

"Salute! Salute! Salute!
One does not go to the palace
To see the king for nothing.
Ever since,
It has never been done;
But with you...
...It can be done.
Who is the king!
You are the king
The king is God
The prince heir is God
The foot of the prince heir is God."

(Ashanti drum)

2) *The founding ancestors*

The cult of the ancestors is a religious tribute that the living ones pay to the spirit of their dead ancestors by sacrificing and offering periodically animals, drinks on well-defined ritual days, and through specific prayers.

> "You, the brave one who
> With your younger brother
> Founded this beautiful village,
> Be glorified!
> Here is your favorite drink.
> Always watch over us;
> Accept my compassion
> And sleep in peace!"
> *(Agni drum)*

Conclusion

It is customary when talking of the religious thoughts of the ancient people of the Middle East to refer to the Bible or the Quran. In the same way the Akan refer themselves to the talking drum in order to quote any discourse related to the sacred. Bible, Quran, and Drum have the same vocation; these are fundamental sacred "books" venerated by their respective peoples. They are monuments of the human spirit because they are timeless. The drum is a tool and an appropriate instrument of knowledge which for a long time was considered as not being accessible to the universe of African traditional beliefs. The discourse of the drum, unchangeable and conventional, is not a discourse of an isolated wise man, but a real ideology of several thousand years which the memory of a whole people preserves with piety from generation to generation.

This paper has evoked for us, through the talking drum, the religious world of the Akan people of a time when neither Christianity nor Islam had penetrated the Gulf of Guinea, that is to say, at a time sadly gone by, when Africa was still African.

Notes

1. The texts used in this paper are excerpts from G. Niangoran-Bouah's book: *Introduction a la Drummologie*. Universite Nationale de Cote-d'Ivoire, Institut d'Ethno-Sociologie (I.E.S.) Sankofa Abidjan, 1981 and from J.F. Amon d'Aby's *Croyances Religieuses et Coutumes Juridiques des Agni de la Cote-d'Ivoire*, Editions Larose (Paris, 1960).
2. Serer myth of Senegal.

8

RELIGIOUS POLITICS AND THE MYTH OF ṢANGO

Akinwumi Iṣọla

Introduction

STUDENTS OF WEST AFRICAN RELIGION may claim to be familiar with the myth of Ṣango, the Yoruba god of thunder. Having been popularized by many eminent scholars,[1] the details of the myth are usually taken for granted. In Hethersett's account in *Iwe Kika Ẹkẹrin Li Ẹdẹ Yoruba*, the most audacious distortion of the myth appears, either by design or by mistake. That the distortion lasted for so long in Yoruba society reveals the disturbing tenacity of the mental enslavement to the printed word of the lettered elite. Once this distortion appeared in print, it was taken as the gospel truth, and no one bothered to check further its veracity from the illiterate adherents of Ṣango worship.

In this investigation, we attempt to examine Hethersett's possible motives, if his distortion was deliberate. We also examine the possibilities of his making genuine mistakes either through ignorance or through indulging in folk etymology. We finally present correct details of the Ṣango myth, fruit of our current research.

Hethersett's Account

According to Hethersett, Ṣango was the fourth Alaafin of Ọyọ, of tempestuous temper, and versed in the art of medicinal charms. In his attempt to eliminate at least one of his two restless war lords, Timi and Gbọnka, causing instability in his domain, he sent Timi to reign at Ẹdẹ and sent Gbọnka to challenge his authority, hoping that the encounter would lead to the death of at least one of them. Instead, however, Gbọnka brought Timi back captive but alive. Alaafin ordered a rematch in his presence and openly supported Timi. Gbọnka, the more powerful warrior, killed Timi and challenged the authority of Ṣango. In his violent reaction, Ṣango killed many of his own people and in his disappointment and frustration abdicated, and left the city of Ọyọ, followed by many of his own people who nevertheless deserted him one by one until he was left with only Ọya his favorite wife. When Ọya also deserted him, he became utterly depressed and hanged himself (ọbaso in Yoruba). His close associates and friends planned a cover-up, because hanging oneself was and still is ignominious among the Yoruba. Anyone repeating the ugly story was seriously punished and soon everybody started saying "ọba ko so" ("the king did not hang").

This is Hethersett's account. Where did he get this story? Before we examine the possibilities open to him, let us first discuss the problems with his account. To start with, he has some historical facts wrong. The episode of the two warlords Timi and Gbọnka did not occur during the reign of the fourth Alaafin of Ọyọ. According to Johnson, it happened much earlier in the history of Ọyọ.[2] Second, the name of the fourth Alaafin of Ọyọ was not Ṣango, according to C. L. Adeoye;[3] he was called Babayẹmi Itiolu. It becomes clearer that Hethersett apparently just pieced together a few facts randomly picked from Yoruba mytho-history to form this potpourri presented as the myth of Ṣango.

There is another misrepresentation: The Yoruba phrase "ọbaa Koso" ("the king of Koso") was translated "ọba ko so" ("the king did not hang"). This is a clear distortion of the word Koso. Koso was where Ṣango reigned. It was the name of a place. But if the word is broken into two separate syllables, the meaning changes: ko means did not, and so means hang. For a mischievous gospeller, the temptation to use this folk etymology might be too great to resist. Hethersett was, by the way, the headmaster of a Church Missionary Society School in Lagos, Nigeria. Perhaps it was through the deliberate juggling of some facts of history and a folk etymological translation of Koso that Hethersett derived his myth of Ṣango according to the Church Missionary Society published in a Yoruba reader meant for use in their Christian schools.

If this is the case, the motives appear clear. The early forties was one of the hottest eras of evangelization in Yorubaland, and every avenue was used to gain converts. Perhaps Hethersett's motives were to popularize a damaging myth of Ṣango and thereby discredit one of the most powerful and feared Yoruba deities. Ṣango is the sworn enemy of liars, thieves, and witches, and his worship is widespread indeed.[4] Hethersett, a headmaster and evangelist, may have believed that the popularization of a degrading myth about Ṣango would do enough damage to his image to cause a decline in adherence. If this is the case, he has succeeded by and large, but his success has been restricted to the circle of the educated elite. The real adherents of Ṣango worship, largely illiterate, have been unaware of the existence of this printed distortion.

The Validity Test

There are two main sources of information about Yoruba myths and history: the Ifa divination poetry and the large body of *oriki* (praise poetry) as contained in the many oral genres.

Various verses of *Eṣẹ Ifa* tell the story of Ṣango. Some tell the story of his deification, others document his nature and military exploits. One in particular, *Ogbetura*, recounts how Ṣango's presence came from Ile-Ife when Ọyọ was founded. Not a single verse in the whole corpus contains anything resembling Hethersett's distortion. Any myth of a Yoruba deity that cannot be found in *Eṣẹ Ifa* is not authentic.

One important characteristic of Yoruba *oriki* is that it tells the whole story of its subject, including *all* the unpleasant details. That is why some scholars have preferred the translation "descriptive poetry" to "praise poetry," because *oriki* is not all praise. For example, in the Onikoyi lineage, the fact that their progenitor was both a warrior and a thief constantly recurs. The *Ọkọmi* lineage similarly "celebrates" the promiscuity of their female members. No fact about a man or a deity, however unpleasant, would be left out of the *oriki*. It is therefore significant to note that a thorough examination of the *oriki* of Ṣango reveals nothing suggesting suicide by hanging.[5] We can safely conclude that Hethersett's account is not accurate.

Perhaps one of the reasons that the distortion has existed for so long is the conspiracy of silence. Apart from the fact that many people are genuinely ignorant of the real facts of the myth, virtually everyone who could read was either Christian or Moslem. It is possible that even if a Christian or Moslem had discovered the distortion, he might prefer to leave it uncorrected for the purpose of religious propaganda.

The Myth of Ṣango

Early in 1983, I was interviewing a *babalawo*[6] (an Ifa priest), and as
background to a question, I quickly retold the myth of Ṣango according
to Hethersett. The old man stared at me, concern written all over his
face. He finally asked: "Learned one, where did you pick up that story?"
When I told him that I read it in a book his surprise increased. He did
not know that a book could contain lies. I too was amazed to discover
that what I had read and believed for so long could be untrue, and so
began the search for the true myth of Ṣango. The babalawo took me
through all the *Odu* that relate to Ṣango in the Ifa divination poetry.
Among the important *Odu: Otua Orikọ* tells the story of Ṣango's
initiation into the Ifa cult and the origins of his powers. *Ofun-eko* tells
of dancing as the main profession of Ṣango. *Ọwọnrinyẹku* narrates how
Ṣango seduced Ọya, Ogun's wife. *Ika Meji* documents many interesting
episodes in Ṣango's life, and *Ogbetura* tells us how Ṣango's presence got
to Ọyọ from Ile-Ifẹ.

All these suggest that Ṣango had existed at Ile-Ifẹ long before the
founding of the city of Ọyọ.

There is no space for us here to recite all the verses that tell the stories
of Ṣango in all the *Odu* cited above. But it is important to our argument
to relate the story in *Ogbetura*, which records how Ṣango's presence was
transferred from Ile-Ifẹ to Ọyọ, in order to reinforce our contention that
(contrary to Hethersett's account) Ṣango could not have been the fourth
Alaafin of Ọyọ.

Summary of the Verse in Ogbetura

It was the practice that every child of Ọlọfin Oodua old enough to
choose a profession would be given the tools necessary to establish
himself in that trade. Jẹgbẹ, one of the children of Oodua, wanted to be
a hunter. His father gave him guns and gunpowder, and he went
hunting. He killed a big elephant and came home to announce it. There
was great joy, and people followed him into the forest to skin the
animal. But the elephant had disappeared miraculously. He killed other
animals which also disappeared before anyone could come to see.
People thought he was lying. Confused and depressed, he went to
consult an Ifa priest. The priest asked him to make a sacrifice in the
forest. It was to be a burnt offering. The fire he made at the site of the
offering in the forest attracted a group of kings who had gone to war
but were lost in the forest. When they found Jẹgbẹ, they asked him to
lead them back to the city. Jẹgbẹ asked for his own share of their spoils

of war and it was given. He led the group to the gates of Ile-Ifẹ, where his father Ọlọfin Oodua was king. He left the group at the gates and went alone to announce the arrival of the group of kings. Because his story was strange, and because of his reputation as a liar, no one believed him. Oodua told him he could keep whatever riches he had gotten, could lead the group he had discovered, and could be their king if he liked. Jẹgbẹ went back to the gates to lead the group into the city on horseback. Everyone was surprised!

But Oodua had given Jẹgbẹ his word and was honor-bound not to change his mind. Oodua therefore asked Jẹgbẹ to lead the group to a new site and be their king. Since the group consisted of kings, powerful men, Oodua gave Jẹgbẹ a "conquering sword" to deal with any revolts and thunderbolts, the symbol of Ṣango, to be his guiding deity. Jẹgbẹ led the group to found a new city: Ọyọ. That was how Ṣango's presence found its way to Ọyọ.

Since Ṣango was there at the foundation of Ọyọ, his origin could not have been as the fourth Alaafin of Ọyọ. Jẹgbẹ, the first Alaafin, established the worship of Ṣango and made it the state religion with himself being the chief priest and Ṣango incarnate.

Who then was the fourth Alaafin of Ọyọ, and why was it possible to confuse him with the real Ṣango of old? As indicated earlier, the fourth Alaafin of Ọyọ was Babayẹmi Itiolu, who was versed in the art of medicinal charms. The important tradition in Ọyọ is to "deify" each Alaafin. When on the throne, he incarnates Ṣango, and when dead, he is deified and becomes Ṣango. In that regard every Alaafin is Ṣango, so the fourth Alaafin could be called Ṣango.

This practice brought about the proliferation of Ṣango that we have today. Apart from the fact that each Alaafin was a Ṣango, other important men in history who were devotees of Ṣango started their own tradition of Ṣango worship. And so today, we have very many "Ṣangos" both in Africa and in the New World. For example, we have Ṣango Ogodo, Ṣango Aganju, Ṣango Afọnja, to mention only a few. But any of these traditions of Ṣango worship must not be confused with the real origin of Ṣango which, according to the Ifa oracle (the main source of Yoruba religious myths), existed in Ile-Ifẹ even before the city of Ọyọ was founded.

Hethersett's mistake seems therefore to have been that he confused Babayẹmi Itiolu (the fourth Alaafin of Ọyọ), himself a passionate devotee of Ṣango, with the original Ṣango in Ile-Ifẹ, whose symbols of worship were brought along in founding Ọyọ.

In spite of the historical inaccuracies in Hethersett's account, the life story he describes may have been similar to that of the fourth Alaafin of

Ọyọ. The fact remains, however, that the real story of Ṣango is simply not there.

Duro Ladipọ's "Ọba Ko So"

Duro Ladipọ's folk opera "Ọba Ko So" ("The king did not hang") is one of the most popular in Yorubaland. The opera actively sponsored by the Institute of African Studies of the University of Ibadan was performed in many of the world's major cities. The play was based on Hethersett's account, and the question has often been asked whether Duro Ladipọ, like other young school boys, fell victim to the presumed authority of the written word and genuinely believed it to be authentic. Later in life he must have discovered the distortion, but perhaps thought it too late to correct. Other scholars believe that even if Duro Ladipọ had discovered the distortion in Hethersett's account, he, a Christian, son of an Anglican catechist, might not have bothered to correct the mistake. He remained a Christian merely using the Ṣango myth for profitable entertainment. Perhaps the truth is that once Duro Ladipọ fell victim to Hethersett's distortion, he did not bother to look any further.

Conclusion

Students of African culture, and of African religion in particular, must continue to re-examine early records that concern traditional religion, especially those recorded during the time that Christian evangelization was being ruthlessly carried out. As we have seen, it is possible for a researcher's work to be weakened either by his own religious bias or simply by ignorance.

Such distorted records may endure mainly because the illiterate but knowledgeable practitioners of African religion cannot read the records in order to knock the bottom out of the falsehoods. The lettered elite that read the records, having been taught to trust written records, rarely venture far enough to question illiterate practitioners. Only dedicated and dynamic questions can bring such distortions to light.

NOTES

1. See Hethersett's account in *Iwe Kika Ẹkẹrin Li Ede Yoruba* (Church Missionary Society, 1981).
   R.E. Dennett, *Nigerian Studies: The Religious and Political System of the Yoruba* (London: Frank Caas and Co. Ltd., 1968), 156–194.
   A.B. Ellis, *The Yoruba Speaking Peoples of the Slave Coast of West Africa* (London: Curson Press (Second Impression), 1974), 46–56.
   Duro Ladipọ, *Ọba Ko So* (The King Did Not Hang) (Ibadan: Institute of African Studies, 1972).
   Judith Gleason, *Orisha: The Gods of Yorubaland* (New York: Atheneum, 1971), 58–78.
2. Samuel Johnson, *The History of the Yorubas* (Lagos: C.S.S., 1981), 155–158.
3. C.L. Adeoye, *Aṣa Ati Iṣe Yoruba* (Ibadan: Oxford University Press, 1979), 27–32.
4. For more information about the worship of Ṣango, see A. Iṣọla, *Ṣango-Pipe: One Form of Yoruba Oral Poetry*, M.A. thesis (Lagos: University of Lagos, 1971). See also B. Idowu, *Olodumare: God in Yoruba Belief* (Oxford University Press, 1970).
5. See Iṣọla, *Ṣango-Pipe*, 1971, for a detailed discussion of the *oriki* of Ṣango.
6. Babalọla Ifatoogun, a part-time instructor in the Department of African Languages and Literatures, University of Ifẹ, Ile-Ifẹ, Nigeria.

9

AFRICAN TRADITIONAL SOCIO-RELIGIOUS ETHICS AND NATIONAL DEVELOPMENT

THE NIGERIAN CASE

Friday M. Mbon

AFRICAN TRADITIONAL SOCIO-RELIGIOUS ETHICS refer to the code of conduct which governed and guided all social and religious actions and interactions in pre-colonial and pre-missionized African societies. The aim of this paper is to show how the application of this ethics could aid and facilitate national development in contemporary Africa in general, with particular reference to Nigeria.

One of the greatest social as well as religious problems facing contemporary Africans is that they are too easily susceptible to borrowing ideologies and *modus operandi* from other cultures usually without thinking carefully and critically enough about the possible consequences and implications of what they are borrowing. Africans borrow, for instance, foreign political and economic schemes, foreign academic programs, foreign religious modes of worship, alien criteria for judging what is right or what is wrong—in other words, they even borrow alien ethics. That kind of uncritical borrowing has led many African countries to what Joseph Kenny has called "identity fluctuation," by which he means the assimilation of new or outside values.[1]

The Nature of African Traditional Socio-Religious Ethics

A quick look comparing both Western secular ethical systems and African traditional socio-religious ethical systems reveals that the former are egoistic, while the latter are less egoistic and more eudaemonistic. Egoism is the theory that the self and not the society is central to social activities. Western ethical systems are generally based on this theory. In African traditional societies, the welfare of the individual was a function and consequence of the welfare of the society, the society being the *summum bonum* of African traditional moral philosophy. Furthermore, African traditional ethics were regulated by a law based on sacred sanctions which had their origin in the world of the spirits and ancestors.[2]

Moreover, African traditional social ethics were communal, not individualistic as Western ethics tend to be. For in African traditional societies, no man lived unto himself. That is to say, what one man did affected, directly or indirectly, other members of his society or community. Harry Sawyer expresses this point thus: "The behavior of the individual without exception is right or wrong according as it affects the group—sometimes a closer, nuclear family group; at other times, a wider circle of extended families and friends."[3] Especially this was true if the act of the individual was one that offended the gods or ancestral spirits.[4]

Examples of social acts that would be offensive to the divine spirits and the society included stealing, cheating, murder, incest or any of the ancestor-sanctioned rules governing and guiding the social and religious life of the community. Violation of any of those rules constituted "sin" in traditional African thinking and ethics, and had to be atoned for immediately, otherwise a group of people in the community or sometimes the entire community might come under the punitive displeasure or curse of the gods or ancestors thus offended.

The punishment or curse could take one of several forms. For instance, it could take the form of bad luck in hunting or fishing, as in the case of the Temna of Sierra Leone where "a plague of mosquitoes or a poor catch of fish was attributed to the displeasure of the national heroes of the affected area."[5] It could also take the form of poor harvest, sickness, or even several deaths in the community. Thus, in African traditional society, one person's "sin" could have serious socio-economic consequences for the entire society, hence the communality of African traditional ethics. It is because of the communal nature of this ethics that the Yoruba of Nigeria, for instance, say proverbially:

> If a member of one's household
> Is eating poisonous insects
> And we fail to warn him (to desist)
> The after-effect of his action
> Would rob neighbours of sleep.[6]

A similar point is made in another African proverb which states that "one wicked person in a state hurts others."[7]

When a member of the African traditional society who had brought disaster or ill luck to the community was known either through personal confession or through divination, he was avoided by the rest of the community until he had made provision for his "sin" to be atoned for, either through personal or communal rituals of cleansing. Only thus could the dangerous consequences of that person's "sin" be averted by the community. Or, if a member of the community had done something that was so shameful (e.g. stealing) that his community's name was dragged into disrepute, that person could be ostracized. "Ostracism," J. Akin Ọmọyajowo has said (speaking specifically of the Yoruba), "is the most dreadful punishment an individual can be given and so, every person tries to keep the norm of the community in order to avoid the shame of ostracism and the embarrassment it will cause other members of his family unit."[8]

It is unfortunate that this form of deterrent punishment—punishment by ostracism—is now unheard of in contemporary African societies, simply because there are no "pure" African traditional societies nowadays. If it were possible for contemporary Africans to turn back the hands of the clock now—that is, to bring back the "pure" African traditional societies, perhaps the fear of ostracism might have served as a deterrent against the many acts of opprobrium which one finds in contemporary African societies, such as burning down public buildings (in Nigeria) in order to destroy official records that might reveal shady deals, embezzling public funds, and other forms of structural or "scientific" official stealing and cheating in public service. One can at least imagine how much money would stay in national coffers to be used for national development were these social incubi deterred by traditional ethical sanctions and concomitant penalties for violation.

In some cases traditional African socio-religious ethics controlled not only the overt acts and behavior of members of the community, but also their very conscience. For example, among the Annang and Ibibio of Nigeria, it was believed that if a member of the community had evil intentions against another member (such as planning to cheat him or planning to have a sexual affair with another's wife), that person's conscience and attitude were an offense against the gods and ancestral spirits. Such an evil planner could come down with some ill luck, sickness, or even death. Among the Riyom and Du of the Plateau areas of northern Nigeria, it is believed that only persons with a clear conscience may enter sacred places.[9]

Also, among the Annang and Ibibio of Nigeria, to harm physically or morally, consciously or unconsciously, one's in-laws (*ukot*) or any person from the village of one's wife or from the village of one's son-or daughter-in-law, or from the village of one's maternal lineage, was to incur divine or ancestral displeasure, the consequences of which displeasure could reach communal dimensions. Whether it was the individual defaulter or his entire community that suffered as a consequence of his or her action, reparation must be made through peace settlement or through ritual sacrifice if normalcy must return to the individual or community concerned. Since through inter-ethnic or inter-community marriages nearly every village or ethnic group is involved in these intricate in-law relationships, if the traditional ethical regulations binding them were still strictly adhered to today by Nigerians, for example, the result would be much greater co-operation and harmony among the ethnic groups in the country. Such cooperation and harmony are certainly essential for national stability and development.

The significance of the in-law relationship is expressed by the people of Ikot Abasi (in Akwa Ibom state of Nigeria) in the proverb: "*Ukot isikide nte ukot akpa*"; meaning "an in-law cannot stand aloof watching his in-law die (or suffer)." The implication of this proverb is that one's in-law is morally bound to defend and protect one in all times and circumstances, even at the risk of one's own life. The consequence of that kind of relationship is that it would be difficult for one to cheat or plan evil against one's in-law for whose defense or protection one would even risk one's own life. Cheating and planning evil against one's compatriots, even against one's in-laws, are the bane of contemporary Nigeria's moral and social development.

I have pointed out the above examples of how African traditional ethics worked, in order to stress the communal nature of these ethics.

In this ethical system, individual members of the society had the interest and welfare of the community at heart. They did not go about acting and behaving as though only they lived in the community. They were careful not to do anything that would bring suffering to other members of the society. In that kind of society, it was unthinkable to see the very rich and the very poor co-existing. Such a situation did not arise because the rich were morally expected to share their riches. This, in fact, was the kind of social condition which President Julius Nyerere of Tanzania had in mind when he wrote: "In our traditional African society we were individuals within a community. We took care of the community and the community took care of us. We neither needed nor wished to exploit our fellow men."[10]

Change in African Traditional Socio-Religious Ethics

Unfortunately, the picture of the nature of African traditional socio-religious ethics which I have painted thus far has changed, much to the detriment of African nations. Contemporary Africans seem to have blindly adopted Western ethical systems which are based on two values, namely, personal comfort and personal affluence. By personal comfort is meant "just being...alone, not to be troubled by the troubles of other people, whether across the world or across the city – to live one's life with minimal possibilities of being personally disturbed...wanting to have my personal life pattern undisturbed in my life time, regardless of what the result will be."[11]

Personal affluence means "an overwhelming and ever-increasing prosperity – a life made up of things, things, and more things – a success judged by an ever-higher level of material abundance."[12]

Value means what is actually liked, prized, esteemed, approved or enjoyed by anyone or by a group of people all the time. Values are the basic measure of prestige and status shared by all or most members of a society. They determine the political, economic, and social behavior of a people. The development or otherwise of a nation to a very great degree depends on the moral and intellectual development or otherwise of its citizens. Hence a country like Nigeria which bases its voting patterns on "tribalism" (ethnicity) and on the "son-of-the-soil" syndrome, is destined to face innumerable problems which inevitably stand in the way of social and political stability.[13]

Furthermore, values form the basis of ideologies which responsible statesmen the world over should explore as a means of promoting and fostering national and international understanding and goodwill among themselves. But if the citizens of one nation live by the selfish and unaltruistic value of making money and more money by all means, chances are that they will use unfair and shady means to maintain this selfish value system, thus making the relationships among themselves and among other countries very difficult. Several third-world nations seem to be facing this dilemma in their international relationships. It is no gainsaying that many nations of the world are extra careful when dealing with one another in matters involving money!

How does a nation like Nigeria expect to develop when through its insatiable lust for money it has come to place itself in a position that makes it difficult for other nations of the world to trust it and deal with it in economic matters? And how has it come to place itself in that unfortunate position if not by its citizens losing sight of their traditional ethical values and virtues such as honesty, sobriety, industriousness, fairplay, concern for the other person — whether that other person belongs to their local community or to the world community?

The kind of ethics that is based on values of money, personal comfort and affluence, greed, and avarice, is for all intents and purposes individualistic and is at variance with African traditional communalistic ethics. Such perfervid individualism paves the way to the selfish way of life. This way of life disturbs the harmony which existed in African traditional societies with their spirit of communal living, the very essence of African traditional communal identity. Furthermore, this way of life destroys the "we-ethos," the "we-law," the "we-logic," and the "we-ethical yardstick" by which the traditional African community measured reality.[14]

It should be stressed here that no nation can honestly and realistically talk of development by reference only to its few privileged, well-placed citizens who have somehow gotten to the top by injuring others and by structural and organized stealing from the national coffers. As Professor Henry Pirenne pointed out several decades ago, national development or progress or its opposite, must be determined on the basis of how well or otherwise the citizens on the lower economic strata are doing, not on the basis of the strata long in possession of wealth and power.[15] This being so, we cannot speak of Nigeria as a "developed" country or even a "developing" country until we begin to see Nigerians being taken care of by the powers that be or shall be; until we see the people provided for in such a way that will enable them to be sure of at least two square meals a day; until we see them begin to enjoy certain essential amenities such as proper health-care, public transportation, water and electricity. It is then, and only then, that Nigeria as a nation can begin to say at least that it has taken a step in the direction of national development.

But such a step will be difficult, even impossible, unless Nigeria goes back to, and begins to put into practice, traditional ethical principles, principles based on the communal concern for the well-being of *all*, and not only for the well-being of a privileged few; principles based on kinship or lineage relationships, and a "big brother" concept, within which configuration those who had more shared what they had with those who had less; principles founded not on the ethics of individualism and human autonomy and selfishness, but on a community-centered, theonomous, theocentric, and ancestor-sanctioned set of ethical criteria. Indeed, many contemporary Nigerians are now beginning to be aware of the need to return to the traditional socio-religious ethics of their fore parents. That is what many of them recently strongly recommended to the Political Bureau, a body responsible for working out the best political structure for Nigeria's next republic. That, too, was the recommendation of President Shagari's Committee on Ethical Re-orientation in 1982 — a recommendation to go back to the African traditional ethical system in which the welfare of the individual was a function and consequence of the welfare of the community; an ethical system in which the individual was happy only if and when the community was happy. The essence of this kind of ethical system was the preservation and integration of social as well as spiritual life. The background of this ethical system was traditional African societies' concern for each other; its goal was to unite members of the community into one great harmonious family in which each one continued to seek the good and welfare of the many.

As a mechanism for achieving the rapid return to African traditional ethical principles and practice, African governments should consider introducing into their legal systems and criminal codes deterrent punitive measures used in pre-modern African societies such as ostracism, public flogging, and other forms of public punishment with the offender in the nude. Moreover, in the religious realm, African traditional ethics, based on the law of karma, should be stressed, while the Christian doctrines of grace and forgiveness are de-emphasized. It seems to this writer that these two Christian doctrines have somehow misled many modern Africans to act and behave shamefully and unethically while hoping to obtain God's grace and forgiveness whenever they repent.

Conclusion

After analyzing insightfully the possible and probable consequences of the diminution of religion in contemporary technocratic, rationally organized societies, the British sociologist, Bryan Wilson, records the following observation:

Contemporary society operates as if affective-neutrality were a sufficient value-orientation for things to work; it may yet discover that there are other necessities, the virtues nurtured essentially in local communities, religious contexts, which in the long run will be shown to be as indispensable to the society of the future as they were to the communities of the past.[16]

Contemporary Africans who are bent on copying the West in every-thing may well heed the warning implicit in this observation and return to their traditional socio-religious value systems. There seems to be no other way through which Nigeria, for example, can come out of her present moral dilemma. No amount of hypocritical and face-saving noise-making about the so-called "ethical re-orientation" or "War Against Indiscipline" will help her or any African country out of the present moral doom. The moral salvation of Africans lies only in their immediate return to their traditional ethics of conscience, the foundation of which is a genuine concern for the welfare of all, predicated on the respect for the Supreme Being, the ancestors, and the deities.

Notes

1. Joseph Kenny, "Religious Movements in Nigeria — Divisive or Cohesive: Some Interpretative Models," *Orita: Ibadan Journal of Religious Studies*, XVI, No. 2 (1984), 122.

2. Cf. Noel Q. King, *Christian and Muslim in Africa* (New York: Harper & Row, 1971), 77.

3. Harry Sawyerr, "Persons in Relationship: An Examination of Three Facets of Tribal Society," in *Les religions africaines comme source de valuers de civilisation* Colloque de Cotonou, 16–22 about 1970 (Paris: Presence Africaine), 190.

4. Cf. Kofi Asare Opoku, *West African Traditional Religion* (Accra: FEP International Private Limited, 1978), 162.

5. Sawyerr, 196–197.

6. Quoted in J.O. Awolalu, "The African Traditional View of Man," *Orita: Ibadan Journal of Religious Studies*, VI, No. 2 (1972), 112.

7. Cited in Kofi Asare Opoku, *Speak to the Winds: Proverbs from Africa* (New York: Lothrop, Lee & Shepherd, 1975), 26.

8. J. Akin Ọmọyajowo, "The Concept of Man in Africa," *Orita: Ibadan Journal of Religious Studies*, IX, No. 1 (1975), 40.

9. Okechukwu Njoku, "The Birom Religion of Nigeria; An Urgent Task for Investigation on Religion, Ritual and Beliefs," *Bulletin of the International Committee on Urgent Anthropological and Ethnological Research*, No. 20 (1978), 58; Cf. Opoku, *West African Traditional Religion*, 162.

10. Julius Nyerere, *Ujamaa: Essays in African Socialism* (Nairobi: Oxford University Press, 1968), 6–7.

11. Francis A. Schaeffer, *How Should We Then Live: The Rise and Decline of Western Thought and Culture* (Old Tappan, New Jersey: Fleming H. Revell Co., 1976), 205.

12. *Ibid.*

13. See O.S.K. Okpo, "Cultural Roots of Nigeria's Political Behaviour," paper presented at the Cultural Seminar of the Cross River State Cultural Centre Board, Calabar, May 22, 1987.

14. These phrases are Korsi Dogbe's; see his "Concept of Community and Community Support Systems in Africa," *Anthropos*, 75, Nos. 5/6 (198), 790.

15. See Henri Pirenne, *Les periodes de l'historie sociale du capitalisme* (Hagyez, Brussel, 1914).

16. Bryan Wilson, *Religion in Sociological Perspective* (Oxford: Oxford University Press, 1982), 52.

10

THE ENCOUNTER BETWEEN AFRICAN TRADITIONAL RELIGION AND OTHER RELIGIONS IN NIGERIA

Joseph Ọmọṣade Awolalu

AFRICAN TRADITIONAL RELIGION (A.T.R.) is the indigenous religion of Africans. It is the religion embraced by the forefathers of the present generation of Africans. In other words, it is that religion which emerged from the sustaining faith held by the forebears of the present generation of Africans and which is being practised today in various forms and intensities by Africans, including Nigerians. It is a religion whose founders cannot be traced, no matter how far we went back into history.

The general pattern of the religion is held to be one with a belief in the Supreme Being, in divinities and spirits, in life after death, and in some mysterious powers. Because the main thrust of this paper is to examine the encounter between African traditional religion and other religions in Nigeria, I would not like to elaborate on the beliefs and practices of this religion at this stage; but these will emerge as we expose the encounter between the indigenous religion and the two imported religions — Christianity and Islam. Nigerians knew and embraced the indigenous religion of their forefathers, and that religion remained intact and uninterrupted before the foreigners of different types and callings came into the country. Among such foreigners were the explorers, the merchants, the administrators, the imperialists, and missionaries. They opened up the country to Western civilization, introducing new systems of government, law and order, and new religions. All these foreign forces mounted vigorous campaigns against the indigenous religion which was regarded as heathenish, paganish, uncivilized, and of the evil one.

Thus, the explorers, the administrators, the merchants, and the missionaries who came from Europe came from a Christian background; and they were convinced that it would be best to have Nigerians converted to Christianity.

> They, therefore, encouraged their home government not only to send capable administrators to maintain law and order but also zealous Christian missionaries to preach the gospel of Jesus Christ. In consequence of this, there was a collaboration among the merchants, the administrators and the missionaries to suppress the indigenous religion and to impose Christianity.[1]

Christianity was introduced into the southern part of Nigeria as a result of the liberation of slaves from the New World toward the end of the 18th century. The liberated slaves who returned to West Africa and who had embraced Christianity in servitude preferred to continue Christian worship rather than return to the old traditional mode of worship. It was they who asked that pastors be sent to them from Freetown, Sierra Leone which was the "home" of the liberated slaves in 1842. In this way, Christianity began to challenge African traditional religion. The missionaries were backed up and given protection by the colonial administrators.

For example, when Governor Carter, the British administrator in Lagos, got to know that Ijẹbu, who were very conservative in their traditional practices, were unwilling to accept Christianity, he used force to introduce "civilization" to the Ijẹbu and to oblige missionaries to establish schools as they had done in Lagos in order to introduce a higher standard of morality and a purer form of religion than was existing among those who were ignorant of the Bible. Eventually, in the famous Ijẹbu Expedition of 1892, the Ijẹbu were defeated, and Christianity was imposed; Governor Carter justified his action on humanitarian grounds because the Ijẹbu, according to him, "were heathens of the most uncompromising description, even hostile to the missionaries who were of their own race."[2] We see here that in their first encounter with non-Christian religion, Christian missionaries were not only negative, they were downright aggressive.

In the case of Badagry, the first town in Nigeria to receive Christian missionaries, it was reported that "there was no open hostility or persecution, but the hold of the traditional religion on the people was very firm. They had welcomed missionaries not because they wanted Christianity but because they were weak and poor and hoped that the missionaries could attract some trade back to the town."[3]

When we turn to the Igbo people of Eastern Nigeria, we discover that the missionaries claimed to have brought the light of salvation to the Nri people. According to Onwuejeogwu, the following occurred:

> Nri people welcomed Western education but resented the method adopted by the Catholics. According to the elders, converts were encouraged to flout authority of the *ozo* men, burn their ritual objects, break the taboos and reveal the secret of the ritual mask....The encouragement of the destruction of traditional objects of worship spread out over all Igboland. In this operation, the educated Christians, who were mostly teachers and pastors, were used. They condemned the traditional title system, marriage, rituals, songs, arts, and labelled them "things of Satan."[4]

The story was not much different among the Isoko people of Bendel State. Christianity came into Isokoland through Patani in Ijoland. According to Obaro Ikime, the "converted" Christians were eager to buy copies of the English Bible which they put under their pillows as witness to God that they had become new people and had joined God's company. Furthermore, such converted Isoko people were encouraged to burn or throw away their objects of worship. "It is well known," observed Ikime, "that the shrines of the ancestors and gods in the Isoko country, as in many other parts of Africa, were repositories of the works of art....The indiscriminate throwing away of such works as a mark of conversion may have filled the hearts of the missionaries with Christian joy! It was doing incalculable harm to the people's cherished heritage. "The tragedy," Ikime further observed, "was that later even carvings which were purely for artistic and decorative purposes were connected with 'juju' and so often destroyed in the fervour that characterized nascent Christianity in the Isoko country."[5]

The greatest and most effective weapon used by Christian missionaries to disrupt traditional beliefs was Western education. As the missionaries claimed that they were working for spiritual salvation of the people, so also did they claim to be working for their material well being. All new converts were taught in the mission houses and were encouraged to look down upon their culture. Later, mission schools and colleges soon sprang up in many places; and men and women were taught the Scriptures and reading, writing, and arithmetic. Eventually those who were educated along this line became converted and bade adieu to the old faith. Some of them who were knowledgeable in the Scriptures became powerful preachers against the 'idolatrous practices' of their people. In this way, traditional life was deeply undermined, and the family structure was disrupted.

In addition to Western education, medicine and technology also came through the missionaries. These improved people's health, reduced infant mortality, put under control diseases and ailments which people dreaded – for example, small pox, malaria, stomach pain and the like – discouraged superstition and fear and brought about better conditions of living.

But the encounter is not to be limited to Christianity, Western education and technology alone; we need to turn to an examination of Islam in the traditional society. Though Islam came into being in the 7th century A.D. in Arabia and was spread quickly in and outside Arabia soon after the death of its founder, Muhammed, in 632 A.D., it did not find its way to the western Sudan until about the 11th century and did not really enter the northern parts of Nigeria until the 14th century. Between the 14th and 19th centuries, it gradually gained a foothold in the north; but it did not penetrate into the wooded southern Nigeria until a much later time. When it did, it did not win as many converts as it won in the far north.

The Muslim approach to the traditional religion was different from the Christian approach. Islam was introduced to the Hausa and Fulani in northern Nigeria by Muslim itinerant traders. They were clever enough not to demand a sudden break with the traditional religion – they won converts gradually, and they made sure that they first enlisted the interest of their leaders. The rulers, in turn, influenced their subjects and encouraged them to say the Muslim confession of faith: "I believe there is no god but Allah, And Muhammed is the prophet of Allah."

Thus between the 14th century and the 18th century very few converts were made among the adherents of traditional religion called the Maguzawa.[6] Those who confessed to the Muslim faith were still practising traditional religion. Sacrifices were offered by the Maguzawa to a number of *iskoki* (spirits) found everywhere – in the sky, forest, hills and bodies of water. *Iskoki* (spirits) do possess worshippers, and such spirit possession is called *bori*. But a radical change came in the 19th century when Uthman dan Fodio, a Fulani born in Gobir who became an enthusiastic Muslim teacher, felt disgusted at the way his fellow Muslims were compromising with the adherents of African traditional religion. He quickly organized some of his followers into a fighting force and waged a holy war (*jihad*) against those who did not accept Islam, or those who were compromising with the traditional religion. In this way, Uthman dan Fodio forced many Hausa to boycott the traditional religion and accept Islam. He, therefore, purified Islam. He conquered the Hausaland and gained a foothold in Adamawa and Nupe areas of the north and got entry into Ilọrin, which is the gateway to the Yorubaland in the southwest.

From the foregoing we observe that Christianity and Islam, when they came in contact with traditional religion, caused a disruption and a division. Both divided the community into two camps — the converts (either Christians or Muslims) who looked down upon the old traditional religion and the loyal adherents of the traditional religion. Thus it can be asserted that from the middle of the 19th century to about the middle of this century, there was a big struggle between the imported religions and the indigenous religion held by Nigerians. As a result of the encounter, the indigenous culture was badly shaken. Many Nigerians became so westernized, Christianized, and Islamized that they came to look down on things indigenous and traditional.

But a dramatic change came about the middle of the 20th century when most countries in Africa became politically conscious and eventually achieved political independence. For example, in 1960 Nigeria attained political independence; and this affected many aspects of Nigerian life, including culture in general and religion in particular. There were many nationalists who associated the foreign religions with imperialism and colonialism and who would like to see Christianity and Islam done away with and have them replaced by the African traditional religion. The only saving grace was that, at the time of independence, there were strong Nigerians who were devoted Christians and Muslims. But Nigerians were forced to reexamine their stand vis-à-vis the African traditional religion. In the wake of the reevaluation of Nigerian culture, indigenous languages, style of dressing, art, music, drumming, dancing, and observances of traditional festivals, among other things, received a boost.

But in no area was the cultural revolution taken more seriously than in that of religion. In consequence of this move, traditional religion came to be recognized as a religion that Nigerians could embrace without a feeling of inferiority among the adherents of the foreign religions. This is to suggest that, with political independence, Nigerians started to become independent not only politically but also in their spiritual heritage. Hence we agree with Bascom and Herskovits when they said:

> Despite the intensity of Christian missionary effort and the thousand years of Muslim proselytising which have marked the various parts of Africa, African religions continued to manifest vitality everywhere. This is to be seen in the worship of African deities, the homage to the ancestors, and the recourse to divination, magic, and other rituals....7

In consequence of the restoration of African traditional religion to a position of honor, the government and the people of Nigeria gave recognition to the existence of three religions in the country, namely African traditional religion, Christianity, and Islam. The Department of Divinity in the University of Ibadan had to change its name to the Department of Religious Studies to convince the government and nation that it was offering courses not only in Christianity and Islam but also in Nigerian traditional religion.

Traditional Festivals which hitherto were secretly observed or were becoming neglected came to be given wide publicity in news media; and Nigerian men and women, whether Christians or Muslims, showed no inhibition or remorse in going to watch or even to participate actively in such traditional festivals.

Ulli Beir, who lived in Ọṣun area of Ọyọ State, was right in his assessment of the attitude of the present generation of indigenous worshippers of Oṣogbo when he observed: "After the first wild abandonment of traditional values, a certain re-adjustment is now taking place. The largest attendance at the annual Ọṣun festival testifies to this. Few people attending the festival would classify themselves as *Oloriṣa*. Yet every person in Oṣogbo, even fanatical Muslims and Christians, knows that they are children of Ọṣun."8

Moreover, instead of shrines with temporary roofs of thatches and grasses and walls made of bamboos and raphias which can easily be blown off by wind or destroyed by termites, there sprang up more permanent shrines with corrugated iron sheets for roofing and cement blocks or burnt bricks for the walls. The Ifa Temple at Ile-Ife, for example, is a huge edifice situated on Oke-Itaṣẹ hill overlooking the city. The huge building compares favorably with any cathedral church in size. Similarly, the Ọṣun shrines in Oṣogbo have been remodeled by Susanne Wenger, a European artist who has accepted traditional religion and who has become a devotee of a number of divinities worshipped in Yorubaland, particularly Ọṣun and Ṣango.

At the introduction of Christianity to Nigerians, newly converted Christians at their baptism must adopt new names which must be Jewish or English to show that they accepted Christianity. Thus we found Nigerian Christians taking such names as Moses, Joseph, Deborah, Keturah, Wellington, Jackson, and the like. With the attainment of independence, the people realized that it was of no spiritual value to take these Jewish or English names, for such names were regarded as colonial. Names given to children during the traditional naming ceremony are now adopted for Christian baptism; and Jewish or English names are now being dropped by those bearing them, and the present generation of children are not given such foreign names. Instead of foreign names people now bear names like Ọmọṣade, Iyabọ, Ọbafẹmi, Ngozi Chukuemeka, and the like.

In 1977, Nigeria made history in cultural revival when it mounted the Festival of Arts and Culture (FESTAC). This was the biggest effort made to call the attention of the world to the rich culture of this nation. Different aspects of traditional religion, in addition to the traditional music, dancing, drama, art, and oral literature figured prominently. Right from the village level to the urban center, Nigerians were encouraged to participate in the cultural revival. Traditional religion was given prominence in both radio and television programs. Adherents of traditional religion now carry out their worship and observe occasional and annual festivals without any inhibition.

Although the traditional religion receives this sort of fillip from the nationalists who organized cultural revival, we must be ready to accept the fact that traditional religion in its old conservative form cannot be practiced as in pristine time. For example, the practices of killing twins and offering human sacrifice in some parts of Nigeria before the advent of Christianity and British rule are gone forever. But some aspects of traditional religion like the use of extempore prayer, drumming, singing, and dancing during worship are already being adopted by Christianity. In this way, there is now healthy interaction between one religion and another in Nigeria. And this is to be expected because in natural life people of diverse faiths live together under the same roof. In other words, brothers and sisters in Nigeria profess different faiths; but they do not cut one another's throat. They instead accommodate one another, upholding the philosophy of "Live and let live."

Notes

1. J. Ọmọṣade Awolalu, "Continuity and Discontinuity in African Traditional Religion," *ORITA, Ibadan Journal of Religious Studies*, XIII/2 December 1981, 7.
2. E.A. Ayandele, *The Missionary Impact on Modern Nigeria* (Longmans, 1966), 56f.
3. J.F. Ade Ajayi, *Christian Missions in Nigeria*, 1965, 34.
4. M.Am Onwuejeogwu, *An Igbo Civilization: Nri Kingdom and Hegemony* (Ethiope Publishing Corporation, 1981), 175.
5. Obaro Ikime, *The Isoko People: A Historical Survey* (Ibadan University Press, 1972), 61–62.
6. For details concerning the Maguzawa, see M. Goriawala in *ORITA, Ibadan Journal of Religious Studies*, vol. IV/2 Dec. 1970, 115–123. See also J. H. Greenberg, *The Influence of Islam on a Sudanese Religion* (New York, 1946), 9.
7. W.R. Bascom and M.J. Herskovits (eds.), *Continuity and Change in African Cultures* (University of Chicago Press, 1959), 3.
8. Ulli Beir, *The Return of the Gods* (Oxford University Press, 1975), 57.

11

TRADITIONAL AFRICAN RELIGION AND CHRISTIANITY

Vincent Mulago

IN THIS CHAPTER, I propose to discuss "traditional black African religion and Christianity."

My contribution will comprise three issues:

The essential elements of black African traditional religion;

The primacy of religion in the life of black Africans;

The encounter between traditional black African religion and Christianity.

The Essential Elements in Black African Religion[1]

To attempt a preliminary description of the religion of black Africans in general and of the Bantu in particular, it might be said that their religion is a complex of ideas, feelings, and rites based on:

- belief in two worlds, visible and invisible;
- belief that both worlds involve community and hierarchy;
- belief in the intersection of the two worlds, the transcendence of the invisible world in no way contradicting its immanence;
- belief in a Supreme Being, Creator, and Father of all that exists.

With this outline as a starting point, we hold that traditional black African religion can be considered as based on four essential elements:

- unity of life and participation;
- belief in the enhancement or diminution of beings and the interaction of beings;
- symbol as the principal means of contact and union;
- an ethic that flows from ontology.

Unity of life and participation. By unity in life or vital union, we understand a relationship in being and life of each person with descendants, family, brothers, and sisters in the clan, with ancestors, and with God who is the ultimate source of all life: *Nyamuzinda* (the completion of everything) according to the Bashi of Zaire, or *Imana* (source of all happiness) for Ruanda and Burundi; and an analogous ontic relation of each with their patrimony, their land, and all it contains and produces, with all that grows and lives there.

If you wish, vital union is the bond joining together, vertically and horizontally, beings living and dead; it is the life-giving principle in all. It is the result of communion, a participation in the one reality, the one vital principal that unites various beings.

This life, with which Africans are preoccupied, is not simply empirical life but also super-empirical life (life beyond the grave) since, in their view, the two are inseparable and interdependent. Two beliefs underlie veneration of the dead: survival of the individual after death and the interchange of relations between the living and the dead. This double belief, which amounts to an axiom, knows no skeptics.

The life of the individual is understood as participated life. The members of the tribe, the clan, the family know that they live not by a life of their own but by that of the community. They know that, if separated from the community, they would lack the means to survive; above all, they know that their life is a participation in that of ancestors, and that its conservation and enhancement depend continuously on them.

For black Africans, living means existing in the bosom of the community; it means participating in the sacred life—and all life is sacred—of the ancestors; it means a prolongation of the ancestors and preparing one's own prolongation through descendants. There is a true continuation of the family and of the individual after death. The dead form the invisible element in the family, in the clan, in the tribe, and this invisible element is the more important. In all ceremonies of any significance, on the occasions of birth, marriage, death, funerals, or investiture, it is the ancestors who preside, and their will yields only to that of the Creator.

Africans believe firmly that there is a living communion or bond of life which makes for solidarity among members of the same family or clan. The fact that we are born into a family, a clan, or a tribe immerses us in a specific current of life, "incorporates" us and molds us to the fashion of that community; it modifies all our being "ontically" and orients us to living and behaving in the manner of that community. So, family, clan, and tribe form wholes in which each member is only a part. The same blood, the same life participated in by all and received from the first ancestor, the founder of the clan, circulates in everyone's veins. For the protection, maintenance, enhancement, and perpetual preservation of this common treasure, it is a duty to work with all our energy, to wage ruthless war against all that is opposed to it, and to support at any price anything that favors it. This is the last word on the customs, institutions, wisdom, philosophy, and religion of Africans.

We have defined vital union, first, as a relation of being or life uniting all the members of one community, and, second, as an analogous ontic relation uniting all its members and all that affects the maintenance or improvement of life, including patrimony and land. This second element also plays its part: all the appurtenances of the ancestors are closely connected with their being; one might refer to these objects that have belonged to the ancestors (spear, drum, diadem, etc.) as instruments of vital union. Life, then, for black Africans, can be understood in two ways: as community in blood, the principal and primordial element, and as community in possessions, a concomitant element making life possible.

Each society, family, clan, tribe, or nation can be considered from the point of view of participation. In fact, the measure of participation in life is the norm of the hierarchy of beings and of social status. An African only counts in their own eyes and in the eyes of society to the extent that they participate in life and transmit life. The logic is quite clear on this point: whoever gives life or any means towards life to another person is to that extent superior to him.

Belief in the enhancement or diminution of beings and in their interaction of beings. If you ask how a man becomes a chief, it is likely that the answer you get will suggest that it happens by simple default, through the death of all elders who had precedence over him so that he remains the oldest person, or else because he has been designated by his predecessor or by the elders of the clan. However, such response is insufficient and even inexact. "A person becomes chief of the clan...by internal enhancement of vital power, raising the *muntu* of the patriarch to the level of mediator and channel of power between the ancestors, on the one hand, and the descendants with their patrimony, on the other."[2]

As the Bantu conceive it, then, there is a change that is ontic, a profound transformation, a new form of being. This new form of being modifies or, better, adapts one's intimate being so that it lives and behaves according to the new situation, that is to say, it behaves like the ancestors so as to be a worthy continuation of them. Investiture conferring on the heir the possessions of his ancestors is the rite which is meant to produce this internal modification.

> The king is not a man...
> He is man before his appointment to the throne;
> But once appointed, he is separated from the ordinary nobility
> And he acquires a place apart.[3]

Yet, before his designation, before the investiture that consecrates and transforms him, the king is no more than a simple mortal, a man like the others. Now that the finger of God and of his ancestors have pointed him out to assume the government of his people, there is produced in him, precisely by this designation that consecrates the investiture, a total change, a change of heart in the Hebrew sense.

What has happened? All the vital energies, all the blood lineage from the ancestors, all the life which God has placed in them so that he can perpetuate it and make it fruitful, have invaded this man and have so strengthened his being—his *ntu*—that he has become a synthesis of the ancestors and the living expression of the Supreme Being and of His divine munificence.

This can be said also, observing due proportion, of chiefs and of sub-chiefs, extending the consideration as far as simple clan chiefs and fathers of families. Succession is always conceived as an ontic modification, a vital enhancement, the "passing over" of something of the deceased parents to their successors. As there can be an increase in being, so also it can happen that being is violently diminished. As the king is no longer a mere man after his appointment, he can also become a simple mortal again when the ancestors, represented by their descendants—the people—simply on account of the latter's interest and well-being, withdraw their confidence.

To underline the representative character of power, the Bashi have instituted an annual feast, the *omubande*, for renewing the royal investiture. So, just as vital union is a relation in being and life with God, with the ancestors, and with the descendants, and a similar ontic relation with the appurtenances that make life possible, similarly vital diminution will be nothing other than the consequence of blocking the flow of the vital current. To bring about a vital impairment of a deceased relative would be to cut off their connection with the living, with the members of their family and of their clan. It is to make sure these connections are never broken that a person strives to live on through descendants. For their part, the living must continue to receive vital influx from ancestors and deceased parents, on pain of seeing their life fade away. Vigor, or life, is the first object of all prayers addressed to ancestors, to deceased parents, and to the spirits of protective heroes, and of all prayers invoking the name and intervention of the Supreme Being.

Life is also diminished by any evil spell: sorcerers are universally detested for that. Equally, it is diminished by any violation of the neighbor's rights. Every spiritual or material injury has its repercussion and influence on life. The evil before all others, the greatest of all injustices is to insult the vital honor of someone. It would be such a case "when a less senior person makes a decision independently, disposing of what belongs to the clan, without recognition of the elders."[4] Just as "every service, all help and assistance, counts as a support and enhancement of life for the one who benefits" and as "its value corresponds exactly to the value of the life that is enhanced," so every injustice, however minimal, will be regarded primarily as a slight on the integrity of being, on the intensity of life. Any injustice is regarded, in the first place, as an attack on the life (that is, on the vital force) of the person who is injured; its malice is related to the great respect owed to human life as God's supreme gift.... It will not be the extent of damage suffered but rather the importance of the violation of life which will be taken as the basis on which reparation of the damage is calculated."[5]

For Africans, beings always retain their intimate ontic relationship to one another, and the idea of distinct beings which happen to be alongside one another but completely independent is quite foreign to their thought. All manifestations of life bring out this element of interaction between beings.

Thus, the black African community forms a vital circuit where the members live in inter-dependence for their mutual advantage. To want to leave this circuit and to escape from the influence of members who are vitally superior would amount to no longer wanting to live.

Symbol: the principal means of contact and union. If the bond uniting the members of a black African community is nothing other than participation, "that is to say, a given solidarity, presenting itself under two inseparable aspects, one personal, the other material,"[6] then the principal — often the only — means available to the members of entering into mutual contact and of strengthening union is the symbol. In order to discover the position and role of symbolism in the life and religion of the black African, we must trace the way life manifests itself from birth to death and beyond the grave, pausing at several stages in life, in particular:

- clan initiation
- spirit initiation
- communion in feasting and the blood pact
- rites of purification, confession, and reconciliation
- marriage ceremonies
- rites concerned with death
- investiture rites

From whatever perspective it is considered, symbolism[7] appears as the striving of the human spirit for contact with power, with the invisible world; it breaks out of the limits of "the fragment which is man in the bosom of society and in the midst of the cosmos"; it is a striving for unification. Hence the three elements belonging to the concept of symbol:

Something tangible: a living being as, for example, the king (symbolizing national unity and divine authority), the patriarch (symbolizing the authority of the ancestors over their descendants), the totem (symbol of clanic unity, etc.), words (like the name of the ancestor or the names of powerful personages, animals, materials, etc.), actions and gestures (like the imitation of the deeds and gestures of someone).

The role of hierophany, or contact with an invisible power. Man, in quest of means of vital enhancement, comes up against the world, against "things" which in reality are not "things." For in truth there are no "things"; there are only channels and reservoirs, which on occasion can contain power. There are two possibilities: either the "things" a man meets with are receptacles to be filled with power, or, on the other hand, the "things" are creatures—creatural. In the first case, there is magic to perform and man appears, somehow, if not as creator of things then at least as creator of powers that confer life. Creatures depend directly on God, and God can at any moment breathe new life into them, provide them with a new potentiality. He makes "things" instruments of his power, he transforms them and creates them anew. So it is that actions, words, or persons can at any time become "powers," either by the competence of the man who by direct force makes it his own power or else by the competence of God the Creator.[8]

So the symbol aims at putting us in contact with invisible powers and

4

forces, by virtue of certain correspondences or resemblances, a relation of connotation or analogy. The mediation of the symbol establishes a current and an exchange of life and vital energies between the being symbolized and the person entering into contact with the being. In this way, the most elementary activity of daily life can be raised to a sublime height when it is discovered "how far it touches on the divine," understanding the "divine" in the sense of all that has power to communicate, to enhance and to influence life in a way that is more than human.

A unifying and effective role. The being symbolized is so present in and so united with its symbol, at least from an operational standpoint, that it becomes possible for it to exercise its actions and influence, as if time and space did not exist. Thus the symbol's action can affect anyone who makes contact with it.

Symbolism appears as a "language" available to all the members of the community but inaccessible to strangers, a language expressing the relationship of the person using the symbol with Society and with the Cosmos, a language which "on the one hand puts the human person in solidarity with the Cosmos and on the other with the community of which he is part, proclaiming before all members of the community his profound identity."9 Symbolic experience signifies "not so much myself and the world but rather myself in the world." It abolishes the duality between man and the world and tends towards unification. Everything created is a gift to people from the Creator to ensure their existence, to contribute to the enhancement and safeguarding of their life.

An ethic that flows from ontology. For black Africans, and for the Bantu in particular, we observe that human life, and so man himself, is the criterion of good and evil; the basis of their moral conscience is connected with their philosophy; they attribute good and evil to several sources. Human life, that is, human persons as the center of creation, is the criterion of good and evil. Black African ethics are an anthropocentric and vital ethics. E.N. Mujynya writes:

> In the world of *ntu*, actions thought favorable to the blossoming of life, capable of conserving and protecting life, of making it flower and increasing the vital potential of the community are, for these reasons, considered good.... On the other hand, any act thought prejudicial to the life of the individual or of the community is judged evil, even where it only attacks the material interests of persons, physical or moral.... To understand this attitude, it is necessary to bear in mind that the Bantu consider human life as the most valuable good and that their ideal is not only to live to a good old age protected from anxieties but above all to remain, even after death, a vital force continually reinforced and

vivified in and through progeny.... In this *muntu* ideal, it is in relation to life and after-life, that every human act is judged.[10]

The basis of moral conscience relates to the black African conception of being, which is essentially synthethizing and unifying. "Being is fundamentally one and all beings that exist are ontologically bound to one another."[11]

In this organic conception, human being, the human *ntu*, is central:

> Above, and transcendent, is God.... Intermediary between God and man are all the ancestors, deceased members of the family and ancient national heroes, all the ranks of the disembodied souls. Below man are all the other beings which, basically, are only means at his disposal to develop his *ntu*, his being, his life. The Muntu world is very extensive but still unified thanks to the relations and interactions between the *ntu*. In this sense, one could speak of a global, cosmic philosophy. The bond is the life of Muntu; to its maintenance and enhancement all the universe, visible and invisible, is summoned to contribute. Everywhere and in all things, there are means of influencing life, and it is important to grasp these and to make their influence beneficent.[12]

Thus the world appears as a plurality of coordinated forces.

> This order is the essential condition of the integrity of beings. The Bantu add that this order comes from God and must be respected.... Objective morality for black Africans is an ontological morality, immanent and intrinsic. Bantu morality holds to the essence of things grasped in their ontology.... We may draw the conclusion that an act or a usage will, in the first place, be qualified as ontologically good by the Bantu and on that ground held to be morally good, and finally, by way of deduction, it will be judged juridically just.... Those are the norms of the good act; obviously the norms for an evil act are parallel to these. Any act or behavior, any human attitude or habit which attacks the vital force or growth or the hierarchy of *muntu* is bad. Destroying life is an infringement of the divine plan and the *muntu* knows that such destruction is, above all, an ontological sacrilege; for this precise reason, it is immoral and consequently unjust.[13]

So the Bantu ethic is an ethic of participation and communion with others.

While Bantu ethics are anthropocentric, it is no less true that God is always conceived as the source of life and of all the resources for existence. Even the names used to refer to the Supreme Being are significant in this regard. The proverbs are even more convincing. If good is attributed directly to God, it is different in the case of evil. This comes from people themselves or from the dead or from personified forces of evil. Evil cannot be from God, except as a "medicinal" resource, a means of mercy and goodness.

The Primacy of Religion in the Life of Black Africans

The study of rites and symbols in the life of black African peoples, and of the veneration they offer to their ancestors, and of their attitude to God, leads us to the conclusion that religion permeates the whole life of the black Africans — their personal, family, and socio-political life. Religion has the psychological and social function of integration and equilibrium; it enables people to understand and value themselves, to achieve integration, to accept their situations in life, to control their anguish. Thanks to religion, the duality between human beings and their world, visible and invisible, is overcome and unification achieved.

In black Africa, "religion permeates everything. Its guiding influence extends to political, social, and family life. In general, the religious spirit prevails over the political."[14]

The essential characteristic of the religion of blacks and of the Bantu in particular resides in the relation between religion and daily life. "Religion is not an abstract principle," writes A. Kagame, "nor even a collection of such principles, but a leaven which makes these principles work, vitally involved as they are with the religious laws and ceremonies which give external expression to this vitality."[15] With reservations cautioning us against certain expressions, he quotes an impressive passage from Bishop Le Roy:

> Religion...in Africa, if it is involved in everything, is also confused with everything: with laws and received customs, feasts, rejoicing, mourning, work and business, events, and accidents of life. It is even difficult at times to distinguish it in practice from medicine, science, superstition, and magic. That is why there is no word to indicate religion in general; it is included under the general expression "customs" — what is received from the ancestors, what has always been believed and done, the practices which must be observed to maintain the family, the village, the tribe, and whose neglect would bring about certain misfortunes — as we have often seen...[16]

"There," comments A. Kagame, "we have a description of a vigorous religion, whose followers blend it with all their activities. What matters is the intention by which nothing is profane. It is only the practitioners of a feeble religion who categorize their service as variously religious or profane. God cannot have intended that one who cultivates the land should cease to be holy during his work, or that one who works on the water should have to wait for the propitious hour for liturgical celebrations in a church, etc. Each person should ensure by his intention that everything, even his walking and breathing, should become religious activities putting him in constant contact with God."[17] Traditional religion does effectively play its role of reassurance and protection.

"Profoundly integrated into social and technical life, it permeates with its ritual all daily activities, and encloses people in a strong network of defenses and certitudes. It plays its part fully in the situations of traditional life."[18] Here we would like to respond to an objection often heard: "Is not African tradition—and to an even greater extent traditional religion—in process of disappearing, through the invasion of technology and industry?" A superficial observer might make this mistake, but for anyone who lives in real contact with Africans, the question simply does not arise.

At Bouake, certain members of the commission on religion in Africa had formulated the same objection. The report of the commission replied that "renunciation of his religion by an African is always artificial and without depth."[19] If Africans readily join religions imported from abroad, that does not in any way imply any split, in spirit or attitude, between their traditional religion and revealed religion. In concrete practice, the former always persists as base and foundation of any subsequent conversion.

This suggests that the future of African religions is not at all problematic for our generation. They have their place and play their role at every level of our societies. If we want to build an integrated and balanced society, to give Africa a chance of remaining true to herself, to develop her culture and traditional civilization in a modern spirit, then religion must be given the first place and must be made the foundation and the top of the cultural edifice of black Africa in general and of the Bantu people in particular.[20]

Encounter of Traditional Religion with Christianity[21]

Any meeting of two different realities incurs the risk of conflict. We do, in fact, observe at times conflict between the cultural heritage of black Africa and Christianity. The "appeal to authenticity" and other such movements and doctrines raise difficult questions for the heralds of the Christian message. Does the latter not appear as a foreign body in our culture and traditional religion? Those who do not know the essence of Christianity are quick to answer in the affirmative. Others who profess to know their Christianity but have only a superficial knowledge of black African religious traditions find that there is no problem: they are convinced that "paganism" must simply give way to Revelation. Whereas those who have an inside knowledge both of the essence of Christianity and of African religious values do not see two realities opposed to one another. God, who is the source of everything positive in our cultural patrimony, is at the same time the author of the Christian revelation. Faithful to himself, he cannot contradict himself. For through the centuries God, as a provident Father, has prepared the way for the Gospel.[22] That is why:

> The Catholic Church rejects nothing that is true and holy in these religions. She regards with sincere respect ways of acting and living, rules and doctrines which, while they differ on many points from what she herself holds and teaches, nevertheless often reflect a ray of truth enlightening all men. Yet, she proclaims and is bound to proclaim without ceasing Christ who is 'the way, the truth and the life' (Jn. 14:6), in whom men must find the fullness of the religious life and in whom God has reconciled all things to himself (cf., II Cor. 5:18–19).[23]

With Vatican II, in the Dogmatic Constitution on the Church, the following is affirmed:

> The one people of God is present in all peoples of the earth, receiving its citizens from all peoples.... But as the Kingdom of Christ is not of this world (cf., Jn. 18:36), the Church, or people of God in which the kingdom takes shape, takes nothing away from the cultural riches of any people; on the contrary, she fosters and takes to herself all the riches, all the resources and forms of life of these peoples in whatever they have of good. She purifies, strengthens, and elevates these resources. She is mindful that she must act as herald for the king to whom the nations have been given as a heritage (Ps. 2:8) and to whose city gifts are brought in tribute (cf., Ps. 71, 72:10; Isa. 60:4; Rev. 21:24). This character of universality adorning the people of God is a gift from the Lord himself; thanks to it, the Catholic church tends to gather up mankind as a whole with all its treasures, under Christ as head, in the unity of the Spirit.[24]

Thus, "the Church, salt of the earth and light of the world (cf., Matt. 5:13–14), is called in a most pressing manner to save and renew every creature, so that all may be restored in Christ and all men may, in him, form one family and one people of God."[25] For in Christ, the Church is "in a certain manner the sacrament, that is, at once the sign of and the means to intimate union with God and to the unity of the whole human race."[26]

It is in this perspective that we take up again the religious values of traditional Africa, her beliefs, and ethics, so as to come to a meeting of these values with Christian faith and morals.

Among black Africans there are para-religious and marginal beliefs and practices, among which the most significant are magic, sorcery, and divination. Blended with religious acts proper (e.g., ancestor veneration and relations with the Supreme Being), these beliefs play a prominent unifying role in symbolism and in expressing the sacred. Comparing these beliefs and practices with Christian faith, it should be said that, apart from what is called "black magic" or "sorcery," most of them, even if they contain errors, belong to the order of philosophy, rather than to religion. Now, Christian faith itself is not a philosophical system. But given that the faith has been handed down to us in philosophical categories that are alien to the black African mentality, difficulties arise.[27]

Belief in survival and in interaction between the living and the dead is the basis of the veneration of ancestors and of the deceased in general. With the veneration of ancestors, we associate the cult of heroes. In certain ethnic groups, we also encounter the worship of genies and of earth spirits. From the viewpoint of Christian faith, we can see absolutely nothing at odds in principle with the practice of making ancestors and other dead persons' beings the object of veneration, or even of a religious cult, provided that this does not exclude the worship due the Supreme Being. Now, in the groups we have studied, the worship of God does often underlie the worship given to the dead.

In all the groups we have studied, the Supreme Being, God, is at the summit. He is conceived as the original source of all life and of all the resources of life, the Father of mankind and of things, who covers everything he has created with his divine providence. If it were not for prejudices and for ignorance of the technical terms indicating the Supreme Being in indigenous languages, there would have been no problem, since the idea of God among black Africans—at least among the Bantu we have been able to study—seems one of the purest ever encountered in the course of history.[28]

Vital participation is the basis of all community and interdependence, of one's interaction with other people and with the environment and cosmos. Communion as participation is the foundation of solidarity, mutual aid, and co-responsibility in being and acting, in possessions, and in work. Thanks to an innate feeling of participation, it is impossible to separate belief in the Supreme Being from belief in survival and in the interaction between the living and the dead, or from para-religious beliefs. This harmony is to be cherished as a black African religious synthesis.[29]

For the Bantu and for black Africans in general, ethics, worship, and law derive from their vision of the world, as we have indicated. Concerning ethics, certain points deserve special attention.

In the encounter between black African anthropocentric ethics and Christian theocentric morals, the herald of the Gospel must know where to situate human person.

Black African ethics are not legalistic or juridical but vitalistic: they are at the service of life and thus totally open to the morality of the Gospel (Jn. 10:10).

Black African ethics are an ethics of communion with others, with people, and with the natural environment— they are global and cosmic ethics. Likewise, Christian morality is based on communion and co-responsibility.

Respect for parents and for hierarchical order is a mark of black African ethics; here they fall in line with one of the Ten Commandments.

Respect for life and for the resources for existence and conservation is another mark of black African culture. It accords here with the Christian message.

Because the ultimate objective for black Africans is to maintain, prolong, and perpetuate life, it is easy to understand how their ethic is indulgent with regard to acts which are contrary to divine law but favor life and the perpetuation of the lineage: polygamy and extra-matrimonial relations in certain cases. In this field, we need more study in order to find the remedy.

Finally, we must not neglect the question of the interior life. In the minds of many black Africans, a desire not brought to realization does not constitute an evil, while, on the other hand, material acts concerning prohibitions and taboos are thought to make the involuntary transgressor guilty. By awareness of interiority and of intention, we should clarify the place of the moral act in conscience and bring freedom to our Christians.[30]

Conclusion

The vital relationship which founds the unity of communities and individuals, this communion as participation in life and the resources of life, this striving for growth and ontological enhancement, is the center and synthesis of family, politico-social and religious life for these people. The role of participation permeates the life of black Africans; and their mentality, purified and perfected, will have its place in the future of humankind. "I would even add," writes M. Blondel, "that to achieve a comprehensive science of thought, this primitive mentality could serve as a source of rejuvenation, against the desiccation and sclerosis that for us masquerades as mental health."[31]

In his October 29, 1967 message "Africae Terrarum,"[32] Paul VI, after having distinguished the constants from the accumulated contributions of present-day ethnology, affirmed that these values are a source of pride for the peoples of Africa. He concluded that the progress which gives access to new forms of knowledge and life ought to consist in making modern Africa, on the basis of these traditional values, both rich in its ancestral patrimony and open to contributions from other civilizations. During his first journey to Africa, in an address of May 6, 1980 to diplomats accredited to the government here in Nairobi, John-Paul II emphasized Africa's role in today's world:

> My fervent hope is that the free nations of independent Africa will take the place that belongs to them in the family of nations. In the search for peace, justice, and international unity, Africa has an important role to play. Africa constitutes a treasure house of so many authentic human values. She is called to share these values with other nations and by so doing enrich the whole human family and all other cultures. But to do this, Africa must remain profoundly faithful to herself; day by day, she must be ever more faithful to her own heritage, not out of any spirit of opposition or antagonism to the others but through belief in the truth....
>
> It will be the glory of this continent and of this nation to create a way of progress for all its inhabitants, fully in harmony with the whole of mankind. The true model for progress is not that which glorifies material values but that which recognizes the priority of the spiritual.[33]

Notes

This paper was translated from the French text by the Center for New Religious Movements, Selly Oak Colleges, Birmingham B29 6LQ, United Kingdom.

1. See V. Mulago Gwa Cikala, "Elements fondamentaux de la religion africaine," in *Religions africaines et Christianisme*, (colloque international de Kinshasa, 9–14 Jan. 1978), 1. *Cahiers des religions africaines*, special number, vol XI, no. 21–22, 1977, pp. 43–62; *La religion traditionelle des bantu et leur vision du monde*, Kinshasa, 133–163; "Religioni traditionali africane Montu: vivere credere," in *Nigrizia*, Feb. 1987, 27–38.
2. P. Tempels, *La philosophie bantoue* (Paris, 1961), 69–70.
3. A. Kagame, *La poesie dynastique au Rwanda* (Brussels, 1951), 53.
4. Tempels, *La philosophie bantoue*, 95.
5. Tempels, *ibid.*, 95–96.
6. J. Przyluski, *La participation* (Paris, 1949), 148.
7. Cf. D.B. Sartore, *Dizionario Teologico Interdisciplinare*, Vol. III, Marietti, Turin, 1977, *sub voce* "Segno-simbolo," 231–242.
8. G. van der Leeuw, *La religion dans son essence et ses manifestations* (Paris, 1948), 353.
9. M. Eliade, *Traite d'histoire des religions* (Paris, 1953), 385.
10. E.N. Mujynya, "Le mal et le fondement dernier de la morale chez les Bantu interlacustres," in *Cahiers des religions africaines*, III, 5, 1969, 63–64.
11. Th. Theuws, "Philosophie bantoue et philosophie occidentale," in *Civilisations* I, 1951, 59.
12. V. Mulago, *Un visage africain du christianisme* (Paris, 1965), 155.
13. Tempels, *La philosophie bantoue*, 80–81.
14. *Traditions et modernisme en Afrique noire* (Recontres internationales de Bouake) Paris, 1965, 94.
15. A. Kagame, *La philosophie Bantu comparée* (Paris, 1976), 304.
16. (Bishop) A. Le Roy, *La religion des primitifs* (Etudes sur l'histoire des religions, no. 1), Paris, 1925, 57–58, quoted by A. Kagame in *La philosophie Bantu comparée*, 304.
17. A. Kagame, *La philosophie Bantu comparée*, 304.
18. J.C. Froelich, *Les nouveaux dieux d'Afrique* (Paris, 1969), 50.
19. *Tradition et modernisme en Afrique noire*, 94.
20. See *Colloque sur les religions* (Abidjan, April 1961) Paris, 1962; *Les religions africaines traditionnelles* (Recontre International de Bouake) Paris, 1965; *Les religions africaines comme source de valeurs de civilisation* (Colloque de Cotonou, 16–22 Aug. 1970) Paris, 1972; *Religions africaines et christianisme* (Colloque International de Kinshasa, 9–14 Jan. 1978). Special numbers of *Cahiers des religions africaines* XI, 21–22, 1977; XII, 23–24, 1978. *L'Afrique et ses formes de vie spirituelle* (Deuxieme Colloque International de Kinshasa 21–27 Feb. 1983). Special number of *Cahiers des religions africaines* XVII, 33–34, 1983. *Mediations africaines du sacre. Celebrations creatrices et langage religieux* (Troisieme Colloque International de Kinshasa, 16–22 Feb. 1986); special number of *Cahiers des religions africaines* XX-XXI, 40–42, 1986–1987.
21. See Mulago gwa Cikala, *La religion traditionnelle des Bantu et leur vision du monde*, 169–177.

22. Cf., Vatican II, Dogmatic constitution on Divine Revelation, *Dei Verbum*, nos. 3 and 4.

23. Vatican II, Declaration on relations with non-Christian religions, *Nostra aetate*, no. 2.

24. Vatican II, *Lumen gentium*, no. 13.

25. Vatican II Decree on missionary activity *Ad gentes*, no. 1.

26. *Lumen gentium*, no. 1. For further developments, see our *Un visage africain du christianisme*, esp. 15–34 ("La theologie et ses responsabilities") and 221–227 ("Conclusion") and the collective work *La pertinence du christianisme en Afrique* (Actes de la Vie Semaine Theologique organisee par la faculte de Theologie catholique de l'Universite Nationale du Zaire, Campus de Kinshasa, 19–23 July 1971), Mayidi, 1972.

27. The remark applies also to the following points.

28. Cf. M. Pauwels, *Imana et le culte des Manes au Ruanda* (Brussels, 1958), 43.

29. Cf. V. Mulago, *Un visage africain du christianisme*, 15–34, 159–227; "Christ-ianisme et culture africaine: apport africain a la theologie" in *Christianity in Tropical Africa*. (Studies presented and discussed at the seventh international African seminar at the University of Ghana, April 1965) Oxford UP 1968, 308–328.

30. We could go on to treat at length the "stepping-stones" in black African ethics in the encounter with Christian morals: hospitality, "values of the heart," etc. We could also lengthen the list of "stumbling-stones": narrowness of the clan spirit, rules of revenge, mystique of authority, etc. We do not go into all this. For those who wish to know more, we suggest, among other treatments, *Ethique chretienne et valeurs africaines* (Report of Colloquium organized by the Lovanium Theological Faculty of Kinshasa 9–11 April 1969) in *Cahiers des religions africaines* III, 5, 1969, 149–159; D. Nothomb, "Possibilite et necessite d'une morale chretienne de type 'ntu'" in *Au coeur d l'Afrique* 5, 1969, 237–252; F. Nyirimpunga, *La morale des non-chretiens et le christianisme au Rwanda* (Fribourg, 1973); Nyeme Tese Munga, *Ethique en un milieu africain. Gentilisme et christianisme* (Rome, 1975).

31. M. Blondel, *La Pensee. I. La génèse de la pensee et les paliers de son ascension spontanee* (Paris, 1948), 324.

32. Paul VI, *Africae terrarum*, AAS 59 (1967) 1073–1097; *La documentation catho-lique*, no. 1505 (1967) col. 1937–1956.

33. AAS 72 (198) 486ff., *La documentation catholique* t 77 no. 1787 (1980) 528ff. (no. 11–12).

12

REVITALIZATION IN AFRICAN TRADITIONAL RELIGION

Rosalind I.J. Hackett

As someone who has been interested for a number of years in religion and social change, particularly in the African context, my attention has focused increasingly on the ways in which traditional religion has adapted to the pressures of modernity.[1] It is well documented that traditional religions suffer institutional decline and diminishing appeal in the face of modernization. In this paper I intend to examine some of the ways in which traditional religious beliefs and practices have found new forms of expression and new avenues of survival in the modern world and study the processes whereby traditional religion remains a cultural, political, economic, and religious force.

These processes, to which I am referring generally as revitalization processes,[2] and which normally lead to some form of continuity and survival (which I shall discuss in the latter part of this paper), I have identified as follows: universalization, modernization, commercialization, politicization, and individualization. (It goes without saying that in reality there may be overlap between the various categories.) I propose

to address each process individually, with relevant examples drawn from
my first-hand experience of the Nigerian situation. This will be followed
by some concluding reflections on future developments of traditional
religion in Africa.

Some of the forms of traditional religious expression to be treated
here inevitably raise the question of where traditional religion ends and
neo-traditional religion begins. In other words, my inclusion of certain
forms of religious expression under the rubric of "traditional" could be
questioned. While I do not claim to treat this question systematically in
the context of the present paper, I am convinced that African traditional
religious beliefs and practices may find continuity in new forms and
contexts.

Before commencing the first section, some comments are in order
regarding the nature of religious change. It is important to note that it
is not the system *in toto* which is altered, but rather various levels,
concepts, practices, and symbols. Fabian views the issue as a "battle of
symbols" rather than of "powers" or "institutions" because "religious
perceptions and solutions are embodied in specific symbols (verbalized
world views, myths, rituals)."[3] Horton, in his article entitled "African
Conversion,"[4] concludes that a change and development of ideas takes
place. As the macrocosmic impinges on the microcosmic, there is a
corresponding de-emphasis on the worship of local spirits, and there is
instead the growth in importance of the cult of the Supreme Being.
Horton's analysis is appropriate in many cases, but we may also find
instances where the process of change which he describes does not
occur, or at least it does not follow the pattern he suggests. Some
societies (for example, Uganda and Ghana) have, rather, experienced a
"multiplication of spirits" in recent years. Other writers have demonstrated that it is the cultic, collective, or calendrical aspects of traditional
religion which are most susceptible to decline and "ordinarily disappear
when a society diminishes in power or loses its identity."[5] Individual or
critical rites, normally associated with healing, divination, and magic,
tend to persist, largely because they continue to meet important needs
in a changing world.

Universalization

The chief characteristic of this process is the attempt to give African
traditional religion a wider appeal and outreach. Contact with other
(world) religions and the desire to "universalize" the African belief
system have often led to the development of the concept of the Supreme
Being, known by the various names in each African culture—Abasi,
Ọlọrun, Chineke, etc. This has generally resulted in the exclusion of the

subordinate deities and spirits, "because only the High God can sanction the codes of conduct required for wider discourse."[6] Movements in this category reflect interaction with Christianity and Islam. One of the most outstanding examples is that of Godianism. This emerged as a neo-traditional movement in Nigeria in 1948, seeking to restore worship of the "God of Africa," and was known as the National Church of Nigeria. Over the last thirty years its founder and High Chief Priest, Chief K.O.K. Onyioha, has reoriented the movement from a political to a more cultural and philosophical bias. In his own words, "Godianism is a philosophical evaluation and appropriate identification of Africa's traditional religious habits and practices capable of universal application."[7]

Chief Onyioha is concerned "to correct the notion that Africa's traditional religion or religious heritage was paganism."[8] He emphasizes throughout his writings and expositions that "our African ancestors spoke to their God directly without passing through any medium,"[9] in contrast to the "foreign religions" of Christianity and Islam. This is an obviously disputable claim since he overlooks the role of religious functionaries in this regard. He refers to a type of reconversion process for both African and Afro-Americans: "The time shall come when future generations of the black world shall achieve through cultural awareness and self-realization to know [sic] that both Christianity and Islam are foreign to them, and drop them in a right-about-turn, to look for true African religion, in origin and content."[10]

The expansion of the field of vision and application (what Horton would call its macrocosmic aspect) of this neo-traditional movement is interesting in two respects. First, there is Godianism's unifying function with regard to all traditional religions of Nigeria—Godianism was to serve as the "coordinating and harmonizing philosophy."[11] The implementation of this vision has naturally been very limited, but we should note the spirit of revitalization and unity generated by Festac 77 and by the Conference of Traditional Religions which preceded it in 1975. The latter conference resulted in a joint Declaration of Traditional Religions of Nigeria[12] which was later adopted in a larger context with the decision to form an Organization of Traditional Religions of Africa.[13] Second, Godianism is conceived of as a "religion for all mankind." As a "practical religion" based on love, universal brotherhood,[14] and a direct and unmediated approach to God, Godianism has come "to give the world an 'ism' which is African both in its origin and content, and synthesized by African intelligence, not only to tell the world that Africa is not after all philosophically void, but also to compromise the conflicting religious philosophies of the various nations and races and return mutual understanding and quiet to the religious front."[15]

Before turning to other examples, we may recapitulate on some of the features which characterize this revitalized form of African traditional religion. Godianism marks an attempt to transcend ethnic, even national, religious boundaries. To this end it has evolved a theology and has incorporated the use of a creed in order to articulate its doctrines. The founder, Chief K.O.K. Onyioha, is active in disseminating information concerning the religion. He travels around in a small bus marked "Godian Religion" and conducted a lecture tour of American universities in 1973. His "intellectualized" approach is further illustrated in his series of publications.[16]

Modernization

The process of "modernizing" traditional religion may take several forms. The "Aquarian Church of the Angels" was founded by Jimmy A. Oparaji of Okuruato in Aboh-Mbaise Local Government Area, Imo State in Nigeria in September 1981. The movement is described by him as "a modernization of the church of our forefathers"[17] and as "a new concept of religion which is almost akin to the traditional worshipping in the ancient times."[18] It is reformative in nature, seeking to propagate those traditional beliefs, practices, and values which are relevant to modern times such as peace and stability, justice, lawfulness, preservation of "our culture and national heritage." This reworked version of traditional religion gives prominence to "the Supreme Being called God" who "lives in the soul of pure people," describing idol worship and juju as "the result of illiteracy." As the name of the movement suggests, various Christian forms have been adopted, but adapted to a more traditional content. Rev. J. A. Opariji explains that "unlike other organizations which comprise bishops, ordained priests, and pastors, the spiritual leaders of the new church would comprise Ezes, Nzes, traditional rulers, and *ofo* title holders as the custodians of traditional religion."[19] We should nonetheless note that the spiritual leader of the church uses the designation of "Reverend."

Further examples may be drawn from western Nigeria. The cult of Orunmila has undergone a radical reorganization (meetings of priests, construction of meeting houses), in an attempt to achieve self-preservation and revitalization through greater organization.[20] Even before the 1940s, "The Church of Orunmila" had grown up with branches in several parts of the country.[21] By 1943, the theory was being propounded that Orunmila was the prophet of God to the Yoruba (or rather the Africans) and that Orunmila was the progenitor of Jesus Christ. The borrowing of organizational forms is again apparent, as in

the case of the Aquarian Church of the Angels, but with the addition of
a reworked synthesis of traditional and Christian myths. Parrinder refers
to their booklet which proclaims a God of Africa who is said to have
been revealed in Ifa and in the God of thunder of Yoruba religion and
of the Old Testament.[22] He notes their borrowing of Christian forms
in order to oppose Christianity, a process that we may note elsewhere.

A well-known festival, the Oke'badan festival of Ibadan, where people worship the hill goddess and celebrate the founding of the town by
Lagelu, constitutes an interesting response to the influence of Westernization, Christianity and Islam, which have taken their toll on the
impact and cultic significance of the festival. Steps have been taken to
institutionalize the worship of Oke'badan (the goddess of the hill of
Ibadan). In a study of the festival, Ola Makinde describes how "a
modern building has been erected for the goddess at a shrine at Oja'ba
where the worshippers worship and hold meetings. The shrine has
electricity and two big loudspeakers like the Christian churches and
Moslem mosques."[23]

The signboard outside the building indicates quite clearly the name
given to this more institutionalized form of Oke'badan worship – "The
Indigenous Faith of Africa" or "Ijọ Ọsẹ-meji." Makinde points out that
Ọsẹ-meji is one of the sixteen principal canons of the Ifa oracle which
was chosen for the founding of the city of Ibadan.[24] In addition, the
wider ramifications and implications of the festival are seen in the public
lectures which are organized by various Ibadan groups, university students,[25] and the Ibadan Municipal Council on topics relating to the
festival, Ibadan, and public health and welfare. This may represent a
"shift in purpose" of which Bennetta Jules-Rosette speaks in her book
on *The New Religions of Africa*.[26] In the case of the Ibadan festival there
appears to have been a weakening of the historical and religious aspects,
counterbalanced by an increased emphasis on the political and cultural
solidarity of Ibadan people, whether specifically Oke'badan worshippers, or Christians, Muslims, or atheists.

Another example of the modernization of traditional modes of worship is the founding by a group of intellectuals known as Orile-Orisa of
a traditional shrine in 1977 on the University of Ife (now Obafẹmi
Awolọlọ University) campus, at Ile-Ife.[27] The shrine represents an attempt to reassert the identity of the traditional worshippers on the
campus, and by providing a place of worship and regular worshipping
times, a community has been constituted alongside those of the Muslims
and Christians, which had come to dominate religious life on the campus. Despite opposition from certain sectors of the university community, the shrine is still active.

We might cite the ubiquitous and resilient Yoruba deity Ogun, who has shown wonderful powers of adaptation to his modernizing environment.[28] This stems partly from his domain of "jurisdiction" as god of iron; he has been able to extend his protection from hunters and blacksmiths to car mechanics, drivers, and even factory workers. At least two well-known factories in Ibadan carry out annual sacrifices to Ogun for the benefits of the workers.

Another interesting example may be drawn from Calabar in southeastern Nigeria. Anansa, believed to dwell in the river around Old Town or Obutong, is still, some would claim, the most prominent of all the Efik deities. Obutong is now virtually uninhabited due to the construction of the Calabar Cement Company (CALCEMCO) and the naval base there, but because, historically, it was the first Efik settlement after Creek Town, Anansa is always given pre-eminence in the list of deities. Her continued popularity and presence are also manifested in and are ensured continuity in the navy vessel named after her – the *S.S. Anansa*, which is permanently moored at the Eastern Naval Command Headquarters in Calabar. A series of accidents during the construction of the new port complex in Calabar in the late 1970s obliged the Nigerian Ports Authority to perform the necessary sacrifices to enable work to continue. Critical events of this nature, such as drowning or ferry accidents, are readily attributed to the *ndem* and their anger at having been neglected. The necessary sacrifices will hurriedly be performed in order to placate the deity in question and restore harmony.

We should not overlook the fact that Christianity may serve as a vehicle for the continuity of traditional beliefs and practices. Notable in this respect are the Nigerian independent churches. These churches, consciously or otherwise, provide an important medium for the continuity and regeneration of African traditional beliefs and practices. Their emphasis upon taboos, "mercy grounds," polygamy, divination, healing, dancing and drumming, and trance-like states and their theories of misfortune and evil have traditional roots, even if justification for some of the practices may also be found in the Old Testament. Many churches, however, are characterized by their complex processes of acceptance and rejection, and, while affirming African modes of worship, may at the same time fervently reject traditional deities and practices. This tension between the old and new, and the attempt to reconcile this through ritual and symbolism, explain why the churches are seen as an important medium in the wider context of social change.

Politicization

Some governments and political organizations still see in traditional religion a potential source of reinforcement and legitimation for their activities. Bennetta Jules-Rosette refers to this as the nationalization of traditional African folklore forms and dances for political use, which is termed political "animation" in francophone Africa.[29] She further describes such modification of traditional rituals: "The format and meaning of the dances retain only some evocative imagery, while the dominant symbols are transformed to communicate a political message."[30]

From my own observations based on field work among the Efik of Calabar, these new opportunities and new roles for traditional religion are encouraged by the traditional rulers and functionaries. The pouring of libations often performed by government figures at the opening of schools and hospitals and other such public functions could also be cited in this regard. It might be argued also that such rites and the appeal to the traditional code of ethics and communitarian values constitute the basis for a "civil religion." This civil, or "transfused," religion, as Mbiti terms it, is well established in Nigeria, for example, particularly since the return to civilian rule in 1979. The new constitution ensures secularity as well as religious plurality, which mirrors the American situation where the concept of "civil religion" was first born.[31] Teaching students in schools and universities the nature of their traditional religious heritage has become a popular activity in recent years, but it is a means of ensuring its intellectual, not its empirical, survival. Moral education is, however, an area where values and attitudes are consciously inculcated into pupils. Traditional values may have their place in the curriculum as long as there is a positive attitude to their role and function. African Humanism, a philosophy, albeit in nascent form, seems bound as it develops to compete increasingly as a viable worldview for modern Africans and offers a medium for the maintenance of selected traditional values.

Nationalism, especially of the pre-independence era, was quite clearly an area in which the spirit of traditional religions could live on. Idowu notes that even before what can be described as nationalism began in Nigeria "there had been signs of revolt against what people had come to regard as foreign religion and culture and voices in the wilderness have been raised as a signal for a return to the old ways and wisdom of the fathers."[32] In the course of two or three decades, however, the political scene has undergone considerable changes. Despite attempts to relate traditional religious symbols and values to the wider political community, the pressures of secularism, revolutionary ideals, and the international community have contributed to the erosion of the role and status of traditional religions.

The secret societies are an important cultural bastion. In Nigeria, these societies have survived the onslaught of government attack and political developments which have undermined their former power and authority, as well as campaigns by the churches. They have nonetheless undergone some internal modifications with a reduction of their religious identity in favor of a more politico-cultural orientation. Allegiance to and recognition of traditional deities is still a feature of these societies, but such practices may be in many cases a mere formality given the additional religious affiliations of initiates in a pluralistic society.

For example, the Ekpe Society, which operates in the Cross River region of Nigeria, is a major vehicle of religious and cultural traditions. It has suffered a considerable loss of political and judicial power, notably in the urban areas, where it has been unable to maintain its authority in the face of modern government and an increasingly pluralistic community. In response to these changes, it has undergone something of a metamorphosis and now styles itself as an "esoteric philosophical society." Some would even describe it as a "gentleman's club," along Masonic lines. Opinions differ as to whether the fraternity is flourishing or declining, but there is no doubt that the majority of leading figures in Efik society are members, for they see Ekpe as the most complete expression of their identity; many others are attracted by the cultural and social benefits afforded by membership.[33] In modern times, the Ekpe society has come to represent a bulwark against political subordination by the Ibibio and Igbo peoples, largely through its ability to build a common denominator and unifying force of the Efik, Qua and Efut peoples, and through its mystical, fearful, and esoteric aspects which are a source of power and authority and of attraction.[34]

Politico-cultural organizations and ethnic associations are areas of cultural revival and potential continuity of traditional religious forms and values. The Pan-Ibibio Language and Culture Association (PILCA), for example, adopted as a theme for its Second Annual Conference held at the University of Calabar in April 1985 "Religion and Cosmology among the Ibibio." What is selected and what survives in these organizations, however, are subject to their usefulness in serving an ulterior cause.

The institution of traditional kingship and chieftaincy in many parts of Africa is an important source for the revitalization of traditional religious beliefs and customs. The king or *obong* of Calabar, for example, represents a continuing focus of Efik cultural identity. Despite his virtual loss of political power, the Obong is still revered as the patriarch of the Efik people. He is considered to be the "living representative of all the spiritual and physical components of the Efik."[35] By virtue of his investiture, it is believed that he becomes more than an ordinary human being — he represents both aspects of existence. He is accorded elaborate funerary rites, as it is believed that he continues to be a man of special eminence in the afterlife. Some of the rites have been modified; for example, human sacrifice has been replaced by the sacrifice of a cow, and the king's possessions are not buried with him as before.

The rituals and ceremonies surrounding the installation and enthronement of the Obong have, in contrast, been carefully preserved. The traditional coronation (*uyara ntinya*) is performed in the ancient shrine of one of the Efik tutelary deities — known collectively as Ndem Efik Iboku. Some ceremonies are performed in the Efe Asaba (shrine of the cobra), which was first used as an Ndem shrine in 1660.[36] The chief priest or priestess is involved in the actual crowning of the Obong and the final salutation by the Ekpe society concludes the traditional king-making process. This demonstrates the complementarity of the two traditional religious institutions: Ndem, with its female and nature associations, and the Ekpe society, identified with the land, the town, and male power, are both necessary components of the making and maintaining of a king, as they are symbols of life itself.

The festivities surrounding the installation of a new Obong, which occur at a later stage over a period of a week, provide an important opportunity for the various traditional societies and masquerades to perform their ritual dances and plays, many of which grew out of the cults of Ndem and Ekpe.[37] It is also a time for other ethnic groups resident in Calabar such as the Bini and the Edo to offer homage to the paramount ruler through fine dances and masquerades. While the religious content may have been lost from many of these traditional forms, or is meaningless to many of the participants and spectators, some traditional religious norms and cultural conceptions are being communicated and perpetuated in this way. The whiteness and rich adornment of the ndem dancers symbolize the attributes of the "mermaids" who inhabit the river and are believed to protect the people of Calabar. The aggressive movements and dark, vivid colors of the Ekpe masqueraders symbolize the fearful *ekpe* forest spirit, which is "tamed" by the initiates to exert their authority over, and maintain law and order in, the community.

In the same area, the cult of Ekpenyong, one of the male ndem, has been revitalized through his role as patron deity of Nka Ekpenyong Nnuk — a cultural and philosophical organization, created in 1979 by the Efik youth of Calabar. In addition to its social and political aims, the group is attempting to stimulate Efik cultural awareness through the use of masquerades and other activities. Sacrifices to Ekpenyong are being revived on an annual basis, during the month of November. Ekpenyong is believed to protect Calabar and in particular his devotees. In popular mythology it is recounted how he temporarily halted the landing of the federal troops in Calabar during the civil war, until the necessary sacrifices were conducted to assure him of their positive intentions.

Commercialization

I understand commercialization to be the process whereby selected aspects of traditional religion are developed and marketed, not just for purely commercial purposes but as a means of promoting African tradition and its core beliefs and symbols.

The role performed by the Austrian artist, Susanne Wenger, in revitalizing the worship of the *Oriṣa*, notably of the river goddess Oṣun in western Nigeria, is worthy of mention here. For over thirty years Susanne Wenger has lived and worked among the people of Oshogbo. Through her art and her initiation into the Yoruba priesthood, she has succeeded in turning the virtually extinct annual Oṣun festival into a popular festival of almost "national" proportions. She has also been instrumental in reviving the interest of the people in their festival and Oriṣa cults, which had suffered decline as a result of the incursion of Islam and Christianity. Susanne Wenger has also sought to break down the barriers between the various cult groups and promote the integration and interchange "necessary for the survival of Yoruba religion under threatening modern conditions."[38]

The role played by the diffusion and distribution of African art in the West should not be underestimated. A magazine such as *African Arts*, for example, provides much ethnographic background and aesthetic analysis of African symbols, artifacts, and beliefs.

Traditional healing methods and pharmacopoeia are now being officially recognized by African governments and are being implemented and institutionalized in some parts of the continent. Herbalists' associations have come to the forefront after a certain disillusionment with Western medicine. This is an area in which traditional theories of evil and sickness may persist.[39]

A more blatant example of the commercialization of traditional religion would be the recreation of traditional cultic practices, masquerades, and festivals for non-religious purposes, i.e., weddings or launching ceremonies. I was told, for instance, in the town of Calabar, that for a reasonable fee, I could witness the performance of *Ndem* dances — traditional cultic dances of the local river gods.

Individualization

Individualization refers to the process whereby those rites which are oriented to individual and critical needs receive greater emphasis over and against more public rituals. The whole area of divination is worthy of mention in this respect, especially perhaps the Ifa divination cult in western Nigeria, for its continuing place in Yoruba society is evidence of the diviner's ability to satisfy certain needs of the individual in a rapidly developing society. These needs are largely "critical," dealing with sickness, death, and misfortune, and the prevention and removal of barriers to individual success or business enterprises. Although closely guarded, largely as a result of condemnation by the churches, some Nigerians talk of their relationship with a diviner in a way that is reminiscent of North Americans talking about their therapists.

Despite the advent of Western medicine, traditional healers continue to serve the needs of many with their ability to deal with "unnatural" or spiritual illnesses. Through their recognition of the agency of witchcraft and the power of traditional symbols, these healers serve to perpetuate traditional beliefs and practices.

Conclusion

In our examination of the processes whereby traditional religious beliefs and practices find new forms and life in the modern world, we can see how some of these examples have arguably outgrown the category of "traditional religions"; but we have included them in our discussion because they are all characterized by their attempt to revive and preserve traditional religious beliefs and practices. There are many factors — geographical, historical, religious, economic, political, cultural, and social — which may account for the variations in response to modernity. Examples from other parts of the world indicate the importance of the orientation of the movement in determining its success and development.[40] Cults or movements which are explicitly "nativistic" and geared to the preservation of traditional religious beliefs and practices have a greater chance of survival. Those movements which allow new forms and ideas to come in (whether occult, Western, or Christian), or view the incorporation of traditional religious features as a means to an end, such as political freedom, are very likely to lose or abandon their traditional identity as circumstances change.[41]

This serves to confirm the general agreement among scholars, in Africa and elsewhere, that distinguishable entities such as "Yoruba" or "Efik" religion are a rapidly disappearing phenomenon. But that does not mean that traditional beliefs, values, and practices may not persist in new areas and new guises.

There is no doubt that external factors such as missionary policies or revolutionary ideologies have taken their toll on traditional religions by questioning their basic premises or outlawing certain practices. Yet such action did not always have the required effect. Some traditional cults derived strength and solidarity (if only temporary) from the attacks on their *raison d'être*, which only serves to illustrate the point that it is virtually impossible to manipulate or predict human, and least of all, religious behavior. The most serious threat to the continuity of traditional religions in the Nigerian context, as elsewhere, is the changes generated by a rapidly changing society and the ability or inability of the religions to respond dynamically to these new needs and new situations. In this article we have tried to highlight the innovative and adaptive capacities of Nigerian traditional religion, as well as account for some of the variations in the creative response. Sometimes the response is characterized by an attempt to bring about greater institutionalization or by the desire to extend, even universalize, traditional beliefs. More frequently, we have noted a type of adjustive process with shifts in emphasis and purpose, as traditional religious leaders and functionaries take stock of their role and function in a modernizing and urbanizing society.

The question of the "survival" of African traditional religions (and it seems appropriate to broaden our vision at this stage) is reminiscent of the discussion surrounding the issue of secularization.[42] Analysis of these processes is affected by subjective attitudes. For instance, for some observers, the continued existence of certain forms, often devoid of content, is not enough to constitute the "survival" of a religious "system" or "tradition" as such. Some writers, influenced by missionary attitudes and political ideologies, document the decline in power and influence of the traditional religious beliefs and institutions, as if it were both necessary and inevitable. Other writers, such as Jules-Rosette, argue that purely "traditionalistic" revivals are impossible. Some, rather, see lingering beliefs in witchcraft, magic, the ancestors, spirits, etc. as superstitious remnants rather than true survivals of living religions.

I prefer to end on the more optimistic note of an African scholar: "But the subconscious depths of African societies still exert a great influence upon individuals and communities, even if they are no longer the only final sources of references and identity."[43] And finally, as we appreciate more fully the historicity of African religions, their capacity to innovate, their capacity to respond even to the challenge of the macrocosmic, so we come to abandon the idea of African religion today as merely a pathetic survival.[44]

Notes

1. Modernity refers to the conditions and way of life issuing from the industrial, technological, and intellectual revolutions in the Western world in the course of the last century. See S.D. Gill, *Beyond "the Primitive": The Religions of Nonliterate Peoples* (Englewood Cliffs, NJ: Prentice-Hall, 1982), 99.

2. This paper is a revised and expanded version of an earlier paper entitled "Innovation and Adaptation among Traditional Religions in Post-Independence Nigeria: Some Observations and Examples," *African Marburgensia*, 15.2 (1982), 31–46. I use the term "traditional" despite the fact that it connotes "unchanging"—a notion which I am seeking to dispel in this essay.

3. J. Fabian, "Religion and Change" in *The African Experience*, J. Paden and E. Soja, eds (Evanston, Ill., 1970), Vol. I, 383.

4. *Africa*, XLI, 2 (1971).

5. M. Titiev, "A Fresh Approach to the Problem of Magic and Religion," in W. Lessa and E. Vogt (eds.), *Reader in Comparative Religion* (New York: Harper and Row, 1972), 432.

6. T. Ranger and I. Kimambo (eds.), *The Historical Study of African Religion* (London: 1972), 15.22.

7. Chief K.O.K. Oyioha, *Godianism: A Series of Papers Presented to the Conference of Traditional Religions of Nigeria*, May 22, 1975, 6.

8. *Ibid.*, 15.

9. *Ibid.* See also the text of his talk "Was the Black Man Ever a Pagan? If No, What Was He?" presented at a Religious Studies and Philosophy Symposium at the University of Calabar, April 4, 1981.

10. *Ibid.*, 1.

11. *Ibid.*, 3. Note also that in 1970 Godianism was registered as a member of the Corporation of World's Major Religions and before that in 1965, a member of the United Nations International Co-operation Council. See Chief K.O.K. Onyioha, *African Godianism* (New York, 1980), 81.

12. *Ibid.*, 2.

13. I am unaware of the fate of this organization.

14. See the Creed of Godianism, *ibid.*, 25f.

15. *Ibid.*, 19. See Chief Onyioha's address of World Disarmament to a special seminar of the General Assembly of the United Nations, May/June 1978.

16. *Christianity, Islam and Godianism in Nigeria* (Enugu, 1964); "The Metaphysical Background to Traditional Healing in Nigeria," in P. Singer (ed.), *Traditional Healing: New Science or New Colonialism? Essays in Critique of Medical Anthropology* (New York: 1977), 203–230; *Godianism* (New York, 1980).

17. *Sunday Statesman*, September 20, 1981.

18. *Ibid.*

19. *Ibid.*

20. E.B. Idowu, *Olodumare: God in Yoruba Belief* (London; Longman, 1962), 212. It has experienced a revival in recent years.

21. *Ibid.*, 214. Despite internal dissensions, Ijọ Ọrunmila is flourishing in several parts of the country. A magazine entitled *Ọrunmila* is being circulated from Lagos.

22. E. G. Parrinder, *Religion in African City* (Westport, CT: Negro Universities Press, 1953), 127.

23. S. Ọla Makinde, "The Cultural, Social, and Religious Significance of Oke'badan Festival," a special (B.A.) Research Project, University of Calabar 1980, 79.
24. *Ibid.*, 81.
25. The Annual Oke'badan Lecture organized by the Historical Department of the University of Ibadan.
26. B. Jules-Rosette (ed.), *The New Religions of Africa* (Norwood, NJ: Ablex Publishing Corp., 1979), 224.
27. See *West Africa*, May 18, 1987, 964 for the document published by Orile-Orisa on the "Seven Tenets of Orile-Orisa."
28. See S. T. Barnes, ed., *Africa's Ogun: Old World and New* (Bloomington, Indiana: Indiana University Press, 1989).
29. Jules-Rosette, 1979, 224.
30. *Ibid.*
31. See R. I. J. Hackett and J. K. Olupọna, "Civil Religion in Nigeria." In *Religion and Society in Nigeria* (forthcoming).
32. Idowu, 1969, 211.
33. Dr. E. Nsan claims that Ekpe membership has increased in recent years, partly due to the cultural revival. Interview, Calabar, June 26, 1983.
34. Interview with Dr. Ekpo Eyo, then Director of the National Museums of Nigeria, who also notes that the former Cross River State Governor, Dr. Clement Isong, (non-Efik, an Ibibio from Eket) sought initiation into Ekpe at Creek Town, as a means of furthering his political career, but the secret plot was foiled at the last minute by preventing the governor and his entourage from reaching the shrine where the ceremony was to have taken place. July 7, 1984.
35. *Ibid.*
36. See *Souvenir Programme of the Coronation Service*, April 21, 1982.
37. See "Efik Dance," *Nigeria Magazine* 53 (1957):164.
38. Ulli Beier, *The Return of the Gods – The Sacred Art of Susanne Wenger* (Cambridge, 1975), 39.
39. Cf., U. Maclean, *Magical Medicine* (Harmondsworth, U.K.: Penguin Books, 1971).
40. Cf., H. W. Turner, *Tribal Religious Movements*, in *Encyclopaedia Britannica*, 1974, ed., Vol. 18, 702.
41. B. R. Wilson, *Magic and the Millennium* (London: Heinemann, 1973), 330. Also K. Burridge, *New Heaven New Earth* (Oxford: Blackwell, 1980), 31.
42. Cf., D. A. Martin, *A General Theory of Secularization* (Oxford, 1979).
43. J. S. Mbiti, *African Religions and Philosophy* (London, 1969), 262.
44. Ranger and Kimambo, 1979, 21.

13

TRADITION AND CONTINUITY IN AFRICAN RELIGIONS
THE CASE OF NEW RELIGIOUS MOVEMENTS

Bennetta W. Jules-Rosette

Introduction

THERE ARE CURRENTLY more new religions in non-Western nations than during any previous historical period. Many new African religious movements (whether they are separatist break-offs or independent developments) are influenced by contact with diverse "unorthodox" Western movements. Additionally, fragmentation and schism are internal characteristics of many of these movements. Government persecution creates further external pressures toward schism. Internally, conditions of plural culture contact and the failure to stabilize leadership roles and patterns of succession promote schism and fragmentation. This development is a byproduct of the decline of customary religious authority and the transposition of many of the functions of religion into the secular domain. It suggests that "subjective secularization," or the manifestation of secularization as a psychological orientation, may be less prevalent in the African context than structural changes resulting in new tensions in the relationship between religion and society.

Africa's dramatic social upheavals over the past two decades have been accompanied by the rise of a variety of new religious movements that are characterized by symbolic protest and the search for cultural continuity. These movements involve a symbolic redefinition of what is perceived to be sacred in society. In this discussion, I shall explore the types and dynamics of new African religious movements as sources for redefining concepts of the sacred and the secular and examine the implications of these conclusions for the present and future state of research in the field.

Africa's New Religions: Major Types and Sources

Over seven thousand new religious movements exist in sub-Saharan Africa. Together they claim more than 32 million adherents (Barrett, 1982:782 and 791). These movements have arisen primarily in areas where there has been intensive contact with Christian missionary efforts. However, prophetic and revitalistic movements existed in Africa prior to extensive European contact. Many movements originated as early as the 1880s. The period from 1914 to 1925 marked a second peak in the emergence of new religions in Africa. A final period may be demarcated from the early 1930s to the present. It is the groups that have emerged during this most recent period which are generally referred to as the new religious movements of sub-Saharan Africa. Some of these movements actually began earlier but did not gain momentum until the 1930s. Many have persisted in largely the same form that they took over fifty years ago. Others have gone underground and resurfaced, often retaining their initial doctrinal and membership requirements.

With reference to doctrinal base, organizational structure, and geographic distribution, three major types of new religious movements in sub-Saharan Africa may be designated: (1) indigenous, or independent, churches; (2) separatist churches; and (3) neotraditional movements. These groups have taken different forms in West, Central, Southern, and East Africa. They blend elements of traditional religion with the influence of historical and modern churches. Many of these groups arose as a result of the political and social domination of colonialism and the sense of psychological dependency that it created. However, in the contemporary period, other sources have stimulated the continued growth of these movements.

Historically speaking, the impetus for the growth of new African religious movements may be traced to five basic sources: (1) The disappointment of local converts with the premises and outcomes of

Christianity led to the growth of prophetic, messianic, and millenarian groups. (2) The translation of the Bible into local African vernaculars stimulated a reinterpretation of scripture and a spiritual renewal in Christian groups. (3) The perceived divisions in denominational Christianity and its failure to meet local needs influenced the rise of separatist churches and community-based indigenous churches. (4) The impotence of Western medicine in the face of personal problems, psychological disorders, epidemics, and natural disasters was a catalyst for concerns with spiritual healing in the new African religious movements. (5) The failure of mission Christianity to break down social and cultural barriers and generate a sense of community have led to the strengthening of social ties in small, sectarian groups. In general, the new African churches have tried to create a sense of community in the new urban environment and in the changing context of rural life.

Among the three groups of new religious movements designated, indigenous churches are the most rapidly growing local responses to Christianity. These churches are groups that started under the initiative of African leaders outside the immediate context of missions, or historic religions. Their membership is estimated to comprise nearly 15 percent of the Christian population of sub-Saharan Africa. Also termed independent churches, these groups have devised unique forms of social and political organization and have developed their own doctrines. Groups as diverse as the Harrist Church in the Ivory Coast, the Aladura Church in Nigeria, Kimbanguism in Zaire, and the Apostolic movements of Zimbabwe may be classified as indigenous churches. Nevertheless, the specific doctrines and the response to government control in each of the churches is distinctive. These groups also vary on the organizational level depending on the extent of their local appeal and the demographic and cultural composition of their membership. Indigenous churches may be divided into three specific subtypes: prophetic, messianic, and millenarian groups. All of these types evidence doctrinal innovation, efforts at spiritual renewal, and a reaction to the presence of mission churches.

Re-Envisioning the Sacred and the Secular

New African religious movements provide an innovative way of re-envisioning the sacred and challenge conventional sociological theories of secularization and the decline of religiosity in contemporary society. Emile Durkheim (1915:52) stated that "all known religious beliefs, whether simple or complex," presuppose the classification of the world into "sacred and profane" domains. For Durkheim, no particular entity, object, or event is considered sacred. Instead, the sacred consists of collective moral and symbolic expressions projected and reinforced by the social group. Social processes are treated as the source for generating and sustaining a sense of the sacred.[1] Durkheim's definition of the sacred refers to ways of seeing and thinking about the world as much as it does a set of social institutions.

This approach contrasts with Max Weber's view that the sacred is embodied in specific religious institutions and must be studied in terms of their relationship to the rest of society (Weber, 1963:207–208). It is from the latter perspective that the opposition between the sacred and the secular as a source of social change has developed as a tool for analyzing historic and contemporary religions. The much-debated problems of secularization and the decline of religiosity, which became major scholarly and popular concerns for Western researchers and theologians in the 1960s and are still a source of controversy, were partially set in motion by Weber's approach.[2]

Recent research has both debated and refined Weber's initial assumptions. In his introduction to the English translation of Weber's *The Sociology of Religion*, Talcott Parsons (1963:lxii) argues that the rise of interdenominationalism and liberal Protestantism in the United States seriously challenges Weber's view of how the secularization process would unfold in contemporary Western societies. In his masterplan for the comparative study of religion, Weber never envisioned the processes of rapid social change and cultural contact resulting from decolonization in the Third World. The notion that the people of modern Africa would have a voice in redirecting the course of religion and institutional change in Europe did not appear as an empirical possibility at the beginning of the 20th century. As movements of protest, many new African religious groups have become vehicles for the creation, exercise, and legitimation of power by their adherents. Those who were formerly powerless have found in religion a means of altering their situation and even reversing their status in both symbolic and social terms. The adherents of these new movements have created and manipulated sacred symbols to attain secular goals. Therefore, the existence of these movements necessarily modifies conceptualizations of the relationship between the sacred and the secular.

A fundamental question lingers when assessing US and European research on African religious movements. This concerns the comparative lens through which such studies are conceived and developed. The church-denomination-sect typology, which has been widely debated since Troeltsch and Weber, probably reached its peak as an analytical tool in the United States by 1970 (Eister, 1967:85–90; Demerath and

Hammond, 1969; Johnson, 1971:124–137; Martin, 1978: 55–82). This typology has done much to obscure research on new religious movements in Africa and elsewhere. This distinction grew out of historical studies of European Christianity. The effects of this typology for research in Africa have been particularly misleading because it has promoted a tendency to view new religious developments as "sectarian" responses rather than as autonomous developments with different cultural and historical roots than those of more established churches and denominations. The wide range of cultural combinations and sociopolitical goals in African groups renders the church-sect typology a relatively weak descriptive device.

Much of the research conducted on African religious movements during the 1950s and 1960s examined them as responses and challenges to colonialism (Balandier, 1955:417–419). In his study of African and other Third World religious movements, Vittorio Lanternari (1963:19) labeled these movements "religions of the oppressed," which he considered to result from "the spontaneous impact of the white man's presence on the native society." The "sacred," in this case, is defined in terms of passive resistance to, and rebellion against, symbols of political and religious domination.

Ten years after Lanternari's book was published in English, Bryan Wilson (1973) developed a typology that compressed African religious movements into two empirical and doctrinal types: the thaumaturgical and the revolutionist, or the magical and the millennial. Although this distinction refers to both world views and specific movements, a concern with supernatural powers — magic, healing, and purification — is, for Wilson, the major thrust of all religions emerging in preindustrial societies. What the sociologist considers "magical" in this context, of course, may be viewed by movement followers as a set of rational alternatives logically derived from tradition or from innovative doctrinal combinations. Wilson's "magic" is actually a description of a wide variety of indigenous customs, beliefs, and new conceptions of symbolic action and protest.

For Wilson, millenarian movements contain much that is "magical" and therefore, have little broad, lasting political or social impact. He cites the case of West African groups such as the Cherubim and Seraphim movement of Nigeria (Peel, 1968:2–9) and some American Indian movements in support of this tendency of millenarian movements to be temporary and localized. When such movements of protest do arise, in Wilson's opinion, they are often so replete with supernatural and other-worldly elements as to be marginally effective as instrumental movements of protest. However, I would argue that a challenge to the existing social order is implicit in many African religious movements, regardless of the specific traditional, cultural, or "magical" elements that are present. In this regard, the meanings and uses of new religious movements for their own group members become central issues for study. One must ask how these group members envision the sacred and the secular and what symbolic challenge they perceive themselves as making.

This point reinforces the methodological concern in some recent studies with defining the cosmology and belief systems in new African religions (Fernandez, 1982; MacGaffey, 1983). On the ethnographic level, this process is essential in order to assess the larger influence of new movements on the societies in which they appear. Building upon a semantic anthropological approach to religion, this line of research suggests that the comparative study of new African religions must be preceded by a schematic interpretive and descriptive treatment of the content of religious doctrines and practice. This suggestion raises key issues of both theological and sociological import. Specifically, how do members of new religious movements conceive of the sacred, of categories of religious belief and practice, and of the distribution of ecclesiastical authority within these groups? Beyond simply noting that these categories challenge or differ from those of Western religious belief and practice, it is necessary to examine the new terms in their own right. I adopted this approach in my own ethnographic and sociolinguistic studies of Apostolic churches in Zaire, Zambia, and Zimbabwe (Jules-Rosette, 1975:21–56).

A Western model of "church" and "state" that neatly separates the sacred and secular domains often does not apply to the history and cultural context of new African religions. For example, Larry Shiner (1966:218) states: "When we apply this spiritual-temporal polarity to non-Western situations where such differentiations did not originally exist, we falsify the data." Yet, if we return to the Lanternari and Wilson theses, we are plagued by the possibility that new religious adherents have used their beliefs as meaningful coping mechanisms and survival strategies. What were previously religions of the oppressed, however, have now become religions of opportunity and channels of upward mobility (Glazier, 1983:16). The sacred vision has been transformed into the secular opportunity.

This latter view builds upon a Weberian model of the emergence of an instrumental rationality that accompanies modernity and change. Indeed, this model has been applied to ethnographic studies of new African religions. A landmark study in this regard is Norman Long's (1968) monograph on the religious and social responses to modernity among the Jehovah's Witnesses of Kapepa village in Zambia. The Weberian view holds that modernity is accompanied by the structuring of religious activities according to secular ideals. Religious motivations for action are rechanneled into the secular domain. Long found a classic version of the Protestant ethic operative among the Witnesses of Kapepa. Most of them were relatively young villagers with little urban experience. They equated hard work and economic success with the process of preparing themselves for the millennium and entry into the "New Kingdom" (Long, 1968:214). Relative to their fellow villagers, the Witnesses made a rapid transition from hoe to plow agriculture with notable commercial success. Long (1968:239–240) remarks "I...concluded that like the correlation that Weber suggested between the Protestant ethic and 'the spirit of capitalism,' there existed in Kapepa a close correspondence between Jehovah's Witnesses and their social and economic behavior....But social, economic, and cultural factors also play their part."

Religion, in this case, helped the Witnesses of Kapepa to adapt to change. They did so by redefining their social world in millenarian religious terms and acting upon these beliefs in their economic lives. Long's study might be used to exemplify the secularization thesis in Africa. However, it also demonstrates the opposite: an increase in religiosity through the involvement of the African Witnesses in a spiritual redefinition of every aspect of their daily lives. Moreover, Long's data on the Kapepa Witnesses are atypical of many Central African groups that developed as offshoots of the Watch Tower movement during the colonial period (Biebuyck, 1957:7–40).[3] These movements tended to exhibit extreme millenarian religious and political responses to European domination without specific social programs for their members or with ephemeral political protest as a result.

The Problem of Secularization in the African Context

Just as the interpretation of the sacred takes a unique form in new African religions, so too does the process of secularization. Peter Berger (1967:171) argues that the worldwide spread of the structures of the modern industrial state triggers religious change in non-Western societies and is an important stimulus for the secularization process.[4] On the other hand, Wilson (1973:499) points to the decline of traditional authority structures and religious beliefs in the face of colonial domination and "Westernization." The implication of both assertions is that tendencies toward secularization are introduced to changing African societies from the outside as a byproduct of the eventual movement of all societies toward industrial and post-industrial socio-economic structures (cf. Parsons, 1966:109–114). These changes are accompanied by cultural pluralization, more frequent contact of diverse social groups, and an increase in bureaucratic forms of organization with impersonal social relationships.

Similarly, Shiner (1966:209–217) has noted three important characteristics of secularization that may be associated with this transition to modernity: (1) desacralization, or a decline in the role of religion in defining the social world, (2) the process of structural differentiation by which religious and secular institutions become distinct and autonomous, and (3) the transposition of religious knowledge and activities into the secular domain. This process of transposition is distinct from the decline of the social influence of religion (Wilson, 1982:149). When applied to new African religious groups, it suggests that followers of these movements retain aspects of customary religion and newly introduced cultural elements without exclusively associating themselves with either alternative. As a result of all three of the processes outlined by Shiner, individuals reorder their religious beliefs in a new way to meet the demands of modern society – a society that Western theologians and social scientists have argued has become increasingly secular.

The combination of the sacred and secular domains in many new African religious movements creates thorny problems when analyzing the process of secularization (Turner, 1974:687–705). In these groups, the political domain has traditionally been defined and reinforced by sacred symbols and beliefs that are fundamental to the communities involved. African movements that draw upon customary religious and political symbolism have often been regarded with a mixture of alarm and suspicion by both colonial governments and new regimes. When these cultural combinations are aggravated by millenarian tendencies in the new groups, the issue becomes even more complex. It is, thus, difficult to disentangle a nostalgic return to traditional notions of the sacred from new conceptions of the sacred developing from changing political and social demands. The decline of old concepts of the sacred and resacralization, or the redefinition of the sacred, in this context, may actually constitute two complementary poles of a single phenomenon. Hence, the concept of secularization offers an incomplete framework for analyzing what actually takes place when old and new symbolic categories are combined.

In defining secularization in the African context, one must also consider the problem of symbolic realism (Bellah, 1970:89–96). How do members of these groups see their own religious claims vis-à-vis the emerging secular society? Peter Berger (1966:8) suggests that recent research on religion often takes for granted the predominance of a universal "secularized consciousness," or total acceptance of a scientific reality, without considering the possibility that, for some people, the standard for cognitive validity may be the sacred, or a non-scientific reality. The quest to regain a sense of the sacred through religious, cultural, and national identity is a common response to social and cultural change in African nations.

Secularization is often assumed to be a linear and uniform process (Lalive d'Epinay, 1981:406). Accordingly, the predictable economic and social changes accompanying industrialization are viewed as making religion marginal in contemporary society. In fact, however, many new religious movements in Africa react to industrial change and the new social orders that accompany it by seeking to create a sense of religious unity and group identity characteristic of pre-industrial communities. Elsewhere, I have referred to this process as the impossible arcadian wish to return to old values and a simpler form of life (Jules-Rosette, 1979:219–229). In this case, the growth of modern social and economic institutions results in an effort to "resacralize" African societies through new religious groups and nationalistic political movements.

Liberation theology is another product of, and reaction to, the world-wide process of secularization and the spread of modern industrial structures to all corners of the globe (Brown, 1974:269–282). Through this approach, theologians operating within established Catholic and Protestant traditions view the Bible as a revolutionary book which documents the processes of religious and political liberation and the goal of freedom. Their objective is to redefine the sacred as a set of moral principles which can be invoked in the wider society to reduce social inequities and injustice. Although liberation theology in Africa and Latin America shares some features with millenarian movements, it differs in its direct equation of secular goals such as social justice with religious ideals.

The example of liberation theology suggests that secular, political goals directly influence the formation and growth of new religious movements. Consequently, it is important to analyze how tendencies toward secularization have actually shaped new religious movements. One method for exploring this problem is to examine tensions in the relationships between church and state in African nations. In many African nations such as Zaire, Zambia, and Malawi, the growth of new religions takes place under close government scrutiny, and many movements (e.g., the Watch Tower spinoffs) are outlawed as threats to nation building. In these cases, new religions are seen as potential sources for weakening civic political commitments by virtue of their ability to mobilize masses of people in activities which are not directly supervised or controlled by the state. Political control attempts to restrict the sphere of influence of the new religious movements in a secularizing society.

A counterbalancing tendency in this secularization process is one toward ecumenical cooperation across the new religious groups. Martin West (1975:142–170) analyzes the rise of ecumenism among South Africa's indigenous churches based upon two large-scale surveys of these movements. He notes efforts toward cooperation among these groups, particularly in education and financial programs but not on the level of doctrine and ritual. Similar tendencies have appeared among indigenous churches in Zambia and East Africa. Some scholars have argued that this process of cooperation ultimately results in the secularization of doctrine and leadership structures within new religious movements. In describing the Apostles of John Maranke, an African prophetic movement which I also studied, Angela Cheater (1981:45) has argued that pragmatic concerns of economic success and secular, social, and family ties have actually altered the interpretation of the sacred within the group and diminished its scope. She sees cooperation with other groups in the larger society as a major force in modifying the doctrinal and organizational structure of the religious group. This controversial argument suggests that social differentiation and change may eventually cause subjective secularization, or a personal decline in religiosity.

Cultural Responses to Secularization

African religious movements and movement types have adopted a variety of cultural and psychological responses to the process of secularization. These responses may be summarized in terms of at least four basic tendencies, according to which several movement types may be classified:

1. Neotraditionalism: retains the myth of an ideal past and is often accompanied by an attempt to reconstruct an authoritative religious tradition. The persistence of traditional religious forms in Africa within the contemporary context is a case in point.

2. Revitalization: introduces new concepts to regenerate the old. On the psychological level, this response is perceived as comprehensive and seeks an explanation of the sacred in both old and new terms. African indigenous churches and prophetic revitalization movements are examples.

3. Syncretism: is the process through which former definitions of the sacred are combined with innovative patterns to produce a satisfying definition of the whole and an expression of core values which is both in line with the past and adaptive to new institutions. Santeriá, Latin American Pentecostalism, and many African movements exhibit this process.

4. *Millenarianism*: creates a myth of the ideal future which attempts to construct a new definition of the sacred and a new social order in ways that yield pragmatically effective results for members of new movements. New African movements and, to a lesser extent, liberation theologies, use this approach. Messianic movements may be included in this category.

Although these four options do not exhaust the cultural and symbolic responses to secularization, they point to ways in which new religious movements in Africa have attempted to redefine the sacred in a secularizing society. In some instances, a direct redefinition of political and social values is involved, as in the case of millenarianism and liberation theology. In other instances, the sacred is revalidated through efforts to preserve customary notions of community and conventional expressive symbols, as evidenced in revitalistic, evangelical, and spirit-type movements. In the latter case, a resacralization of dominant traditional symbols occurs, often in reaction to the decline of religious values and institutions in the rest of society. In spite of the resacralization process, some scholars like Robin Horton (1971:107) have argued that religion in modern Africa will ultimately move in an increasingly secular direction in terms of its doctrine and organization and will survive primarily "as a way of communion but not as a system of explanation, prediction, and control." At present, however, a more prevalent trend in African religious movements is the attempt to create cohesive forms of community in which religious values are more coherent and exercise a larger, direct influence on social life. Dynamic religious movements throughout Africa are redefining the psychological, religious, political, social, and cultural aspects of life that interweave the sacred and the secular.

The Future of the New African Religions

An important concern in the field of African religious studies centers around the extent to which new movements may be considered stable over time. It has been argued that the new religions develop through a process of schism and renewal. They break away from the influence of both missions and newly established churches to develop bonds of family and community that are particularly strong at the local level. Utopian ideals and fundamentalist interpretations of scriptures reinforce the initial break and the sense of spiritual renewal in these groups. Schism may be regarded as a sign of doctrinal ambivalence and organizational weakness. At the same time, it is the hallmark of spiritual experimentation and renewal. There is a combination of customary symbols and the new values characteristic of cultural pluralism. Many newer groups stress that their religions form interethnic and transcultural associative networks.

Although some of the new Christian groups of Africa originate in ethnically homogeneous areas, most emphasize the potential and even the necessity for cultural sharing through overarching symbols and doctrine. This sharing does not mean that an external system is imposed on, or destroys, old cultural forms. These processes of cultural combination and symbolic protest allow the members of new religious movements to acquire a reflective stance toward their immediate problems and to preserve past cultural ideas. The types of religious responses vary widely with respect to a group's attitudes toward tradition and to the degree of change which individuals consider to be possible in a particular society. The four types of movement responses mentioned above resolve social and cultural clashes through blending old and new interpretations of the sacred.

At the same time, a question of stable leadership and its institutionalization arises. The death or demise of a leader creates an important challenge to the viability of a group. Often several branches of an indigenous church or separatist movement exist in a single area because of the inability of members to resolve a crisis in leadership succession or to integrate competing doctrinal variations. Thus, schism continues to threaten the stability and survival of new religious movements after they have established autonomy from missions or historic churches. This problem has led some scholars to speculate that the new African religions are unstable and highly mutable and that their appearance merely marks one phase of social, political, or religious protest in the emergence of Africa's new nation-states. Nevertheless, historical evidence suggests that these groups have considerable longevity in spite of their shifting leadership structures, new membership, and fluctuations in popular appeal. The persistence of groups like the Bwiti cult in Gabon and the Kitawala movement in Zaire and Zambia from the turn of the century to the present follows this trend.

Another important tendency contributing to the eventual stability of the new religious movements is the shift toward ecumenism. Churches such as the Kimbanguists and the Aladura, which have endured for practically half a century, have made attempts to become international in outlook and to associate themselves with worldwide ecumenical movements. Several indigenous churches affiliated themselves with the World Council of Churches between 1969 and 1981. They include: The Church of the Lord Aladura in Nigeria, the Kimbanguist Church in Zaire, the African Israel Ninevah Church in Kenya, and the African Church of the Holy Spirit in Kenya (cf. Perrin Jassy, 1970:86–77). Other indigenous churches and cults have made efforts to join together in local, national, and all-African cooperative associations which represent them as united political and cultural groups.

Local voluntary associations formed by these churches attempt to retain the doctrinal autonomy of each group while developing joint fundraising, educational, and cultural efforts. This type of cooperation is evident in the African Independent Churches' Association formed in 1965 in South Africa and in similar ecumenical councils and associations that have formed in Zambia and Kenya (West, 1974:121–129). Although such associations do not solve the problem of internal group conflict and leadership succession, they do appear to reinforce cooperation and political stability within the independent church movement.

The Cultural and Social Contribution of Africa's New Religions

Many of Africa's new religious movements arising from the 1920s to the present have started as religions of the oppressed and later have become movements of protest, opportunity, and mobility. Their protest has often been expressed as a challenge to the authority and liturgy of mission churches. Several of these groups, including the early Watch Tower movement inspired by Kamwana in Nyasaland, Kimbanguism in Zaire, and the Harrist Church in the Ivory Coast, have also led to, or supported, movements of political liberation and national independence. The close relationship between political and religious conceptions of freedom and human rights has contributed to this development.

The social influence of Africa's new religions, however, is not limited to the political sphere. The new images and ideal of community promoted by these groups offer alternative lifestyles to their members and to others who come into contact with the new movements. Through tightly knit communities and internal support structures, Africa's new religions establish claims to loyalty. Culturally, they promise a popular religion that is not alien to the "masses." Nevertheless, some of the contemporary groups emphasize the ultimate attainment of rewards promised in orthodox doctrines. This goal is accomplished through social insulation, withdrawal, and strict personal adherence to the Bible or to the Qur'an. The literal interpretation of sacred writings serves to create alternative types of social relationships. In some instances, this return to fundamentalist doctrines within the African context has had the effect of triggering charismatic renewals and new forms of proselytizing within established mission churches.

The more insulated religious movements still adamantly retain a radical separation from some aspects of the contemporary societies in which they appear. Nevertheless, their attitudes toward work, toward the role of women, and toward new forms of cultural expression, such as discourse and dress, permeate other sectors of social life that are not directly associated with their religious origins. Religious language and imagery, such as the Jamaa teachings and Apostolic or Zionist sermons and ritual, have now entered common parlance as aspects of urban popular culture (Fabian, 1971:202). The study of Africa's new religious movements, therefore, leads to a broader exploration of new cultural forms.

Conclusions

Because religion involves a high concentration of innovative and restorative symbols, it is a wellspring from which these new expressions are transmitted to a wider society. Through Africa's new religious movements, conventional cultural and symbolic forms are revived and reinterpreted. Taken from their original source, some of these religious beliefs have been applied to secular life. The ultimate viability of these new religions may, in fact, reside in the capacity of their beliefs and practices to become more fully integrated into the mainstream of modern Africa's social and cultural life. The greatest impact of these groups may, thus, take place through cultural diffusion and sharing rather than through the spread and historical evolution of any particular movement.

The processes of fragmentation and redefinition of leadership roles and goals in Africa's new religions take place under unique cultural conditions (cf. Sinda, 1972:111). Often, these processes involve redefining the sacred as part of a new search for collective identity and reinterpretation of tradition. Paradoxically, these redefinitions may challenge conceptions of the sacred in Western religious traditions. Heterodoxy, however, is not always synonymous with secularization (Berger, 1980:23-38). Through suggesting novel ways in which the sacred may be integrated into contemporary life, Africa's new religions offer an empirical challenge to sociological theories that propose that secularization is an essential feature of the incorporation of Third World communities into the industrial and post-industrial social orders.[5]

Notes

1. Durkheim considered the concept of the sacred to refer to the symbolic, categorical, and moral aspects of social life. His view has been refined and re-emphasized in contemporary studies of the social institutions that support religious world views and concepts of the sacred (cf. Berger, 1967: 33–34; Douglas, 1966:21).

2. Peter Berger's presidential address to the Society for the Scientific Study of Religion in Boston (1966:3–16) summarizes the influence of the secularization thesis on contemporary theology before the impact of new religious movements and the rise of the new evangelical Christianity in the United States had been fully assessed by researchers. Larry Shiner (1966:207–220) presents an excellent overview of the problems of using the concept of secularization in empirical research. Although many new empirical developments had taken place since Shiner's article was published, the methodological issues that he proposes are still important contributions to the discussion of secularization.

3. Norman Long's example of the Zambian Jehovah's Witnesses who, according to him, fit neatly into a Weberian model of social change is atypical. For example, the Watch Tower movement that began in 1908 under Elliot Kamwana may be viewed as a powerful millenarian response to the colonial regime of Nyasaland (Barrett, 1968:29). Although this movement resurfaced later in other forms, it never assumed the characteristics of the Zambian group described by Long.

4. Along these lines, Ted Solomon (1977:1–14) suggests that the transposition of concepts of the sacred into the secular domain and the bureaucratization of religious movements may be productively analyzed through the new religions of Japan including Sokka Gakkai, Rissho Kosei-Kai, and PL Kyodan. These groups have been politically active and have used Nichiren Soshu Buddhism to reshape the expression of Japanese nationalism.

5. This article is reprinted with permissioin from James A. Beckford and Thomas Luckmann, eds., *The Changing Face of Religion* (Sage, 1989:147–162).

References

Balandier, George, 1955 *Sociologie Actuelle de l'Afrique Noir*. Paris: Presses Universitaires.

Barrett, David B.,1968 *Schism and Renewal in Africa: An Analysis of Six Thousand Contemporary Religious Movements*. Nairobi, Kenya: Oxford University Press.

Barrett, David B., ed., 1982 *World Christian Encyclopedia: A Comparative Study of Churches and Religions in the Modern World, A.D. 1900–2000*. New York: Oxford University Press.

Bellah, Robert, 1970 "Christianity and Symbolic Realism." *Journal for the Scientific Study of Religion* 9 (Summer):89–96.8.

Berger, Peter L., 1966 "A Sociological View of the Secularization of Theology." *Journal for the Scientific Study of Religion* 6 (Spring):3–16.

1967 *The Sacred Canopy: Elements of a Sociological Theory of Religion*. Garden City, New York: Anchor Books.

1980 *The Heretical Imperative: Contemporary Possibilities of Religious Affirmation*. Garden

City, New York: Anchor Books.

Biebuyck, M.O., 1957 "La Société Kumu Face au Kitawala." *Zaire* 11:7-40.

Brown, Robert McAfee, 1974 "Reflections on 'Liberation Theology'." *Religion in Life* 43 (Fall):269–282.

Cheater, Angela, 1981 "The Social Organization of Religious Differences Among the Vapostori weMaranke." *Social Analysis* 7:24–49.

Demerath, N.J., III and Phillip E. Hammond, 1969 *Religion in Social Context*. New York: Random House.

Douglas, Mary, 1966 *Purity and Danger: An Analysis of Concepts of Pollution and Taboo*. New York: Praeger Publishers.

Durkheim, Emile, 1915 *The Elementary Forms of Religious Life*. Joseph Ward Swain, trans. London: Allen and Unwin.

Eister, Allan W., 1967 "Toward a Radical Critique of Church-Sect Typologizing: Comment on 'Some Critical Observations on the Church-Sect Dimension'." *Journal for the Scientific Study of Religion* 6, (Spring):85–90.

Fabian, Johannes, 1971 *Jamaa: A Charismatic Movement in Katanga*. Evanston, Illinois: Northwestern University Press.

Fernandez, James W., 1982 *Bwiti: An Ethnography of the Religious Imagination in Africa*. Princeton, New Jersey: Princeton University Press.

Glazier, Stephen, 1983 *Marchin' the Pilgrims Home: Leadership and Decision-Making in an Afro-Caribbean Faith*. Westport, Connecticut: Greenwood Press.

Horton, Robin, 1971 "African Conversion." *Africa* 41 (April):85–108.

Johnson, Benton, 1971 "Church and Sect Revisited." *Journal for the Scientific Study of Religion* 10 (Summer):124–137.

Jules-Rosette, Bennetta, 1975 *African Apostles: Ritual and Conversion in the Church of John Maranke*. Ithaca, New York: Cornell University Press.

Jules-Rosette, Bennetta, ed., 1979 *The New Religions of Africa*. Norwood, New Jersey: Ablex Publishing Corporation.

Lalive d'Epinay, Christian, 1981 "Popular Culture, Religion, and Everyday Life." *Social Compass* 28, 4:405–424.

Lanternari, Vittorio, 1963 *Religions of the Oppressed: A Study of Modern Messianic Cults*. Lisa Sergio, trans. New York: Alfred A. Knopf.

Long, Norman, 1968 *Social Change and the Individual: A Study of the Social and Religious Responses to Innovation in a Zambian Rural Community*. Manchester University Press.

MacGaffey, Wyatt, 1983 *Modern Kongo Prophets: Religion in a Plural Society*. Bloomington, Indiana: Indiana University Press.

Martin, David, 1978 *A General Theory of Secularization*. New York: Harper and Row.

Parsons, Talcott, 1963 "Introduction." In Weber, Max, *The Sociology of Religion*. Ephraim Fischoff, trans. Boston: Beacon Press, pp. xix–lxvii.

Parsons, Talcott, 1966 *Societies: Evolutionary and Comparative Perspectives*. Englewood Cliffs, New Jersey: Prentice-Hall.

Peel, John D.Y., 1968 *Aladura: A Religious Movement Among the Yoruba*. London: International African Institute.

Perrin Jassy, Marie France, 1970 *La Communanté de Base dans les Eglises Africaines*. Bandundu, Zaire: Centre d'Etudes Ethnologiques, Series II, Vol. 3.

Shiner, Larry, 1966 "The Concept of Secularization in Empirical Research." *Journal for the Scientific Study of Religion* 6 (Spring):207–220.

Sinda, Martial, 1972 *Le Messianisme Congolais et ses Incidences Politiques*. Paris: Payot.

Solomon, Ted J., 1977 "The Response of Three New Religions to the Crisis in the Japanese Value System." *Journal for the Scientific Study of Religion* 16 (Spring):1–14.

Turner, Harold, 1974 "Tribal Religious Movements, New." *The New Encyclopedia Britannica*, XVIII:697–705.

Weber, Max, 1963 *The Sociology of Religion*. Ephraim Fischoff, trans. Boston: Beacon Press.

West, Martin, 1974 "Independence and Unity: Problems of Cooperation Between African Independent Church Leaders in Soweto." *African Studies* 33:121–129.

West, Martin, 1975 *Bishops and Prophets in a Black City: African Independent Churches in Soweto, Johannesburg*. Cape Town, South Africa: David Phillip.

Wilson, Bryan R., 1973 *Magic and Millennium: A Sociological Study of Religious Movements Among Tribal and Third-World Peoples*. New York: Harper and Row.

Wilson, Bryan R., 1982 *Religion in Sociological Perspective*. Oxford University Press.

14

PERSEVERANCE AND TRANSMUTATION IN AFRICAN TRADITIONAL RELIGIONS

Evan M. Zuesse

THERE IS NO DENYING THE POWER of traditional religious attitudes in Africa. In marketplaces in Nigeria handbooks to the Book of Psalms circulate, instructing the reader on which verses to read to cure boils and which verse to chant to destroy a rival trader. Rituals to assuage ancestors are enacted in the mining towns of Zaire and amid drilling rigs in South Africa. The former "Emperor Bokasa" of the Central African Empire, now a republic, is brought to court for conforming all-too-well to the stereotype "bad sacral king" of African mythology and cult, even to the practice of cannibalism. The recourse to Islam and Christianity can be added to this brief catalogue of traditionalist paradoxes, for it can be persuasively argued that the modern African interest in direct worship of God is a traditional African response to catastrophic change (Horton, 1971; Zuesse, 1979:100ff, 163f. etc.).

My instances are selected to stress the traditionalism of contemporary "religious innovations." Everyone admits the continuing strength of traditional religions in the villages and among the most conservative "pagans;" but more significant for the future, possibly, are the evidences of the preservation of the past in the midst of the most striking innovations.

In this, Africa follows more universal laws of history. The chief fact of our own age, as of all previous ones, is not its unprecedented changefulness, but its tenacious conservatism. Even the most self-consciously revolutionary regimes repeat the forms of the past, and often their content, right down to the details. For example, as recent disclosures made under Gorbachev have revealed, the resemblances between the Soviet Union and Czarist Russia have all along been extensive and deep: it is doubtful whether the personal autonomy or the power relations of Soviet communal farm workers have really been any different from those of estate serfs of the last century, and the political manipulation of anti-Semitism (as "anti-Zionism") and of imperial ideology until recently could hardly be distinguished from that of earlier centuries. Even such specific institutions as the Gulag and the KGB have been directly indebted to Czarist models, despite the "October Revolution."

Similarly, despite all Mao Tse-tung's explicit goals, his own teachings were used as a substitute Analects — with his own encouragement! — and now the *Analects* is respectable again in its own right (cf. Thompson: 231–41; Bonavia, *et al.*:24–32; Levenson; and *Newsweek*, 12/10/81:15). A paradigm instance of rapid modernization is Japan, yet the more enthusiastic the Japanese "imitation" of the West, the more evident the distinctively Japanese form of modernity that has resulted. Secularism in India, too, has appeared in a thoroughly Indian and even Hindu variety, despite Max Weber's prognostications (cf. Weber; Singer, 1973, 1976).

Rather than indulging in such paradoxes, however, it may be more useful to demonstrate the power of tradition by tracing some main themes in Persian traditionalism, for here we have documentary evidence of an unusual kind which spans four millennia. The relevance of all this to Africa and its future will soon be made clear.

Around 4,000 years ago, Iran, or Persia, was inhabited by Indo-European pastoralists and farmers, who shared a worldview in which the gods and spirits fought together ceaselessly to sustain (on the one side) or destroy (on the other) the cosmic order. The creation myth was also a war myth, for this world was said to have emerged from a struggle between a warrior-god and a magician/cosmic serpent. The warrior won, and instituted human culture, but the primal battle had to be refought endlessly, in battles against human enemies and in cultic rituals.

Humanity was divided into the good and pure "us" and the evil, polluted "them." Zarathustra, in perhaps the seventh millennium B.C.E., added an explicit moral dimension to these ideas, stressing the power of the good creator Lord on High, Ahura Mazda; the sedentary farmer-herders of the valleys, worshippers of Ahura Mazda, served *Artha*, "Truth," and thus sustained the world order through social and moral behavior, herding and tilling, while the highland nomadic raiders and killers of cattle and humanity worshipped the *daevas*, the "devils," and their master Angra Mainyu, the "Evil Spirit": theirs was the path of the Lie, *Druj*. Some scholars maintain that Zarathustra was a monotheist, but as his reform spread through Iran and became the official religion of the Babylonian, and later the Parthian, Empire, it came to repeat in a more elaborate way the strongly dualistic conceptions of the pre-Zoroastrian period, with Satan (Ahriman) and the Lord (Ahura Mazda or Ohmuzd) twins born of an impersonal Endless Time (Zurvan—see Zaehner).

These structures lay deeper than any specific religion. In the third century C.E., Mani, a Persian, repeated them in his own worldview, giving rise to Manichaeanism. In this religion, a mystical realm of light and supernal deities are pitted in cosmic battle against the lower material realm of coarse darkness and the brutal powers governing this world. The followers of truth are a secret movement oppressed by this world and its rulers. From age to age, the Emissary of Light reincarnates himself as world saviors such as Moses, Buddha, Jesus, and finally Mani (the motif of reincarnation was no doubt an influence from Buddhism).

The same ideas turn up again when Persia becomes Muslim, but now in Muslim guise. It is interesting to observe that during the first centuries of Shi'ism, this sect was of little interest in Iran; instead it was promulgated by the Abbasid rulers of Iraq and Egypt and stood for a much more rationalistic, philosophical and tolerant aspect of Islam than that of the Sunni Muslim jurists and ascetic preachers. But once its worldly failures drove Shi'ism underground and encouraged its sense of a world dominated by evil powers, the Shi'ite faith took hold in Iran and gradually became dominant there. Most of the structural features of Manichaeanism mentioned above are reproduced in this form of Islam, even the doctrine of reincarnation of the emissary of light, embodying the Deity itself, in various perfect Savior figures (Muhammad, Ali, Husain, and all the Imams). These dualisms were brought into everyday life through a symbolism of purity and pollution: non-Muslim travellers were excluded from Shi'ite villages in Iran, for example, throughout the pre-modern period, on the grounds that their presence polluted the faithful.

Today, the generally rather quietistic Shi'ite faith has become activistic again and has been inspired by a topical re-application of its war-myth, the story of the passion of Husain at Qarbala, to struggle not only against the Shah, but also against the Great and Little Satan of the "Christian" United States and the "Jewish/Zionist" State of Israel. The deep structure of the worldview remains the same as in pre-Zoroastrian times, but the topical application is different. Perhaps ten years from now the "Great Satan" will be Russia.

As we shall see, African religions stress unity and integration as much as Iranian religions stress polar opposition and conflict. Yet Iranian religious history can teach us much about the future of African traditional religions.

We learn, for example, that there is what I have called here a deep spiritual structure to religion, which may remain the same even when the "religion" itself changes, and the divine names and symbolisms are replaced by other names and forms. There is a level of a civilization's religion that runs deeper than "religion." Thus we find a commonality to the spirituality of Iranian civilization, whether its religion is tribal, Zoroastrian, Manichaean, or Shi'ite. The specific names given to the forces of light and of darkness may change, but the structural opposition persists and grows in intricacy.

(These structures are not genetic: through the massive incursions of Babylonians, Arabs, and central Asiatic peoples, the Iranians today are not the same as the ancient Indo-Europeans. If a source must be found, it most probably lies in the worldview of childhood, generated by the patterns of child-rearing, intimate kin interaction, and local neighborhood play patterns, which immigrants would insensibly pick up and conform to.)

So we may insist that there is a deep spiritual structure in African religions, which underlies them regardless of the specific names and forms of the divine powers or the varying forms of cult. It is not enough, in order to characterize traditional African religions, to present detailed catalogues of particular gods, spirits, cultic practices, and myths. Long after such specific details shall have been lost and forgotten, African traditional religion and spirituality will survive in other forms, as yet unimagined. Whether "pagan," "Christian," "Muslim," "Marxist," or some other religious ideology dominates in the future, the deep structure will surely retain a family resemblance to the spiritualities of the past.

We may, in fact, derive from our reflections on Iranian and other religions the conclusion that there are at least four levels of traditional religion: 1) deep structure; 2) folk practices; 3) actual names and symbolisms; and 4) intellectual rationalizations. Of these the latter levels are progressively more transient. For example, we need only recall how many different theologies of Christianity have followed each other down through the ages, to see how little intellectual rationalizations endure; yet Christianity insists above most other religions on the eternal necessity of getting its explicit doctrines right!

Today it is common to find impressive historical or philosophic constructions of "African thought"; these are presented by intellectuals who are seeking to define, and so to preserve in a modern setting, "negritude" or "the African contribution to modern civilization," etc.[1] There can be no doubt that this is a necessary exercise and will contribute to maintaining the viability of African spirituality by showing it to be contemporary or relevant, but inevitably most of these reconstructions are extremely transient. Their very self-consciousness (and sometimes their defensiveness or their topicality) dates them.

As for the specific names of divine powers and the forms of tribal cult, it is obvious merely from surveying the many hundreds of localized religions that these cannot contain per se the essential identity of African spirituality: they embody it, but do not wholly possess it. The names differ from tribe to tribe, but the commonalities are often so evident that the specific cults seem to be symbols of deep structures, rather than utterly distinct and unique forms. We do not, after all, encounter in African religions the radically opposed variations in attitudes to the self, to salvation, and to the cosmos, that we discover separating Paul Tillich or a Presbyterian banker from the monks of a Coptic monastery in the Egyptian desert. Despite the variety of names and forms, African religions do genuinely exhibit an astonishing uniformity of emphasis which make of them merely local variations on a few axiomatic themes, to a much greater degree certainly than we find in Christianity or others of the world religions such as Hinduism.

Thus even the folk practices seem to have a more enduring form than that of specific cultic names and symbols. It is not just a matter of emphasis, but of actual practices that continue to be acted out in a wide variety of environments, for they evidently possess a hidden "rightness" that goes beyond the immediate "reason" for the enactment: they conform to the deep spiritual structure, the common emphasis that we have just mentioned.

As an example, we might mention the importance of spirit mediumship throughout African religions; this persists today even in urban settings and overseas, in Brazil, Haiti, or in the south of the United States, within such different "religions" as Catholicism, Protestantism, Islam, and explicitly "pagan" cults (see Bastide, 1978; Bourguignon, 1973; Simpson; Verger; Walker). Spirit mediumship "says" something important about African spirituality; it testifies to that "deep structure" of meaning that we have already pointed to. It has often been remarked that witchcraft and healing practices persist in urban environments in Africa even when so-called "higher" forms of traditional religiosity disappear. According to our thesis, this suggests on the contrary that these practices preserve some very deep and profound spiritual assumptions about the nature of reality and the way that Africans experience it. The same holds for other persisting practices, such as divination, ancestral cult, and so on.

Let us, then, try to describe some of those deep structures, which are likely to appear in African forms of religion even a thousand years from now, in some form or another.

But first it is necessary to define what we mean by such structures. They are clearly not identical with folk practices, or even specific cults, and they also differ from intellectual rationalizations, from "philosophies" of African worldview, in some way. Are they perhaps what Claude Lévi-Strauss spoke of as cognitive structures?

According to Lévi-Strauss himself, the kinds of cognitive structures that he so brilliantly described in his many books and articles have nothing to do with religion (Lévi-Strauss, 1966:221, 223–8). He merely wished to understand how the human mind, in *all* cultures, organizes data; the processes are the same in all cultures even if the specific data are not. Thus his researches were hardly calculated to reveal uniqueness in spirituality or culture, but were directed to universal operations of thought. Moreover, as he wrote in one essay on mythology, it was his hope to put all the data groupings and permutations in American Indian or Greek mythology on computer cards (Lévi-Strauss, 1963: 228–9).

It is intuitively quite clear to us that religion cannot be captured in this way. We might ask ourselves why. The simple answer is that religion is not about data, as such, at all. It is about the ways in which these data are understood. It is, in short, and right at its origins, about meanings, existential meanings, that apply to this quite real person that I am, in my actual situation. Luc de Heusch helps make the point very clear for us, for he applied Lévi-Straussian methods to deciphering the esoteric, "inner" teaching of Luba religion, in his *Le roi ivre, ou l'origine de l'etat: mythes et rites Bantous* (Paris: Gallimard, 1972), and in subsequent works. He organizes an astonishing mass of material, the data of countless myths and cults, to arrive at the "real religious ideas" of the Luba and its neighbors. However, as I have shown elsewhere, de Heusch's reconstruction gives us not the slightest idea of the actual religion and values of a neighboring culture that we actually do have information on, for we have from it an ethnographic analysis of its initiatic cult (Zuesse, 1978; 179:3–13; cf. Biebuyck). The essence of the Bwami cult of the Lega is not the correlation of a great deal of data, but the inculcation of a kind of poise, a stance towards life, a way of looking at things. It accomplishes this solely through the teaching of thousands of proverbs. The teaching of any single proverb is trivial, and indeed non-initiates know most of the proverbs that the initiate learns. It is the total impact of the proverbs that finally matters, as their teachings are worked deep into the initiate through countless repetitions, through dancing, singing, and artwork.

Another way of putting the same point: two scientists may know the same range of facts about the stars. For one, these facts are merely data to be studied and re-arranged in experiments. The other beholds in them the "ineffable mysteries." The data are the same. Both, let us say, are fine scientists. But we may speak of religion in regard to one alone.

To penetrate, therefore, to the kind of deep structures that are important in religion, we must decipher the *existential meaning* that ties together a wide variety of folk practices in different cultures. The remarks that follow attempt only a beginning at such a cryptanalysis. We cannot, for example, pursue the topic into a detailed survey of particular cultures, nor trace existential meanings back into the complex world of childhood, as we would like to do.

Some Themes in Traditional African Spirituality

Perhaps the most central and pervasive concern of traditional African religions is the maintenance of life as the integral interflow of relationships. This has several key aspects. Reality is not *being*, contrary to the prevalent Christian idea, but is *relationship*. The more one ties things together, the more power and transcendence, for power flows through relationships. The goal of life, then, is to maintain and join the cosmic web that holds and sustains all things and beings, to be part of the integral mutuality of things. As a result, one does not seek to separate oneself from the world, but to integrate oneself with it. The normal round of things is a main focus of religion and sacred effort; to flourish as family member and farmer is certainly a valid expression of spiritual concern. There is nothing "inauthentic" in such a spirituality (contrary to such theorists as Horton, 1960; 1964; 1967; 1973; Jensen, and others). What some other religions consider "secular" concerns are entirely appropriate spiritual concerns in African religions, and rightly so according to their logic. We might therefore expect that secularity in future African civilizations will still preserve authentically African forms of spirituality, and that there might be less conflict between political and religious forms than in the West where separation of "church and state" is found.

We might note right at the start that this view of things is almost the logical opposite to the Indo-European Iranian viewpoint we have discussed earlier. As a consequence, the African attitude to "evil" will be characteristically very different from the Iranian one, just as *integration* is different from *separation*, and consensus is different from polarization.

But before dealing with such matters let us seek to understand the consequences of such attitudes for the view of God in traditional African religions. The kind of language so dear to the salvation religions, in which one is urged to abandon lesser things and join one's isolated, inner, "true" self to the cosmic Self, unite Atman and Brahman, or attach the soul to God, is alien to African values. The relative material world is not the imperfect nor the compromised. It is the sole realm of reality and is good. God is concerned above all to cooperate in maintaining a world in which crops will grow and health will abound. But because of this, God is not the usual center of worship. Indeed, it is an expression of his continuing benevolence that he has withdrawn his overwhelming power and presence *behind* the intermediary beings he has appointed to govern the modulated realm of specific beings. God does not involve himself too directly in the world that he sustains, for too particular and intense an involvement might destroy the fabric of the divine order he sustains. It is a peculiarity seldom mentioned by students of African religions that we often encounter prayers to God *to keep away* from the petitioners and to permit the intermediaries and "refractions" of the spirit that maintain the differentiated realms of the universe to exist. Throughout east, central and southern Africa it is believed that illness, madness and even death come from God's nearness. God is present above all in the catastrophic thunderstorm and the lightning that kills, in the earthquake that levels houses and the epidemics that depopulate regions. It is at such times that one petitions God directly and not through intermediaries, but these petitions are above all appeals to God that he return his alien remoteness to a distance, that he have mercy and restore the network of the divine order as it had been.

When sickness, madness, and death afflict the Konde, they say that God is near. "Hence what the people desire above all things is that God should go away again. 'Go far hence, O God, to the Sango, for thy house is very large,' is a prayer not seldom heard on the lips of the Konde when they think God is near." (Frazer:189)

Many Nilotic peoples erect shrines to those who are struck by lightning, believing them to be chosen by God to dwell close to him and to act as intermediaries for the living, but the same peoples dread the lightning and plead with God not to punish them with such an election. Their prayers during storms are filled with confessions of sins and pleas for mercy. Likewise, during storms the Zulu rain-doctors used to shout from their compounds, "Move away thou Lord of lords, move away, thou greatest of friends, move away, thou Irresistible One!" (Smith, 1966:109). Aidan Southall has extended the insight afforded by such remarks to a more general one, when he suggests that the shrines and possession cults of the Nilotic Alur represent a kind of exorcism of Jok (the Supreme Being whose refractions are the many spirits), by means of which Jok is expelled from the sick, the unlucky, and the disturbed (each of these is said to be afflicted by Jok) into a specific shrine and ritual or into a patterned mediumistic possession (Southall:255). The same might well be said of many African religions.

This is not to ignore that many African religions do include a cult specifically to the Supreme Being. Perhaps there has been too much stress on the *deus otiosus* theme in the literature, so as to contrast this to the active presence of God as taught in Christianity and Islam. The conception of God and experience of his presence in Nuer religion, for example, has to be called biblical in its power and directness (Evans-Pritchard, 1956). The same could not only be said of certain other Nilotic religions, but of a good number of other African religions.

But implicit in the comments made above is the conclusion that God is worshipped above all through obedience to the specific imperatives and everyday relationships of the normal course of things; reverence to the intermediary beings is reverence to God (see Zuesse, 1979:98ff). There is, moreover, a direct cult to the Supreme Being that is widely spread through Africa, but which has been oddly ignored in the literature, and that is the cult to one's personal destiny, which may be part of a general divination ritual complex. Many traditions identify God and the personal destiny soul, even to the point of using the same term for both. The Ruanda, for example, assert that each person has a personal *imana* which can be cultically worshipped. One might say on a lucky day, "My imana is good," or "I have a good imana." But Imana is also the name for God, and the traditional Ruandese insist that there is no distinction between Imana and the imanas (Guillebaud: 184, 188, 190, etc.). The Fon of Dahomey often refer to the personal destiny soul as *se* or *mawu*, but these terms also apply to God (Maupoil:14,388). The divinatory cult in these and other instances is in effect a cult to the Supreme Being.

Power unmediated is terrific and breaks the boundaries. Power as it is disseminated in the articulated divine order is good. This has moral repercussions. Those who most embody the direct power of God, such as sacral kings, must show this through transcendence of the norms and restraints that maintain health and goodness for the rest of us: they are permitted, and even obligated, to indulge in immoralities and excesses that would destroy lesser beings. Indeed, it is a kind of madness: mourners at funerals may even have to act out this madness that comes from too close proximity to the sublime, so as to honor it and exorcise it. Rituals of reversal, of madness and upside-down behavior, immoral and destructive, mark most ritual occasions when the mediated divine order breaks down and the primal powers draw too close, when God is near and there are no longer the boundaries between the living and the dead, the ancestors of the past and the living of the present (cf. Norbeck; Zuesse, 1979:108–32).

We cannot be surprised, then, if African rulers are often expected to behave in an extreme fashion during New Year's festivals and interregnums, and that this is viewed with a certain satisfaction, as if by such behavior they demonstrate their sacral right to their positions. Although, like God himself, they traditionally are withdrawn behind (and their direct power is checked and balanced by) the multitude of groups and individuals that administer the kingdom and represent all its major groupings (such as the regional village councils and chiefs, the queen-mother, rain-maker and other priests, and the various aristocratic lineages: cf. Evans-Pritchard and Fortes:11–13), on occasion they step forward and demonstrate their transcendence of ordinary life. When one is that close to the primordial sources of the divine, one can behave outside any particular category of the divine order, just because one is to a degree the summation of all categories.

God too derives his transcendence from this fact: he "presents" and is the synthesis and totality of the divine order, and so must be beyond any particular category in it. The more esoteric versions of African religions make this dialectic explicit. Fon *Fa* divination (like the nearly identical Ifa divination of the Yoruba of Nigeria) breaks down reality into a primal alternation of male and female potencies, which double and redouble to create first the opposition of light and dark, heaven and earth, etc., and then the four cardinal points with all the traits associated with each (the fourfoldness of life), then sixteen elemental powers, and finally 256 elements, each with its own characteristic qualities. These generate the world. The first two elements, however, out of which all the rest come, are Mawu and Lisa, the female and male modes of God. That is, God is the divine order in its totality — and thus what transcends all things including the world merely as such. As the rabbinic sages of the Talmud put it, God is the "Place" of the world — and this very term, "Place," *Makom*, signifies to them God's uttermost transcendence of all the universe together with God's full presence at every place within the universe. Only if God utterly transcends the world can he be equally present at every point and time in it (Schechter: 26, 34, 46). In such a perspective, terms such as "transcendence" and "immanence" must lose much of their oppositional quality.

It is therefore no proof of God's remoteness from the worshipper, that one appeals only to his lesser agents in cult, for we see the same thing before sacral kings and chiefs: one addresses them only in the third person and even through their ministers, even when standing in their awesome presence. The Akan king, like so many others, had to be veiled, lest the power of his direct glance and presence destroy his subjects. Such reference to the "refractions" of Deity (and of kingship) affirms the importance of the relationships and distinctions of the divine order which are the chief evidences of God's benevolence. The lesser powers maintain the specific realms and distinctions that permit a universe of sanctified hierarchies. In a world of power, relationship, and mediated mutualities, after all, hierarchy is a positive good.

But this is a dynamic hierarchy, not a static one: in a world where relationships are the key, even being is dissolved into modes of action — God himself is acted on by invoking those mediatory beings which are his specific modes of acting in the world. To a remarkable degree, these assumptions are also borne out in terms of the concept of the self. Here we penetrate to what may be called the psychological correlate of the metaphysical notions and attitudes we have already discussed.

In a penetrating review article, John Beattie suggested that there appear to be four main themes in the African view of personhood or the self: first, that the context defines the self (the context consisting of the group or relationship that is dominant in that particular situation); second, that the self is composite, not unitary; third, that arising out of the integration into a multitude of contexts the composite self may be seen as open and extended into its surrounding environment rather than being closed in upon itself — the self is an arena rather than an independent center; and finally, as the relationships and contexts vary, so does the intensity of the self's essential qualities (Beattie:314). To these insights we may add that the openness of the self to its environment puts all of its relationships into a kind of dynamic flux, in which it is fully possible for the self in at least one of its multiple modes, and perhaps all of them, to be taken over and *possessed* by the superior power of other beings. From this danger arises a sixth main theme, that the most desireable goal of personal development and social interaction (for the two are one, as we shall see) is to attain to a condition of tranquil equilibrium of interacting forces within the self and between the self and its environment: this is a condition frequently characterized as being "cold" rather than "hot" (unstable, excitable, dangerous, intense). In this collected state the self dominates.

Perhaps the elementary assumptions underlying even these six main themes of personhood are just two in number, and we should start with these: first, that the self is actional in nature; and, second, that the self is composite and not unitary. It is evident that these traits are structurally identical to those that we have found in the African view of God.

The Krobo of Ghana can even pray to aspects of their selves (Huber: 139):

> My *kla Kwao* (thursday soul: people differ in traits and even in destiny in accordance with the day of the week in which they are born), you too come and drink (of the offering to the ancestors)! As we are celebrating our ritual, let our right hand draw fortune, let our left hand draw fortune, let us stay in good health! You, my *gbetsi* (spiritual anima, alter ego), stay calm that we may get rich and bear many children!

The prayer is actually made to various semi-independent aspects of the petitioner who therefore speaks of himself as a multitude: "we." The ancestral spirits from which he stems still have an intimate affect on him and presence in him; his destiny soul, his spiritual anima or guardian spirit, even his right hand and his left hand, all have a kind of autonomy and all must be in accord if he is to be successful and content. One's life is an unending dynamic process of seeking equilibrium, of negotiating one's way even within the "arena" of the self.

The Ila of Zambia have the expression, upon hearing good news, "The ear-*bupuku* are delighted!" Every organ in the body as its own energizing spirits, visualized as tiny serpents, *bupuku* (Smith and Dale, I:225). In addition, the person's name has a specific spiritual identity, relating to a similarly named ancestor; the personal will is produced by a specific soul, the *mozo*; the shadow is a distinct soul-entity which is part of the self and is called the *chingvule*; the inner personality is the *musedi* soul; the vital breath is the *muwo*; and life itself is *bumi* (*ibid.*, II:161f.). Each of these spiritual entities is engaged not only with the self, but also with an entire stratum of reality beyond the self: the ancestor is engaged with the name, and in different ways with the vitality of the *bumi* and *muwo* (with male and female ancestors contributing different qualities and being present through them); these also interact with natural forces; the *chingvule* objectivates, so to speak, the body and represents its involuntary participation in a world of physical things and so on. To maintain harmony in the self, it is necessary to be on good terms with one's entire social and spiritual world. This requires appropriate actions such as reverence to one's parents, kin, and ancestral spirits, observance of cultic obligations, maintenance of social relationships, and respect for natural forces.

(As a result, health depends on more than merely readjusting the physical operation of the body, or surgery, etc.: it requires attention to the entire network of interrelations between the self and other powers and presences, from the family and neighbors to the spirits. African medicine has always been aware of the psychosomatic nature of illness. E.g., see Appiah-Kubi.)

J.V. Taylor has suggested a general synthesis of African (West African and Bantu) soul-concepts, in which the blood, given by the mother and her line, contains the life-soul (the vitality), the bones or flesh embody the individual soul stemming from the father and his line (the personality), while the shape of one's life is determined by the destiny soul, as I have called it, or transcendent-soul, in Taylor's terminology, which comes directly from God (Taylor:59ff). Clearly there can be many different ways of organizing such diverse and culturally variable data (cf. also Hochegger, and especially the essay by Thomas, together with the other contributions to the same symposium). But it is clear that with such a worldview to participate in the ancestor cult, to revere the nature-spirits, and to keep on good terms with living kin and neighbors, is not only a matter of external good relations, but of inner health and tranquility, for all these presences are both external and internal. *Hospitality* is a key value resonating in many aspects of life.

In such a world, the more relationships one establishes with others the more one's own spirituality is enhanced, and the homage of many friends and dependents increases one's own charismatic power and strengthens one's souls. The village headman is assumed to be a powerful magician, quite rightly and logically from such premises, while a person who is friendless and without relatives is almost a non-person and is unable to resist the dark powers of evil ghosts and sorcerers. Village politics may often be regarded from a religious angle as the struggle to obtain and hold more soul-power and so to be more "real." By entering into networks of solidarity, such as kinship and locality, and rising to a central position in them, the self achieves density of existence, "weight," and stable power. Leaders have "heavy" souls.

In order to "be," then, one must act, or rather interact, with others. A powerful threat to both the self and the cosmos, it is clear, is social conflict. Many anthropological studies of African ritual have interpreted it to be directed to the reconciliation of contending parties and therefore largely social in purpose. But the fusion of social and spiritual concerns is evident in all accounts and is strikingly borne out in the study by

Grace Harris, *Casting Out Anger* (Cambridge: Cambridge University Press, 1978). The Taita of Kenya make of *kutasa*, the ritual purgation of anger, the central act of religion. Kutasa particularly works on the secret resentments and frustrations that arise in the course of life; open anger and conflict can be dealt with and dissipated in ordinary village politics, but the hidden angers are what destroy individuals and society spiritually. The cult is about deep harmony.

There are, it would seem, four main models of interpersonal relations in traditional African folklore, mythology, and ritual symbolisms. These are *kin* reciprocity, the complementarity and creative fusion of *sexuality*, the dominance and enslavement of *war*, and finally the destruction and absorption imaged in *sacrifice*. In these, the relationship between the self and the other is progressively less and less equal, until in sacrifice one of the two is absorbed into the other. The importance of possession trance in African religions shows that the radical dominance found in myths of war have a direct expression in personal spiritual experience – so radical is the dominance, in fact, that mediums are often treated as sacrificial offerings in their initiations (cf. Zuesse, 1979:185, 191, 202, 205n.52).

While reciprocity and sexual complementarity are the preferred models for interaction, then, outright conquest and even personal obliteration are openly accepted spiritual possibilities. These are not seen as evil per se, for there is not a concept of the inviolable, isolated self apart from all social-spiritual contexts. Enslavement and obliteration are evil only if they are fundamentally destructive of the larger social and divine order as such.

We can understand, therefore, why witchcraft and zombi-states are so fearful and dreaded possibilities. They are the negative possibility of approved and even experienced realities. In witchcraft, the overall harmony of society and the cosmos is destroyed, as humans, who should be kin or neighbors, mystically hunt, fight, and kill each other; the witch sacrifices others for his or her own self-aggrandizement, instead of behaving as normal and good people do, and sacrificing from his or her own self (own chickens, goats, or other things that participate in the self) to divine and social others. The distinctively African nightmare-condition of the zombi embodies the evil potential of enslavement, which is otherwise a traditionally accepted part of African realities.

For it is part of the spiritual vision of things that we find in African religions, that all things must participate in and give themselves up to the dynamic interchange of things, the vital web that constitutes the divine order. Unlike more dualistic worldviews, tormenting and disruptive spiritual forces are not excluded from the self or society by a process of separation, but attempts are made instead to include them in the self and harness them for society by a process of accommodation and incorporation. Possession trance phenomena in African religions make the logic very clear. Victor W. Turner has drawn our attention to the widespread "cults of affliction" that we find in east, central and southern Africa (Turner, 1968). In these cults, the illness or misfortune afflicting a person or a family is interpreted as the sign of a spirit that has been thwarted in its attempt to commune with its human servants. Due to negligence of its cult, or disregard for its laws, human beings have distorted the easy flow of spiritual vitality between the spirit and humanity. So the afflicted person must honor the spirit, and learn its laws and obey them; then the affliction will stop, and the intervention of the spirit will be able to speak from time to time.

The logic applies not only in Bantu cults, but elsewhere in Africa, and to other phenomena. The wildness and impulsiveness of Eshu/Elegba, the often-demonic trickster of Fon and Yoruba religion, may force those who are possessed by him to attack women sexually, cause fights, and create general disturbance; but the other face of the same reality is Fa/Ifa itself, personified wisdom, and the divinatory system that cures all upheavals in the divine order (Zuesse, 1979:208f.) One common way of curing witchcraft is to make the witch enter into participation with his or her victim, by sharing a feast with the victim, spitting on the victim (sharing exuviae), or joining in a common cult — henceforth, if the witch should attempt to harm the victim, the evil would also rebound on the witch. Only drastic evil, therefore, must be expelled from the community. Whereas in Christian Europe spirit possession was itself seen as demonic and was responded to by seeking to exorcise the spirit, in Africa spirit possession, although heralded by illness and misfortune, is integrated into a cult which then works toward healing and good fortune. The mark of irredeemable evil is above all the refusal to accommodate in any way, not to share with the oppressed victims at all. Thus "evil," like the "self" and like "God," is not a state of being, nor is it a matter of abstract moral rules, but it is a characteristic of a certain mode of interaction with other persons and with the divine order itself. What builds up the divine order is good and what acts to destroy it is bad. The measure, therefore, is not so much a personal one as it is cosmic.

In this essay, I have been trying to consider traditional African spirituality on a level and in a context that may seem an unusual one. I have sought to define some of the characteristics of the "deep structure" of this spirituality, a structure, that is, of existential experiences of life, that underlie a wide range of "folk practices" such as spirit mediumship and witchcraft, sacral kingship and myths of conquest. I would maintain that long after specific religious cults disappear, and even a thousand years into the future, so long as there is an African civilization at all, these deep structures will continue to shape African spirituality and worldview.

These reflections have consequences for the moral and socio-political order of present and future African cultures, as well, although we cannot pursue such ramifications here; besides, the forms these will take are surely beyond the imagination of those alive today: unless divinely inspired, no one is a true prophet, the Bible tells us, and I make no claim to divine inspiration.

Neither is it claimed that deep structures cannot be modified by the internal evolution of a civilization or the influences of others. The specific forms that the worldview of Iranian civilization has taken testify to the possibility of significant modifications and re-orientations brought on by such influences as the Buddhist doctrines of transmigration and reincarnation of the world savior, or the Manichaean conception of the opposition of world rulers (divine and human) to the human bearers of the true teachings, etc. African spirituality, too, shall undoubtedly slowly evolve and change.

But we may be sure that the dynamic and joyful quality of African spirituality will survive, in whatever future reincarnation it appears.

Note

1. African intellectual journals, such as *Odu*, or *Presence Africaine*, frequently feature such essays. An important theme of many of these and other such constructions is to establish a certain primacy vis-à-vis Western and Middle Eastern cultures and religions; as Amar Samb put it (Samb: 136):

    Comment le Noir a-t-il réagi devant d'autres religions? Que ce soit le Judaisme ou le Christianisme ou l'Islam ou l'Hindouisme, le Noir africain ou dravidien ou de tout autre lieu s'est conduit comme s'il avait été le créateur de ces religions.

    At the same time, there is an attempt to distinguish what is unique in African spirituality and *unlike* other spiritualities. And as Samb's own essay goes on to demonstrate, the key to both is often claimed to be ancient Egypt. Such themes, however, are not those only of native African intellectuals. Many other reconstructions of African spirituality echo them. Leo Frobenius was a notable early voice, often cited in contemporary essays.

    However, such claims generally relate to intellectualistic viewpoints or folk practices and symbols; they may or may not be accurate, but in any case do not touch the level of "deep spiritual structures" that we are interested in in this essay. I believe these to be distinctive to African cultures; they predated Egypt, and it is doubtful that Egyptian ideas modified them. An interesting recent attempt to articulate an overarching African philosophy in terms of the ethnographic data is that of Zahan. However, despite that author's great learning and insight, one gets the feeling that too much is claimed for the mystical theosophy we know of from the Dogon and Bambara esoteric myths. Yet there is no denying that many of the Mande mythic folk ideas are found in African religions very far from the Mande cultures (cf. Zuesse, 1987). It is clear that many current attempts at painting "the African philosophy" are heavily indebted to the work of the Griaule circle.

References

Appiah-Kubi, Kofi. 1981. *Man Cures, God Heals*. Totowa, NJ: Allanheld, 1981.

Bastide, Roger. 1978. *The African Religions of Brazil: Toward a Sociology of the Interpenetration of Civilizations*. Translated by Helen Sebba. Baltimore: The Johns Hopkins Press.

Beattie, John. 1980. "Review Article: Representations of the Self in Traditional Africa," *Africa*, 50/3:313–20.

Bonavia, David; Welch, Holmes: *et al.* 1980. "China After Mao: Back to the Old Beliefs," *Far Eastern Economic Review*, August 15, 1980:24–32.

Bourguignon, Erika (ed.). 1973. *Religion, Altered States of Consciousness and Social Change*. Columbus: Ohio State University Press.

Evans-Pritchard, E.E. 1956. *Nuer Religion*. Oxford: Clarendon Press.

Fortes, Mayer. 1940. "Introduction." In *African Political Systems*, eds. Evans-Pritchard and Fortes. London: Oxford University Press.

Frazer, Sir James. 1926. *The Worship of Nature*. London: Macmillan & Co.

Hochegger, H. 1965. "Die Vorstellungen von Seele und Totengeist bei Afrikanischen Völkern," *Anthropos*, 60:273–339.

Horton, Robin. 1960. "A Definition of Religion and Its Uses," *Journal of the Royal Anthropological Institute*, 90:201–26.

.... 1964. "Ritual Man in Africa," *Africa*, 34/2 (April) 85–103.

.... 1978. "African Traditional Thought and Western Science," *Africa*, 37/1&2 (January & April) 50-71, 155–87.

.... 1971. "African Conversion," *Africa*, 41/2 (April).

.... and Finnegan, Ruth (eds.). 1973. *Modes of Thought: Essays on Thinking in Western and Non-Western Societies*. London: Faber & Faber.

Huber, Hugo. 1963. *The Krobo*. Studia Institute Anthropos, 16. St. Augustin: Anthropos Institut.

Jensen, Adolf. 1963. *Myth and Cult among Primitive Peoples*. Chicago: The University of Chicago Press.

Levenson, Joseph R. 1958, 1964, 1965. *Confucian China and Its Modern Fate: A Triology*. Berkeley: University of California Press.

Lévi-Strauss, Claude. 1963. *Structural Anthropology*. New York: Basic Books.

.... 1966. *The Savage Mind*. Chicago: University of Chicago Press.

Maupoil, Bernard. 1943. *La Géomancie à l'ancienne Côte des Esclaves*. Travaux et Memoires, 42. Paris: Institut d'Ethnologie.

Norbeck, Edward. 1967. "African Rituals of Conflict." In *Gods and Rituals: Readings in Religious Beliefs and Practices*, edited by John Middleton. 197–226. Garden City, NY: Natural History Press.

Samb, Amar. 1981. "Dimensions socio-culturelles et religieuses," *Presence Africaine*, no. 117–118:130–37.

Schechter, Solomon. 1961. *Aspects of Rabbinic Theology*. New York: Schocken.

Simpson, George E. 1978. *Black Religions in the New World*. New York: Columbia University Press.

Singer, Milton. 1972. *When a Great Tradition Modernizes*. New York: Praeger.

............, ed. 1973. *Entrepreneurship and Modernization of Occupational Cultures in South Asia*. Durham, North Carolina: Duke University Press.

Smith, E.W. and Dale, A.M. 1920. *The Ila-Speaking Peoples of Northern Rhodesia*. 2 vols. London: Macmillan & Co.

Southall, Aidan, 1969. "Spirit Possession and Mediumship among the Alur." In *Spirit Mediumship and Society in Africa*, edited by John Middleton and John Beattie. London: Routledge & Kegan Paul.

Taylor, J.V. 1963. *The Primal Vision*. Philadelphia: Fortress Press.

Thomas, Louis-Vincent. 1973. "Le pluralisme coherent de la notion de personne." In: *La notion de personne en Afrique Noire*, edited by Germaine Dieterlen, 387–419. Paris: Editions du Centre nationale de la Recherche Scientifique.

Thompson, Lawrence G., ed. 1973. *The Chinese Way in Religion*. Encino, CA: Dickenson Publishing Co., Inc.

Turner, Victor W. 1968. *The Drums of Affliction*. Oxford: Clarendon Press.

Verger, Pierre. 1957. *Notes sur le culte des Orisa et Vodun*. Mémoires de l'Institut Francais d'Afrique Noire, 51. Dakar: I.F.A.N.

Walker, Sheila S. 1972. *Ceremonial Spirit Possession in Africa and Afro-America*. Leiden: E.J. Brill.

Weber, Max. 1958. *Religion in India*. Translated by H. Gerth. New York: Free Press.

Wilson, Bryan R., ed. 1970. *Rationality*. London: Basil Blackwell & Mott.

Zaehner, R.C. 1961. *The Dawn and Twilight of Zoroastrianism*. New York: G.P. Putnams' Sons.

Zahan, Dominique. 1979. *The Religion, Spirituality, and Thought of Traditional Africa*. Chicago: University of Chicago Press.

Zuesse, Evan M. 1978. "Action as the Way of Transcendence: The Religious Significance of the Bwami Cult of the Lega," *Journal of Religion in Africa*, 9/1:62–72.

.... 1979. *Ritual Cosmos: The Sanctification of Life in African Religions*. Athens, Ohio: Ohio University Press.

.... 1987. "(African) Mythic Themes." In: *Encyclopedia of Religion*, edited by Mircea Eliade, vol. 1:70–82. 16 vols. New York: Macmillan Press.

Contributors

Wande Abimbọla, Professor and Former Vice Chancellor, Ọbafẹmi Awolọwọ University, Ile-Ifẹ, Ọyọ State, Nigeria.

Joseph Ọmọṣade Awolalu, former Professor, Department of Religious Studies, University of Ibadan, Ibadan, Ọyọ State, Nigeria and Chairman Post Primary School Management Board, Ondo State, Akure, Nigeria.

Rosalind I.J. Hackett, Associate Professor, Department of Religious Studies, University of Tennessee, Knoxville, TN, USA

Akinwumi Iṣọla, Professor, Department of African Languages & Literature, Ọbafẹmi Awolọwọ University, Ile-Ifẹ, Ọyọ State, Nigeria

Bennnetta W. Jules-Rosette, Professor, Department of Sociology, University of California, San Diego, California, USA

John S. Mbiti, Professor, Evangelical Theological Faculty, University of Bern, Bern, Switzerland

Friday M. Mbon, Senior Lecturer, Department of Religious Studies, University of Calabar, Calabar, Cross River, Nigeria

Rev. Father Vincent Mulago, Professor, Faculty of Catholic Theology, University of Kinshasa/Limete, Zaire

Georges Niangoran-Bouah, Professor Emeritus, Universite Nationale d'Abidjan; Director of the Department of African Musicology, Laboratory of Drumology, Abidjan, Ivory Coast

Jacob Kẹhinde Olupọna, Senior Lecturer, Department of Religious Studies, Obafẹmi Awolọwọ University, Ile-Ifẹ, Ọyọ State, Nigeria

Joseph Akinyẹle Omoyajowo, former Professor, Department of Religious Studies, Ọbafẹmi Awolọwọ University, Ile-Ifẹ, Ọyọ State, Nigeria and Secretary, Anglican Church of Nigeria, Lagos.

Gerhardus Cornelis Oosthuizen, Project Leader, Research Unit On New Religions and Indigenous Churches, University of Zululand, Durban, South Africa

David B. Westerlund, Associate Professor, Department of Comparative Religion, University of Stockholm, Stockholm; Senior Research Fellow, Department of Cultural Anthropology, University of Uppsala, Sweden

Evan M. Zuesse, Senior Lecturer and Head of Department, Department of Religious Studies, South Australian College of Advanced Education, Underdale, South Australia, Australia

Index

A

Abasi 136
Abbasid 169
Accommodation 181
Acholi 65, 67
Actions 124–125
Adam 68
Adaptability 3, 27, 31
Africae Terrarum 131
African
    artefacts 144
    beliefs 7, 144
    Christianity 22
    Church of the Holy Spirit 161
African civilizations
    secularity in 173
African
    cosmology 46
    cultures 44, 182
African deities
    worship of 116
African ethics 102, 104–105, 107, 125,
    131, 134n
    communality of 103
African folklore 180
African folklore forms
    nationalisation of 141
African humanism 141
African Independent Churches
    Association 161
African
    medicine 179
    mythology 167, 180
    philosophy 182, 183n
    prophetic movement 158
    religio-cultural identity of the 54
African religion(s)
    comparative study of 154
    cultural integration of 22
    historical dimension of 22
    historicity of 146
    phenomenological-hermeneutical
        interpretations of 3
    social influence of 161
    spiritual structure of 170

    spirituality of 68
    view of God in 174
African religious
    beliefs 3, 92
    experience 2
African religious life
    essence of 28
African religious movement
    (as) revolutionist 153
    (as) thaumaturgical 153
African ritual 179
    ritual symbolisms 180
    social ethics 8
African societies
    patriarchal nature of 5
African
    spirituality 2, 10, 12, 170–171,
        181–182
    symbolic systems 21
    symbols 144
African tradition
    core beliefs and symbols of 144
African
    value systems 8
    wisdom 63
African worldview 3–4, 64, 182
    philosophies of 172
Agni 85
Ahriman (See Satan)
Ahura Mazda 169
Ajẹpọ 57
Ajẹra 57
Akamba 61, 64–65, 68
Akan 22–23, 74, 83–85, 92
    king 177
Akposso 60
Ala 75
Alaafin of Ọyọ 94, 97
Aladura Church 151, 160
Ale 75
Ali 169
Al-Jahilliya 1
Allah 114
Allegory 28
Analects 168
Analogy 125

187

Analysis 3
Anangaman 88
Anansa 140
Ancestor(s) 40, 42, 46, 53, 58n, 82–83,
    87, 91, 102, 108, 113, 120–123,
    126–127, 137, 146, 167, 176, 178
    cult of 55, 92, 179
    homage to 116
    spirits of 17, 82, 89
    symbiotic union with 41
    worship/veneration of 12, 54,
        127, 129–130
Ancestral
    cult 172
    displeasure 104
    ritual purgation 180
    spirits 179
Angra Mainyu (Evil Spirit) 169
Ani 75
Animism 20
Annang 104
Anomie 4
Anthropological
    investigation 3
    model 29
Anthropologist(s) 15–18, 21–23, 29
Anthropology 1, 19–20
Apostles of John Maranke 158
Apostolic
    Churches 154
    movements 151
    sermons and rituals 162
Approach(es)
    biblical 43
    case study 12
    holistic 16, 44–45, 48
    limitative 22
    liturgical 48
    modernist 39
    mythic 28
    phenomenological
    post-modern scientific 39
    religio-phenomenological 16
    scientific and technological 39
    semantic anthropological 154
    structuralist 20
    traditional 41
    traditional medical 48
Aquarian Church of the Angels 138–139
Arabs 170

Archival materials 31
Arguments 4
Aro 69
Art(s) 2, 30, 113, 115, 117
    works of 113
Artha (Truth) 169
Artist 7
Artwork 173
Asae Yaa 74
Ashanti 62, 69
Ataja 57
Atheists 139
Atman 174
Authority structures
    decline of 155
Awijare 57
Awoupadi 88
Awure 57
Aya Olua 76

B

Babalawo 96
Babayẹmi Itiolu 94, 97
Babylonian Empire 169
Babylonians 170
Badagry 52, 113
Baganda 61
Bambara myths 183n
Bambuti Pygmy 62
Bannerman 59, 64, 66–68
Bantu 119, 122, 125–128, 130
    cults 181
    ethic 126
    soul-concepts 179
Banyarwanda 69
Banyoro 61
Baoule 86
Baptism 116
Bashi 120, 122
Basoga 70
Being(s) 41, 173
    African conception of 126
    enhancement or diminution of
        120–121
    increase in 122
    integrity of 123
    interaction of 120, 123
    intimate 122
    new form of 122

Beir, Ulli 116
Belief(s) 22, 26, 40, 82–83, 85, 111,
    119–120, 129–130, 162
        marginal 129
        para-religious 129–130
        patterns 47
        (in) survival 130
        system 48, 154
        theistic 27
        truth-claims 29
Bemba 61
Berger, Peter 155, 156, 163n
Bible 41, 82, 92, 112-113, 151, 182
        personal adherence to 161
        (as) revolutionary book 157
Biblical knowledge 40
Bini 143
Birth 41, 61, 121
Blondel, M. 131
Blood 6, 121, 179
        community in 121
        lineage 122
        pact 124
Boa 85
Bori 114
Brahman 174
Brotherhood 137
Buddha 169
Buddhism 25, 169
Buni 178
Bupuku 178
Bwami cult 172
Bwiti cult 160

C

Cannibalism 167
Capitalism 155
Carter, Governor 112
Carvings 113
Catechism 40
Catholic(s) 113
        Church 129
        modernism 18
        tradition 157
Catholicism 171
Celebrations 76
Ceremonies 12, 82, 121, 127

Charismatic
        power 179
        renewals 162
Cherubim and Seraphim Movement 153
Chief 40, 121–122
Chieftaincy
        institution of 142
Childhood
        worldview of 170
Chineke 137
Chingvule 178
Christ 129
Christian(s) 5, 52–56, 58, 95, 98, 113,
    115–116, 131, 139, 170
        baptism 117
        doctrines 107
        evangelization 98
        faith 129–130
        fundamentalism 9
Christian groups 160
        spiritual renewal in 151
Christian
        message 128
        missionaries 81, 113
        missionary effort 116, 150
        missions 43
        morality 131
        morals 129
        myths 139
        revelation 128–129
        theocentric morals 130
        theology 43
        worship 112
Christianity 1, 3–4, 8–11, 18–19, 22,
    26, 31–32, 43, 51–52, 56, 82, 92,
    112–117, 119, 128, 137, 139–140,
    144, 151, 167, 171, 175
        essence of 128
        European 153
        theologies of 170
Christianization 22
Church(es) 129
        African Israel Ninevah 161
        community-based
        independent 11, 32, 150
        indigenous 4, 150, 161
        Kimbanguist 161
        (of) the Lord Aladura 161
        Missionary Society 94
        modern 150

Church and State
    tensions in the relationship
        between 157
Church-sect typology 11
Church(es)
    separatist 11, 150–151
Circle 41
Civil religion 141
Clan 120–121, 123
Cognitive structures 172
Collective identity 162
Colonial domination 155
Colonialism 18, 115, 150
Commercialization 135, 144
Committee on Ethical Re-Orientation
    107
Communal
    concern 107
    identity 106
Communication 83
Communion 120, 131, 159
    (in) feasting 124
Community 40–41, 45, 102–104,
    106–107, 119–121, 123, 125, 130,
    139, 159, 161
    (in) possessions 121
    sense of 4, 47–48, 151
    vital potential of 125
    welfare of 105
Comparative
    research 16
    studies 16
Conference of Traditional Religions 137
Confession(s) 103, 124, 175
Conflict 170
Conscience 104, 125–126, 131
Consciousness
    transformation of 38
Conservatism 168
Contact
    (with) invisible power 124
Conversion 3, 128
    marks of 113
Converts 4, 113–114
    divided 115
Cooperation 158
Core values 159
Correspondences 125
Co-responsibility 130–131
Cosmic battle 169

Cosmic web 173
Cosmological symbolization 28
Cosmologies 2, 154
Cosmos 28, 125, 171
Council of World Religions 1
Creation 5, 83, 85, 88, 91
    myth 168
Creativity 38
Creator 17, 120–121, 125
Cryptanalysis 173
Cult(s) 53–54, 161, 170, 180
    (of) affliction 181
    nativistic 145
    object 82, 85
    (of) Orisa 4
    retention of 52
Cultic
    names 171
    obligations 179
    practices 5
    rituals 168
Cultural
    awareness 137
    change 157
Cultural continuity
    search for 150
Cultural
    diffusion 162
    heritage 7
    heterogeneity 35, 36
    idioms 30
    integration 22
    materialism 20
    patrimony 128
    pluralism 160
    pluralization 156
    revival 117
    revolution 115
    riches 129
    sharing 160
Culture(s)
    "half caste" 43
    heterogeneity of 21
    oral 26
    Western 45
Curse 102
Customs 127

D

Daevas (devils) 169
Dances 143
    format and meaning of 141
Dancing 41, 76, 115, 140, 173
Darkness
    forces of 170
Darwin, Charles 42
Dead
    veneration of 120
    worship of 130
Death 5, 41, 55, 61–63, 70, 91,
    103–104, 121, 126, 174
    life after 111
    penalty 87
Decolonization 152
Declaration of Traditional Religions of
    Nigeria 137
Decontextualization 16
Deity(ies) 10, 27, 31, 39, 53-55, 75, 77,
    87, 95, 108, 140
    exclusion of 137
    experience of 78
    feminine 6, 73
    Hebrew concept of 6
    "refractions" of 177
    worship of 74
Denominational Christianity
    divisions in 151
Desacralization 156
Descendants 120–121, 123
Deus Absconditus 40
Deus otiosus 175
Development 1, 10, 101, 104, 106
Diachronic analysis 3, 30
Dialogue
    interfaith 26
    inter-religious 1
    intra-religious 1
Disease(s) 61-62
Disembodied souls 126
Divination 46, 53, 116, 129, 136, 140,
    172
    Ifa 52, 103, 145
    poems 8
Divinatory
    cult 175
    system 181
Divine 40, 125

Being 28
    displeasure 104
    law 131
    names 170
    order 174–177, 180–181
Divine powers 170
    specific names of 171
Divine
    primordial sources of 176
    providence 130
Diviners 4, 47–48, 77
    (as) sociologists 48
    therapeutic methods of 45
Divinities 17, 23, 55, 75–76, 80n,
    89–90, 111
Doctrinal
    ambivalence 160
    autonomy 161
    innovation 151
Doctrine(s) 26, 129, 151, 158
Dogma 29
Dogmatic Constitution of the Church
    129
Dogon myths 183n
Dopamu 56
Druj 169
Drum
    (as) living institution 2
Drumming 115, 117, 140
Drumology 7
Du 104
Dualism 169
Duality
    between man and the world 125,
    127
Durkheim, Emile 11, 16, 19, 151–152,
    163n
Dyanif 84

E

Earth Spirit 74-75
    worship of 130
Ebora 76
Ecclesiastical authority
    distribution of 154
Ecological issues 46
Ecology 30
Economic development 39

Ecstasy 76
Ecumenical
    cooperation 158
    Councils 161
Ecumenism 158, 160
Edanga 88
Edangaman 88
Edo 143
Education
    Western 4
Efe Asaba 143
Efik 141, 143
    cultural identity 142
    deities 140, 143
Efut 142
Egoism 102
Egungun 53, 55, 58n
Eka-Abassi 60
Ekao 60
Ekpe
    cults of 143
    society 142–143
Ekpenyong
    cult of 143
    sacrifices to 144
Ẹla 54
Elders 45, 76, 113, 121, 123
    council of 87
Eliade, Mircea 30
Emancipation 11
Emissary of Light 169
Empathy 18
Endless Time (See also Zurvan) 169
Enslavement 180
Epistemological issue 40
Equilibrium 127, 177, 178
Ẹṣẹ Ifa 95
Eshu/Elẹgba 181
Esoteric Philosophical Society 142
Essence
    community of 41
Essuman 86
Eṣu 55
Ethic(s) 12, 27, 101–102, 125, 129,
    130, 141
    anthropocentric 125–126, 130
    communal 102, 104, 106
    (of) communion 131
    (of) conscience 108
    cosmic 131

global 131
(of) participation and communion
    126
societal 10
vital 125
Ethical criteria
    ancestor-sanctioned 107
    community-centered 107
    theonomous 107
Ethical
    principles 107
    regulations 104
    sanctions 104
    system 105
    values 106
Ethnic associations 142
Ethnical groups 36, 104
Ethnocentrism 17
Ethnographic level 154
Ethnologists 16
Ethnology 131
Etiology 47
Eve 68
Events 42–43
Evil 104, 181
Evil act
    norms of 126
Evil
    African attitude to 174
    criterion of 125
    nature of 12
    (as) "medicinal" resource 126
    origin of 5
    spell 123
    theories of 140
Existence
    homogenization of 45
    personalization of 44
Experience 3
Extra-marital relations 131
Ezes 138

F

Fa/Ifa 181
Faith(s) 27, 111, 117
Family 41, 45–46, 107, 120, 123, 127,
    129, 131, 179
    bonds of 159

monogamous 65
polygamous 65
solidarity of 121
structure 114
Father
of all 120, 130
Feelings 119
FESTAC (See also below Festival of Arts
and Culture) 137
Festival(s) 4–5, 52–55, 144
Annual Yam 76
(of) Arts and Culture 9, 117
Ibadan 139
New Year 87, 176
Ọmọjao 76–77
Oke'badan 139
Ọṣun 116
traditional 115–116
Fides (belief) 40
Fiducia (trust) 40
Fire 61
Flogging 107
Folk
etymology 93
practices 12, 170–172, 182n
Fon 175
Fon Fa
divination 176
religion 181
Force 124
Ford Foundation 30
Forgiveness 107
Founder 121
Fragmentation 149
Freedom 131, 157
political and religious conceptions
of, 161
Freud, Sigmund 19
Fulani 114
Functionalism 20
Fundamental doctrines
return to 162
Funeral(s) 121
ceremonies 56
Funerary rites 143
Future 4, 42–44
anxiety toward 57

G

Gbọnka 94
Genealogy 87
Genesis 5
Genies
worship of 130
Genius 89
Gestures 124
Ghetsi 178
Ghosts 179
Gift 125
Gikuyu 64–67
God 17–19, 23, 27, 40, 60-63, 68–71,
82, 84–85, 87–91, 113, 120, 122,
124, 127–129, 137–138, 174–176
(of) Africa 137, 139
African concept of 74, 178
alien remoteness of 174
attitude to 127
(the) Creator 86, 88, 125
female and female forms of 176
feminine concept of 74
masculine concept of 74
patriarchal image of 78
(as) provident Father 129
rationality of 40
separation from 62
transcendent 126
Western concepts of 28
worship of 130, 167
Goddess 75, 85
Godian Religion 138
Godianism 137–138, 147n
Good
criterion of 125
Good act
norms of 126
Gospel 129–131
Government intelligence reports 31
Grace 107
Great Mother 74
Group(s) 39
dependency 46
messianic 151
millenarian 151
prophetic 151
sectarian 151
Guardian spirit 178

H

Harrist Church 151, 161
Hausa 114, 115
Healer(s) 4, 46–48, 57
    (as) psychotherapist 48
Healing 40, 45–47, 68, 136, 140, 153, 181
    holistic 38, 47
    methods 144
    practices 172
    traditional 4, 57
Health 47, 179
Heathens 113
Herbalist(s) 4, 10, 56
    Associations of, 144
Heritage 5, 113
Heroes 91, 123, 126
    cult of 130
Heterodoxy 162
Hierarchical order 131
Hierarchy 119, 177
    (of) beings 121
Hierophany 124
High God 137
Hinduism 25, 171
Historical approach
    significance of 3
History 27, 30, 54, 59
History of religions
    hermeneutical concern of 30
Holistic disposition 37
Hospitality 179
Human beings
    origin of 60
Human
    rights 161
    sacrifice 117, 143
Humanism 29
Humanity 44, 49
Husain 169–170

I

Ibibio 23, 60, 104, 142
Ideas 119
Identity 41, 125
    fluctuation 102
Ideology(ies) 49, 92, 101, 105, 170

Idol worship 138
Idolatrous practices 114
Idowu, E. B. 17–18, 54
Ifa 53
    divination 176
    divination poetry 95–96
    oracle 97, 139
    temple 116
Iferan 57
Igbo 54, 61, 74–75, 113, 142
Ijebu 112–113
    expedition 112
Ijo Orumila 147n
Ika Meji 96
Ikot Abasi 104
Ila 61, 178
Ile-Ife 52, 58n
Ill-luck 5, 103–104
Illness 174, 181
    psychosomatic nature of 179
Imagination 38
Imam 169
Imana 120, 175
Immanence 12, 177
Immortality 41, 61-62
Imperialism 9, 115
Incorporation 181
Incubi 104
Independent Church Movement 161
Indigenous
    beliefs 153
    culture 115
    customs 153
    Faith of Africa 139
    languages 115
    religion 112
    worshippers 116
Individual 45, 102
    survival after death 120
Individualism 41, 106–107
Individualization 135
Individuation 145
Indo-Europeans 170
Industrialization 157
Initiatic cult 172
Initiation(s) 180
    clan 124
    spirit 124
Injustice 123
In-law relationship 104

Institutionalization 146
Integration 127, 170, 174
Intention 131
Interaction
        (with) cosmos 130
        (with) environment 130
        (between the) living and the dead
            130
Interdenominationalism 152
Interdependence 130
Interior life 131
Intermediaries 174
Intermediary beings 17, 175
Intuition 37–39, 45
Investiture 121–122
Invisible world
        immanence of 120
        transcendence of 119–120
Involvement 4, 41
Iran 168–169
Iranians 170
Iranian civilization
        religious history 170
        spirituality of 170
Iṣarun 76
Islam 1, 3–4, 8–9, 19, 22, 25, 31-32,
    51–52, 56, 74, 82, 92, 112, 114–116,
    137, 139, 144, 167, 171, 175
Islamic
        fundamentalism 9
        New Religious Movements, 11
Isoki 114
Isoko 113
Israel 170
Iya 75

J

Jamaa teachings 162
Japanese nationalism 163n
Jehovah's Witnesses of Kapepa 155
Jẹgbe 96–97
Jesus (Christ) 74, 112, 138–   139,
    169
Jihad 9, 115
John Paul II, Pope 10, 132
Jok 175
Juju 113, 138

K

Kamwana, Eliot 161, 163n
Karma
        law of 107
Kimbanguism 151, 161
Kimbanguist(s) 160
        Church 161
Kimilu 65
Kin reciprocity 180
King 40, 87, 91, 122
        (as) symbol of divine authority
            124
        (as) symbolizing national unity
            124
Kingdom
        (of) Christ 129
Kingship 107
        institution of 142
        sacral 7
Kitawala movement 160
Kla Kwao 178
Knowledge 3
        catechetical 4
        scientific 4
        scriptural 4
Konde 174
Koso 94
Krobo 178
Kutusa 180
Kwotto 61

L

Ladipọ, Duro 98
Lagelu 139
Land 120–121
Law 130
Leadership 160
Leadership roles 149
        fragmentation and redefinition of
            162
Leadership succession 161
        crisis in 160
Lega 173
Legend(s) 54, 60, 82
Levi-Strauss, Claude 172
Levy-Bruhl, Lucien 38
Libations 141

Liberation 11
    Theology(ies) 157, 159
Life 60
    communion of 121
    creative process of 63
    empirical and super-empirical 120
    enhancement of 123
    force 47
    goal of 173
    (as) integral flow of relationships
       173
    mysteries of 61–62
    soul 179
    unity of 120
    violation of 123
    wholeness of 45
Life-giving principle 120
Light
    forces of 170
    mystical realm of 169
Liminality 20
Lineage
    perpetuation of 131
Lisa 176
Litany 69
Literature 2
Liturgical
    celebrations 127
    events 5
Liturgy 7, 11
Living and dead
    interchange of relations between
       120
Loss 62
Love 137
Lovedu 74
Luba religion 172
Lugbara 64–66, 68
Luhyia 61
Luo 61

M

Maasai 63, 67, 69
Macrocosm 31
Madarikan 57
Madness 174, 176
Magic 5, 17, 39, 56–57, 116, 124, 127,
    129, 136, 146, 153
    "black" 130

Maguzawa 114
Maitatsine Muslim uprising 9
Makom 176
Male domination 73
Man
    (as) creator 124
Mande folk ideas 183n
Mani 169
Manichaean 170
Manichaeanism 169
Marriage(s) 113
    ceremonies 124
    inter-ethnic and inter-community
       104
Marx 19
Marxism 29
Marxist 170
Masquerades 143–144
Matriarchal system 75
Mawu 175–176
Mbiti, J. S. 17–18, 59–72
Mbothior 83
Meaning(s)
    existential 172–173
Medicine 4–5, 47, 56–57, 114, 127
    women 77
Mediator(s) 40, 122
Mediatory beings 177
Medium(s) 68, 77, 180
Mediumnistic theory 23
Membranophone 81, 83, 85, 87
Memory 87, 92
Menstruation 69, 80n
Mental illness 48
Messianic movements 159
Metaphysical
    forces 40, 45
    world 38, 41, 47
Metaphysics 37
Method 3, 27, 29
Methodological concern 154
Methodology 2–3
Microcosm 31
Millenarian
    movements 153, 155, 157
    tendencies 156
Millenarianism 11, 159
Millennium 155
Miracles 37
Misfortune 181

Mission Churches
    challenge to (their) authority and
        liturgy 161
Mission schools 114
Missionaries 112–114
Missionary
    papers 31
    policies 146
Modernity 31, 147n, 154–156
    pressures of 135
Modernization
    1, 135, 168
Monotheism 27–28
Monotheistic traditions 1
Moral education 141
Morality
    ontological, immanent and
        intrinsic 126
Moremi 54
Moses 169
Moslem (see Muslim)
Mother goddess 75
Mother of mankind
Motherhood 64
Movements of opportunity 161
    prophetic and revitalistic 150
    (of) protest 153, 161
Mozo 178
Muhammed (or Muhammad) 114, 169
Muntu 122, 126
Musedi soul 178
Music 30, 115, 117
Muslim(s) 5, 9, 12, 52–56, 58, 95,
    114–116, 139, 169–170
    proselytising 116
Muwo 178
Mysterious 36–37, 39
Mystery 38, 44–45, 82, 173
Mystic 28
Mystical 39
    thinking 38–39
    philosophy 183n
Myth(s) 20, 54, 60–63, 82, 170
    (of) conquest 181
    distortion of 93
    (of) ideal future 159
    (of) ideal past 158
Mythology(ies) 5, 59, 172

N

Nation 121
    building 157
National
    Church of Nigeria 137
    identity 157
    independence 161
Nationalism 19, 141
Nationalist(s) 115
Nationalistic political movements 157
Natural forces 178–179
Nature 40, 45
    order in 40
    relationship of African religion to 4
    spirits 17, 179
Ndebele 74
Ndem 140
    cults of 143
    dances 144
    Efik Iboku 143
    shrine 143
Negritude 171
Neo-traditional movements 11
Neotraditionalism 11, 158
New Religious Movements (NRMs) 11,
    32, 149ff, 150, 153, 157, 158
    doctrinal base of 150
    geographic distribution 150
    impetus for 150
    organizational structure of 150
    (as) responses to colonialism 153
Nichiren Soshu Buddhism 163n
Nigerian independent churches 140
Nilotic
    Alur 175
    peoples 174
    religion 175
Nka Ekpenyong Nnuk 143
Nomenclature 2
Non-rational 4
Nri 113
NRMs (See New Religious Movements)
Ntu 122, 125–126
Nuba 74
Nuer religion 175
Nyame 88
Nyamuzinda 120
Nyankonpon 88
Nyerere, Julius 105
Nzes 138

O

Ọba 55, 75
Ọba ko so 94, 98
Ọbaa koso 94
Ọbalufọn 76
Ọbatala
Objectivity 4, 40
Obligations 12
Obong 142
        enthronement of 143
Obumo 60
Odangaman 88
Odoumandan 88
Odoumandaman 88
Odu 96
Oduduwa 6, 54, 58n, 75
Odu Ifa 7
Odumunga 88
Ọfọ 138
Ofosi 75
Ofun-eko
Ogbetura 95–96
Ogun 53–54, 140
Ogun Obinrin 77
Ohmuzd (See Ahura Mazda)
Ọja'ba 139
Okomi lineage 95
Old Testament 139–140
Olodumare 53
Ọlọfin Oodua 96-97
Olokun 75
Olorisa 116
Ọlọrun 53, 137
Olọsa 75
Oluasarun 76
Oluorogbo 54
Omuvande 122
Onikoyi lineage 95
Ontic
        change 122
        modification 122
        relation 120–121, 123
Ontological
        enhancement 131
        harmony 41
Ontology 120, 125
Onwuejeogwu 113
Onyioha, K. O. K., Chief 137–138
Oogun awọn agba 57

Oparaji, Jimmy A. 138
Opposition of world rulers
        Manichaean conception of 182
Oral
        history 60
        literature 7, 117
Organization of Traditional Religions of
        Africa 137
Origin
        myths of 61–62
Oriki 95
Orile-Orisa (association) 10, 139
Orisa 52, 75, 144
Orisa-oko 55, 75, 77
Orisanla 53
Oro 55
Ọrunmila 55
        cult of 138
Ọsẹ-meji 139
Oshogbo 144
Ọshun 116
Ossein 88
Ostracism 103, 107
Ọsun 75, 116, 144
Otchre Kwaou Aba 88
Otua Oriko 96
Ovabo 74
Owe 75
Owonrinyeku 96
Oya 55, 75, 77, 94, 96
Ọyọ 95–98
Ozo 113

P

Pagan(s) 168, 170
        cults 171
Paganism 1, 128, 137
Pan-Ibibio Language and Culture
        Association (PILCA) 142
Pantheon 53
Paradise 5, 61
Parrinder, E. G. 16, 139
Parthian Empire 169
Participation 4, 39–40, 120–121, 123,
        130–131
        vital 130
Past 42, 43
Patriarch 122
        symbolizing authority of ancestors
        124

Patrimony 120–122
Paul VI, Pope, 131
Paul, Saint 74
P'Bitek, O. 18, 63, 65
Peace settlement 104
Pentecostalism 159
Persia (See also Iran) 169
Persian Traditionalism 168
Personal
    affluence 105–106
    comfort 105–106
Personal destiny
    cult to 175
Personal
    development 177
    involvement 40
    obliteration 180
Personality 41
Personhood 12, 178
    African view of 177
Pharmacopoeia 144
Phenomenological-anthropological
    models 29
Phenomenological-hermeneutical
    investigation 28
Phenomenology
    hermeneutical 29-30
    morphological 29
Philosophy 125, 130
    global and cosmic 126
Pirenne, Henri 106
PL Kyodan 163n
Plural culture contact 149
Poet 7
Polar opposition 170
Political
    commitments 157
    community 141
    control 158
    independence 115
    liberation 157, 161
    message 141
Political values
    redefinition of 159
Politicization 135
Politico-cultural organizations 142
Polygamy 66, 131, 140
Polytheism 27
Possession(s) 12, 76
    cults 81

trance 180, 181
Power 12, 82, 124, 175
    channel of 122
    creation, exercise and legitimation
      of 152
    numinous 47
    (through) relationship 173
    representative character of 122
Pra 90
Practices 130
Prayer(s) 5, 47, 59–60, 68–71, 92, 123,
    175
    extempore 117
Preachers 114
"Pre-logical" mentality 38
Present 42
Pre-Zoroastrian times 170
Priest(s) 46, 48, 53, 68
Priestess(es) 68, 75–77, 80n
Primal
    battle 168
    powers 176
Primal traditions
    study of 2
Profane 28, 127, 151
Progeny 126
Progress 42, 106, 132
Prohibitions 131
Prophets 47
Prophetic revitalization 158
Protestant
    ethic 155
    theology 18
    tradition 157
Protestantism 152, 171
Proverb(s) 2, 5, 7, 59, 60, 63, 65,
    67–68, 103–104, 126, 173
Psychological dependency 150
Punishment 102-103, 107
Purification 153
Pygmies 69–70

Q

Qua 142
Quran (or Qur'an) 82, 92
    personal adherence to 161

R

Rainmaking ceremonies 69
Rational dimension 3
Reality 173
      nature of 172
Reason
      crowning of 40
Reciprocity 180
Reconciliation 124
Reconversion process 137
Records 8
Reductionism 16, 22
Reductionists 22–23
Reincarnation 169
Rejuvenation 61-62
Relation
      (of) connotation 125
Relationship(s) 12, 40–41, 173, 179
      (in) being and life 120
Religion
      African scholars of 18
      anthropology of 29
      civil 19
      comparative study of 2, 21
      (as) experimental phenomenon
         27–28
      historians of 2
      history of 1, 2, 30
      "inside" and "outside" views of 23
      limitative approach to the study of
         21
      monotheistic 26
      (of) opportunity 154
      (of) oppressed 154
      phenomenological approaches to
         the study of 2
      phenomenologists of 18
      phenomenology of 26, 30
      (as) preparatio evangelica 22
      primal 25–26, 30
      primitive 26
      reductionist concept of 17
      revealed 128
      secular concept of 22
      social function of 16, 127
      socio-functionalist approach to 2
      theological approach to 2
      Western scholars of 18

Religiosity
      decline of 152, 158
Religionwissenschaft 2–3, 26, 30
Religious
      acculturation 32
      awareness 4
      beliefs 151
      cult 130
      doctrine 154
      domination 153
Religious group
      doctrinal and organization
         structure of 158
Religious
      heritage 141
      imagery 162
      innovations 168
      institutions 152
      language 162
      laws 127
      liberation 157
Religious phenomena
      symbolic analysis of 29
Religious
      plurality 141
      practice 154
      studies 19
      symbols 141
      syncretism 32
      unity 157
Religious worldview
      African traditional 3
Renewal 159
Reparation 104, 123
Resacralization 156
Resemblances 125
Resilience 3, 27, 31
Respect
      (for) life 131
      (for) parents 131
Resurrection 61–62
Revelation 10, 128
Revitalization 10–11, 135, 158
Revolutionary
      ideals 141
      ideologies 146
Rissho Kosei-Kai 163n
Rite(s) 29, 119, 122, 127, 136, 141,
      143, 145
      death 124

funeral and burial 55
investiture 124
(of) purification 124
Ritual(s) 5, 12, 22, 26, 82–83, 113,
116, 140, 158, 167
cleansing 103
dances 78
mask 113
modification of 141
public 145
(of) reversal 176
sacrifice 104
Riyom 104
Rood Sane 84
Ruanda 175

S

Sacral
kings and chiefs 176–177
kingship 181
right 176
Sacralization 85
Sacrament 129
Sacred 2-3, 6–7, 11, 27–28, 82–83, 85,
88, 92, 130, 150–157, 159, 163n
effort 173
interpretation(s) of 158, 160
life 120
new definition of 159, 162
places 104
sanctions 102
Sacred symbols
manipulated, 152
Sacred writings
literal interpretation of 161
Sacrificial meals 41
Sacrifice(s) 43, 78, 114, 140, 180
Sacrilege 126
Saints 17
Salvation 12, 44, 13, 171
moral 108
religious 174
spiritual 113
Ṣango 7, 8, 55, 93–98, 116, 174
Afǫnja 97
Aganju 97
Ogodo 97
Satan 113, 169
Great and Little 170

Savior figures 169
Se 175
Shangana 64
Schillebeeckx, E 43
Schism 11, 149, 159, 160
Science 37, 41–45, 49, 127
development of 40
"spiritualization" of 44
Scientific worldview 3–4
Scripture(s) 114
fundamentalist interpretations of
159
reinterpretation of 151
Secret
movement 169
societies 142
Sectarian responses 153
Secular 11, 150, 152, 154, 156, 159
Secularism 35–36, 38, 141, 168
Secular ideologies 29
Secularity 141
Secularization 11, 41, 146, 151–152,
155–158, 162
cultural and symbolic responses to
159
subjective 149, 158
thesis 155, 163n
Secularized consciousness 157
Self 177–180
attitudes to 171
cosmic 174
Self-realization 137
Senghor, L. S. 43
Separation 174
Serpent
magician/cosmic 168
Sexual complementarity 180
Sexuality
creative fusion of 180
Shagari, President 107
Shi'ism 169
Shi'ite 170
Shona 74
Shrine(s) 113, 116
Sickness 5, 104
Sin 102–103
Singing 41, 45, 76, 78, 117, 173
Skepticism 36, 37
Slaves
liberation of 112

Smart, Ninian 28
Smith, Wilfred Cantwell 25
Social change 1, 140
    Weberian model of 163n
Social
    differentiation 158
    insulation 161
    integration 56
    interaction 177
    justice 157
    processes 152
Social relationships
    alternative types of 162
Social status 121
Social values
    redefinition of 159
Society 102, 125
Sociology 1
Sokka Gakkai 163n
Solidarity 123, 179
SOMB 83
"Son-of-the-soil" syndrome 105
Songs 113
Ṣọnpọnna 55
Sorcerers 123, 179
Sorcery 17–18, 129–130
Soul 38
    destiny 179
    life 179
    power 179
Source criticism 21, 22
Space 125
Spirit(s) 18, 82-83, 87, 102, 111, 146,
    179
    ancestral 102, 104
    divine 102
    mediumship 171, 181
    "multiplication" of 136
    possession 68, 76, 181
    world 69
    worship of 136
Spiritual
    anima 178
    entities 41
    experimentation 160
    healing 151
    heritage 116
    illnesses 145
    life 107
    priority of 133

renewal 151, 160
    structures 182n
Spirituality 71, 179
    African forms of 173
Stories 60
Structural differentiation 156
Succession 122, 149
Successors 122
Suffering 61–63
Sunni Muslims 169
Supernal deities 169
Supernatural
    powers 46, 153
    world 39
Superstition 127
Supreme Being(s) 10, 12, 28, 40,
    83–84, 108, 111, 120, 122–123, 126,
    129–130, 138, 175
    cult of 136
Supreme deity 27, 31
Supreme God 75
Swahili 65
Symbol(s) 31, 123, 125, 127, 136, 159,
    171, 182n
    customary 160
    innovative 162
    mediation of 125
    overarching 160
    (as) means of contact and union
        120
    resacralization of 159
    restorative 162
Symbolic
    challenge 154
    experience 125
    meaning 29
    protest 150, 160
    realism 156
Symbolism(s) 124, 130, 140, 156, 170
    (as) language 125
    (of) purity and pollution 169
Symbologies 30
Syncretism 11, 158
Systems
    meaning-giving 29

T

Taboos 113, 131, 140
    menstruation 6
Taita 180

Talmud 176
Tano 90
Tchre 86
Tchreman 86
Technology 8, 43–44, 49, 114
Technology and Industry
    invasion of 128
Temna 103
Ten commandments 131
Theology(ies) 2, 29, 30
    (as) human discourse on God 27
Theory 27–29
Therapy 46
Theravada Buddhism 28
Things
    (as) channels and reservoirs 124
    (as) creatures 124
    mutuality of 173
Thought
    universal operation of 172
Tillich, Paul 171
Time 4, 42–43, 125
    cyclic concept of 42–43
    (as) linear movement 43
    two-dimensional concept of 42
Timi 94
Togetherness 41
Totem
    symbol of clanic unity 124
Tradition
    reinterpretation of 162
Traditional
    beliefs 145–146
    cults 146
Traditional deities
    recognition of 142
Traditional
    medicine 52
    Medicine Societies 10
Traditional religion(s)
    commercialization of 144
    erosion of 142
    intellectual rationalizations of 170
    structure of 170
Traditional religious beliefs
    revitalization of 142
Traditional symbols
    power of 145
Transcendence 2–3, 12, 27–28, 173,
    176–177

Trance 12
Transmigration and reincarnation
    Buddhist doctrines of 182
Tribal cult 171
"Tribalism" 105
Tribe 60, 120–121, 127, 171
Troeltsch, E. 11, 152
Trust 40
Truth(s) 27, 59, 129
    followers of 169
Tsonga 64, 66
Turkana 60
Tusi 60–61
Tutelary spirits 77
Typology 153
    church-denomination-sect 152

U

Ukot 104
Unification 125, 127
    striving for 124
Union 129
Unity 129, 170
    (of) communities 131
Universality 129
Universalization 135
Universe 45, 82, 126
    God's full presence within 177
Urbanization 8, 36
Uthman Dan-Fodio 9, 115
    Jihad of 52, 58n
Utopian ideals 159
Uwolowu 60
Uyara ntinya (Traditional coronation)
    143

V

Value(s) 105, 131, 141
Value systems
    traditional socio-religious 108
Vatican II 129
Village politics 179–180
Vital
    circuit 123
    current 123
    diminution 123

enchantment 124
energies 122
enhancement 122
force 123
impairment 123
influx 123
Vital power
enhancement 122
Vital
relationship 131
union 120–122

W

War 180
myths 168, 180
Warrior-god 168
Watch Tower Movement 155, 157, 161, 163n
Weber, Max 11, 152, 155, 168
Weberian
model 154
view 155
We-ethos 106
Western
civilization
education 113, 114
Western medicine 144–145
impotence of 151
Western
religious traditions 162
secularism 8
Westernization 139, 155
Wisdom 44, 59, 141
literature 5
Wise sayings 7
Witchcraft 5–6, 12, 17–18, 145–146, 172, 180
Wives
plurality of 56
Women 59ff
role and image of 2
Words 124
World Council of Churches 161
World(s)
intersection of two 119
(as) plurality of forces 126
World savior
Buddhist doctrines of 182

World(s)
visible and invisible 119
Worldview(s) 23, 31–32, 36, 38–39, 46–47, 63, 82, 136, 141, 153, 168–170, 179
analysis 29
dualistic 180
(of) Iranian civilization 182
post-modern 4, 35, 49
Worship 37, 48, 54, 117, 130
African models of 140
modernization of modes of 139
objects of 113
traditional mode of 112

Y

Yemoja 75
Yoruba 4, 51ff, 61, 103, 138, 145, 176
myths 53
priesthood 144
religion 144, 181
rites 53

Z

Zarathustra 169
Zionist sermons and rituals 162
Zombi-states 180
Zoroastrian 170
Zulu rain-doctors 175
Zurvan 169